IMAGES
of America

OKLAHOMA CITY FILM ROW

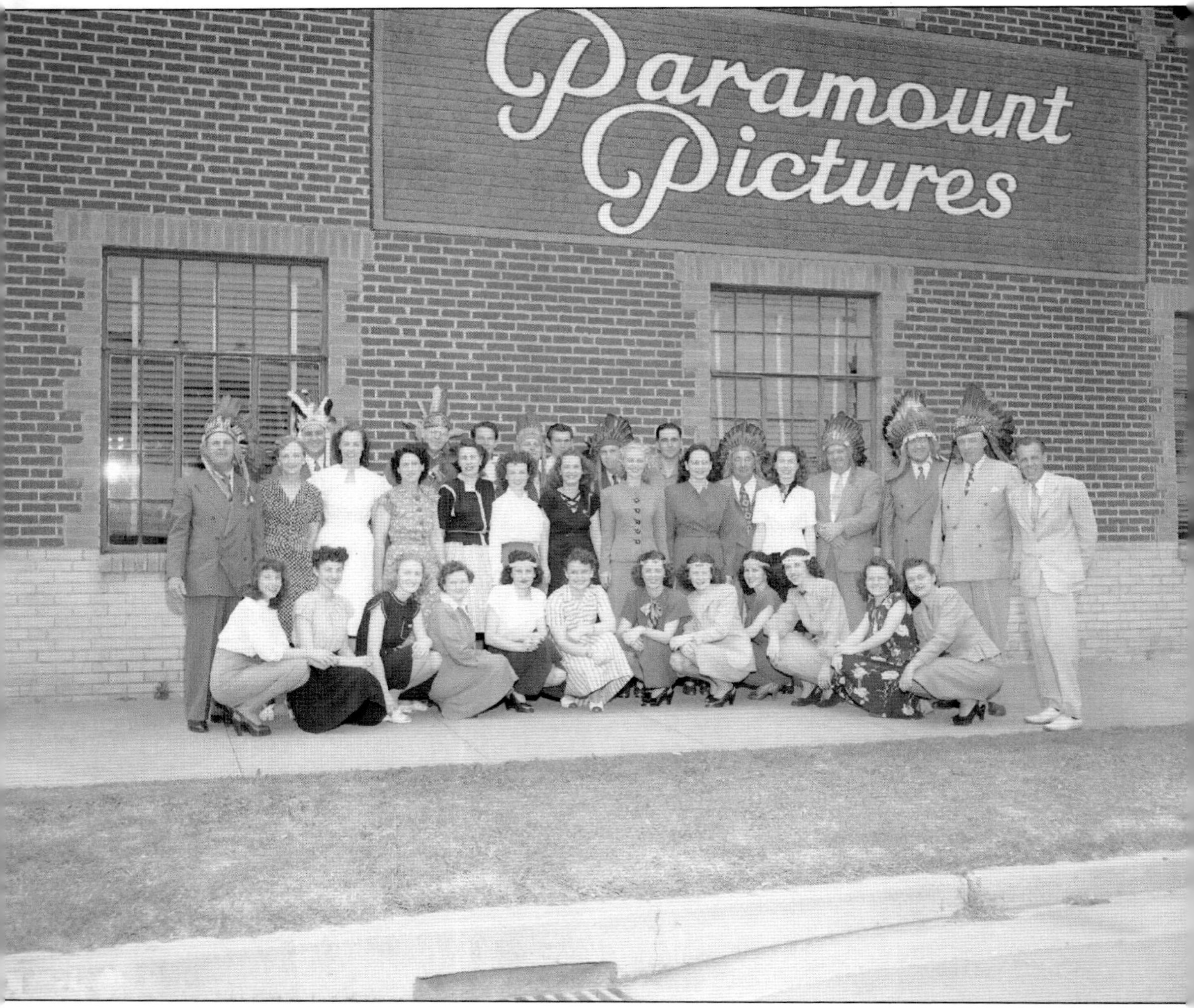

ON THE COVER: The image on the cover and pictured above was taken in 1947 of the Paramount Pictures Film Exchange management and staff. The image is looking at the southeast corner of the building and its painted logo at 700 West Grand Avenue. Branch manager Carl Howard Weaver stands at the far left. Duke Clark, Paramount's distribution chief for the western United States, stands on the far right wearing a headdress. Oklahoma became a state in 1907, and the Native American headdresses worn here are most likely commemorating the state's 40th birthday. Restoration efforts on the Paramount building in 2010 uncovered the logo pictured above after removing decades of old paint layers. (Courtesy of the Oklahoma Historical Society.)

IMAGES
of America

OKLAHOMA CITY FILM ROW

Bradley Wynn with
foreword by Steve Lackmeyer

ARCADIA
PUBLISHING

ISBN 978-0-7385-8381-5

Published by Arcadia Publishing
Charleston, South Carolina

Printed in the United States of America

Library of Congress Control Number: 2010924254

For all general information, please contact Arcadia Publishing:
Telephone 843-853-2070
Fax 843-853-0044
E-mail sales@arcadiapublishing.com
For customer service and orders:
Toll-Free 1-888-313-2665

Visit us on the Internet at www.arcadiapublishing.com

I dedicate this book to my beautiful wife, Kristina, and my amazing son, Cameron, who both unconditionally love and inspire me. I did it!

In memory of Eldon and Maxine Peek of the former Oklahoma Theatre Supply Company: thank you for staying.

Contents

Acknowledgments

The Oklahoma City Film Exchange and Historic Film Row are unique, as they appear to remain standing with most of their historical buildings, film vaults, a screening room, and period architecture in place. The row also retained, for 74 years, the Oklahoma Theatre Supply Company, an original business from that bygone era, complete with artifacts and owner Maxine Peek's eyewitness memories. The supply company closed in July 2004.

In 2003, the rediscovery of Film Row inspired staggering efforts and investment toward its revitalization. The volunteers of untold hours toward this endeavor are too numerous to list, but there are a select few who should be mentioned and who had a direct hand in or inspired this book that now records the history time nearly erased.

First, this book would never have been possible without the generosity and support of the Oklahoma Historical Society and its dedicated research staff. As a result, most of the images shared here are being published for the first time. I am also extremely grateful to fellow historian and writer Steve Lackmeyer, whose foreword and amazing dedication to Oklahoma City's past adds to Film Row's amazing story. Without him, our city's past would be long forgotten. I want to thank the estate of J. Eldon and Maxine Peek, historians Larry Johnson and Doug Loudenback, George Verstraete of First Rate Images, Rachel Mosman, Dr. Dale Metzler, Bonnie Countess Hewes, James Murati, Robert Mulzet and Brian Kenny of the Barco Library Cable Center, Leith Adams and Steven Bingen of Warner Brothers, and the USC Cinematic Arts Library for their photographs, contributions, and support.

I also wish to thank a special core group of amazing individuals who sacrificed so much for a dream that both preserved and changed the cityscape forever: Chip Fudge, David Wanzer, Brett Johnson, Robbie Kienzle, A.J. Kirkpatrick, Russell Claus, Dr. Lane Peyton, Tyler Peyton, Robbin Davis, Susan Urbach, Dr. Donna Carlon, Ted Ryals, Ann Simank, and Jim Roth.

I also want to thank Wesley Horton, Monte Wilson, Lori Cross, Mary Gerarda Kelcy, Bill Moore, Hayden Hewes, Ted Ryals, Jeff McKenzie, Rob Smith, John Gilbert, Oscar and Shiron Butterfly Ray, Darrell McAllister, Branson Young, Jeffery Chapman, Max Alvarez, Darren Brown, Nathaniel Hardy, Carl Rose, Roger Albright, Mrs. Carlton Weaver Jr. (Beverly Jane), Don Stephens III, David Callahan, Dean Slatev, Dr. Deborah Carmichael, Ed Poole, Fred Godwin, Randy Titus, Dan Straughan, Sharon Allen, Debbie Neece, Toyscapes, Inc., the Exchange, IAO Gallery, Joey's Pizzeria, and the staff of the International Crystal Manufacturing Company for all they contributed to the preservation and story of Historic Film Row.

I also want to say thank you for the immense support of Joe Walker, Ted Gerstle, Winnie Rodgers, and the awesome staff of Arcadia Publishing who believed in this work and me!

To my loving wife and son, who journeyed with me through everything: thank you!

Please note that when applicable, the historic spelling of "theater" is "theatre" for the purposes of this book and many addresses throughout appear on Grand and Sheridan Avenues. In 1961 Grand Avenue was renamed Sheridan.

The story continues! If you or someone you know has more information and images about Film Row, please contact the author, Bradley Wynn, at P.O. Box 711; Oklahoma City, OK 73101-0711.

FOREWORD

As of this writing, Oklahoma City is enjoying a $2-billion renaissance in its urban core; the story cannot be told without highlighting the revival of old historical business districts that include Bricktown, Automobile Alley, and Deep Deuce.

The history of all three of these downtown neighborhoods has been well documented in history books, including titles released by Arcadia Publishing. But one such downtown strip has been ignored by various authors—until now. The Film Exchange District is certainly of interest to historians, film buffs, and observers of urban planning and Art Deco architecture.

In its heyday, the Film Exchange was home to branches of most if not all of the major Hollywood studios. Trains would deliver films into these offices along West Grand Avenue (now named Sheridan Avenue), and theater owners and operators from throughout Oklahoma gathered in small screening rooms along Film Row to decide which movies would entertain audiences back in their hometowns.

These film exchange operations were housed in buildings that mostly reflected the modernist, Art Deco vision of the 1920s through the 1940s. It was the heyday of the movie industry, and a walk through some of these buildings today is an opportunity to relive those moments when Clark Gable and Cary Grant could be relied on to pack even the largest theater for weeks on end. Sidewalks here were even shared by numerous stars and starlets as they promoted their films with local audiences in many of downtown Oklahoma City's theaters and film exchange offices.

As key as this district was to Oklahoma City's early-day commerce and theaters throughout the state, the Film Exchange District simply doesn't show up much in newspaper archives. With the demise of such districts throughout the country, this stretch of West Sheridan Avenue became the city's "skid row"—an area city boosters wished to ignore.

"Film Row," as it's referred to now by locals, needed a historian of its own to tackle the task of assembling the sort of photographs featured in this book. Bradley Wynn, a self-described film buff, began to delve into the area's history before the last of its old-time residents like Maxine Peek passed away. He listened to their stories, preserved their memories, and continued to hunt for remnants of its past even as the district raced forward to a new future.

Finding photographs wasn't an easy task for Bradley. The Oklahoma Historical Society was a great place to start, especially for photographs of the statewide theatrical community. As president of Retro Metro OKC, I was happy to open up the group's online photographic archives to Bradley (Retro Metro OKC is a nonprofit dedicated to working with the Oklahoma Historical Society and other organizations to making the city's past more accessible). By studying Retro Metro OKC's photographs, Bradley not only found rare images for his book, he also helped us better identify those same materials for our online audience.

The result of Wynn's efforts is a great reflection of not just the Film Exchange District but also of the state's movie industry. We see the area's proud beginnings, its sad demise, and its triumphant revival.

His photographs show not just buildings but the people who proudly came to work, ensuring that in a state stuck halfway between the two coasts, the same movies drawing in audiences in New York City and Los Angeles also entertained crowds in Oklahoma City and Ponca City.

When Bradley Wynn first began documenting the history of the Film Exchange District, it was still a sad tale, a crumbling neighborhood whose population consisted of vagrants and homeless patrons of nearby shelters. As this book is published, a new 50-story Devon Energy Center tower looms large over the neighborhood—a community that is now home to a popular restaurant, art gallery, and several creative firms.

The Film Exchange District is a great tale of triumph over tragedy, of great dreams realized again and again. It's the sort of tale that could make for a good movie—and certainly a good book.

Bradley Wynn has given Oklahoma City a great gift by making that book a reality.

Steve Lackmeyer is an award-winning reporter and columnist with the *Oklahoman* and has covered urban development in Oklahoma City since 1996. He is author of three books about the Oklahoma City's history—*OKC Second Time Around*, *Skirvin*, and *Bricktown*, the last with Arcadia Publishing. Currently, Steve is working on a book about the history of the Central Oklahoma YMCA and another on the construction of the Devon Energy Center.

INTRODUCTION

Starting in 1907, entrepreneurs created the first film exchange offices in Oklahoma to cash in on public demand for moving pictures. These exchanges would negotiate with young filmmakers and studios for rights to distribute and show movies to the numerous venues materializing all over. As the years passed, exchanges scattered all over the city, from Northwest Twenty-third Street to Southwest Fifty-second Street and Robinson Avenue, until they consolidated along Grand Avenue, a street then on the very outskirts of the downtown area.

Each exchange office did the promoting, renting, and shipping of its films to theaters within its area, and exhibitors from across Oklahoma and surrounding states frequented the two-block area to screen films. Screening became a requirement under some regulations to ensure that content shown to the public was free of indecent acts, which was problematic during the early decades of filmmaking. Ancillary businesses and theatre supply showrooms along the same street offered a variety of concessions, carpeting, seating, lighting, sound, posters, lobby cards, and supplies that representatives could acquire for their theatre houses. This one-stop shop and stretch of Grand Avenue became "Film Row."

Film Row became a hub from which the business of film was always at work. Exchange personnel took breakfast and lunch in one of two Film Coffee Shops. Movies screened daily from one of four screening rooms at the 20th Century Fox in 10 North Lee Avenue; the Paramount Pictures, Griffith Theatres, and Video Independent Theatres in 701 West Grand Avenue; the Metro-Goldwyn-Mayer (MGM) at 629 West Grand Avenue; and the Simplex on the Film Exchange building's second floor at 702 1/2 West Grand Avenue.

From 1932 through 1941, the Film Exchange sponsored a baseball and softball team made of volunteers from all the exchange offices and semi-professional players. The team competed in numerous sandlot charity games with other businesses and city offices, usually at Wheeler or Wiley Post Parks. Many followed the games in the daily newspapers. In 1932, the Film Exchange baseball team nearly won the state championship from the City of Antlers after playing against 16 teams over 10 days. The entry of the United States into World War II in 1941 appears to have ended future games.

In the late 1940s and early 1950s, the massive Griffith Theatres chain split into Video Independent Theatres and the Video-Vumore Company. Both resided at 11 North Lee Avenue until Video-Vumore acquired the former Paramount Pictures building at 701 West Grand Avenue around 1953. From its offices at 11 North Lee Avenue, Video-Vumore created a cable venture offshoot conceived by Pres. Henry Griffing known as the Bartlesville Experiment, a first-run movie experiment in Bartlesville, Oklahoma, starting in 1955. The exercise was an idea before its time, lasting from September 3, 1957, with Doris Day in the *Pajama Game* to June 6, 1958, and it would become a precursor to pay television, better known as cable television.

Business boomed along the row until the early 1960s, when advances in technology, transportation, and economics changed filmmaking, studio, and distribution practices. One by one, exchange offices closed in cities across the nation. Oklahoma City renamed Grand Avenue to Sheridan Avenue in 1964 (and almost changed it again to Myriad Avenue in 1979). Film Row became a collective of eclectic businesses and empty office spaces dominated by numerous bars, prostitution, and drugs by the 1970s. In 1971, the Columbia Pictures Film Exchange was the last studio to close its doors along Film Row after 43 years of operation at 702 West Grand Avenue.

Video Independent Theatres and Vumore TV, subsidiaries of the massive Griffith Theatres chain, continued operations from their 11 North Lee Avenue and 701 West Sheridan Avenue offices, but decades-long monopoly lawsuits against Griffith, revenue shortages, overreaching, and sudden changes in both management and operations forced closure. On May 3, 1983, Martin Theatres (later renamed Carmike Cinemas) acquired Video Independent Theatres and closed its Oklahoma City home offices immediately, ending Film Row.

Oklahoma City further faced a crisis of blight and economic shortfalls through this period, and years of urban renewal laid waste to much of its downtown cityscape, as promises of something better fell far short of their goals. Many familiar landmarks, like the Criterion Theatre and Biltmore Hotel along Main Street and Sheridan Avenue, were razed by wrecking ball or explosive demolition. Amazingly, "Skid Row," as Film Row became known, escaped destruction.

The only surviving business from the exchange era was the Oklahoma Theatre Supply Company, operated by J. Eldon and Maxine Peek since 1930. The company was responsible for bringing sound to Oklahoma and surrounding states through its installation of theatre sound systems and in later years over a million drive-in movie speakers. According to owner Maxine, the company also provided everything a theatre needed and even "kept an entire projection room in stock, because one would burn down every few months or so due to flash fires." Oklahoma Theatre Supply lost much of its business in the mid-1980s due to ongoing theatre closures. Most of its sales were limited to popcorn and concessions for schools. It closed in July 2004 after 74 years of single-owner operation. Maxine Peek passed away eight months later.

It would take more than 30 years before this lost gem along Sheridan Avenue was rediscovered. In 2004, early advocates for the area's preservation and revitalization approached the city's planning department and proposed a bold new plan. The plan asked the area to be designated a new business district, inspired by its past.

Within months, generous assistance in planning and large private investment saved many of the key structures from destruction. In 2006, the city declared the 42-block portion, from Walker Avenue to Classen Boulevard and Southwest Second Street to Northwest First Street and Colcord Drive, the Oklahoma City Film Exchange District. In addition, private efforts successfully listed the 600–700 blocks of Sheridan Avenue in the National Register of Historic Places, thus creating Historic Film Row.

From 2005 to 2011, property owners accomplished what many said was impossible, as they brought their historic buildings back from the brink. New businesses immediately moved into the spaces and occupied nearly every structure along the 600–700 blocks by the end of 2010. These new businesses and efforts brought much-needed attention to the area, and streetscaping soon began transforming the landscape into a myriad of new designs never implemented before in the city. These ranged from colorful crosswalks featuring giant filmstrips at intersections with large Hollywood motifs to new landscaping and public works.

The Oklahoma City Film Exchange District has become a unique addition to the downtown cityscape and its growth. When looking upon the revitalized colony of structures along Film Row today, it is difficult to believe its story began over 100 years ago and continues to this day.

One

Lights! Camera! Theaters!

Oklahoma City was settled on April 22, 1889, and during the 18 years leading up to statehood, the city and its citizens were far from idle. Every avenue of commerce was springing up from the efforts of enterprising entrepreneurs. The most popular among them were entertainment venues. As the city grew, so too did its sophistication with the 1903 Overholser Opera House at 217 West Grand Avenue. The beautiful theatre presented professional live performances and vaudeville acts for more than 20 years. In 1928, the Warner Brothers Film Exchange acquired and renamed it the Orpheum. Later, it became the Warner, and it remained Oklahoma City's oldest theatre until it closed in 1964. Today's cityscape has incorporated the structure into the Center City parking garage and lot.

Only one year after constructing the Overholser Opera House, filmmakers were busy capturing the state's unique history and landscape. In 1904, a Thomas Edison Manufacturing Company film crew shot *A Brush Between Cowboys and Indians* at the famous 101 Ranch near Bliss, Oklahoma. The ranch was home to the 101 Wild West Show, and many of its performers became well-known western movie stars.

As the popularity of filmmaking across the nation grew, so too did the need for venues and distribution of movies being made. By 1910, more than 100 film exchange distributors were operating in the United States. Exchanges were usually located near a railhead and would negotiate with film studios for the rights to a completed film production and then distribute the product to nickelodeon venues. By 1928, nearly 30 exchanges were operating throughout Oklahoma City, starting with the Oklahoma Film Exchange Company at 221 West California Avenue in 1907, the year of statehood.

In 1920, the Vitagraph Film Company constructed a Film Exchange building at the corner of Reno and Hudson Avenues that housed approximately 29 separate film exchange offices. This was followed by another Film Exchange building constructed at Southwest Fifth Street and Robinson Avenue for Metro-Goldwyn-Mayer (MGM), Paramount Laskey, Universal, RKO Pictures, Pathe, Vitagraph, Warner Brothers, and Fox Films.

This was only the beginning.

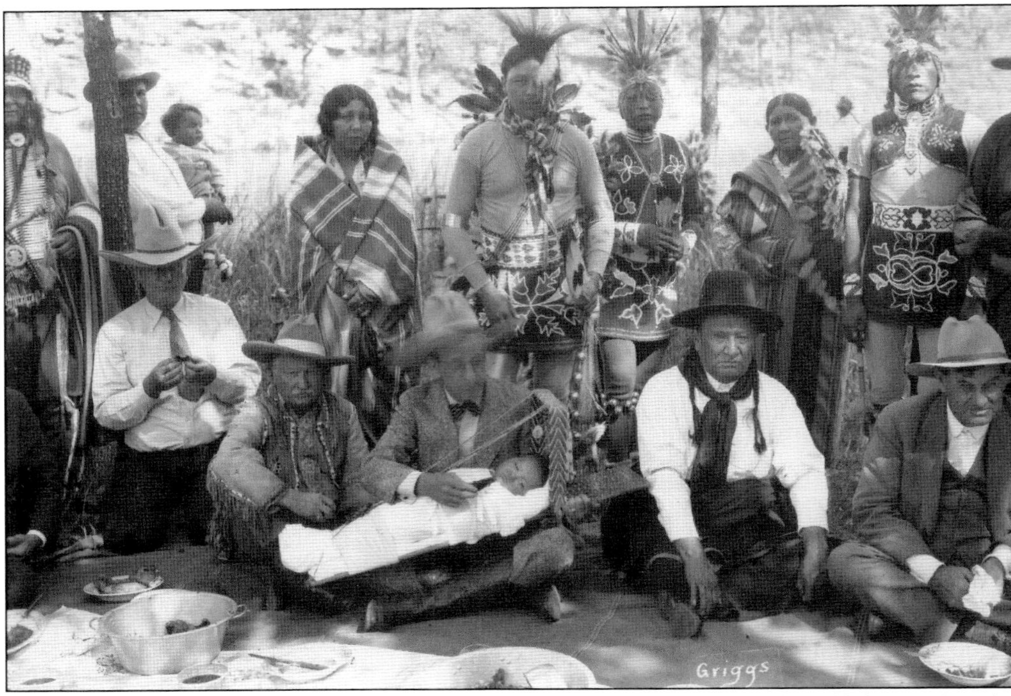

This image above shows members of the 101 Wild West Show near Bartlesville, Oklahoma. From left to right, standing, are Po-so-top-a, unidentified, infant, Mary Lookout and husband Jean Standing Bear, unidentified, Julia Lookout, and unidentified. Sitting in front are, from left to right, Col. Zach Miller (101 Ranch), Gordon "Pawnee Bill" Lillie, Frank Phillips, Standing Bear's baby, Fred Lookout, and Francis Revard. The 110,000-acre 101 ranch became very popular, hosted numerous visiting dignitaries—including US presidents and famous celebrities—and became home to some of the first western movies in filmmaking. Among the earliest was *A Brush Between Cowboys and Indians* in 1904. The image below depicts the ranch's "White House." (Both, courtesy of the Oklahoma Historical Society.)

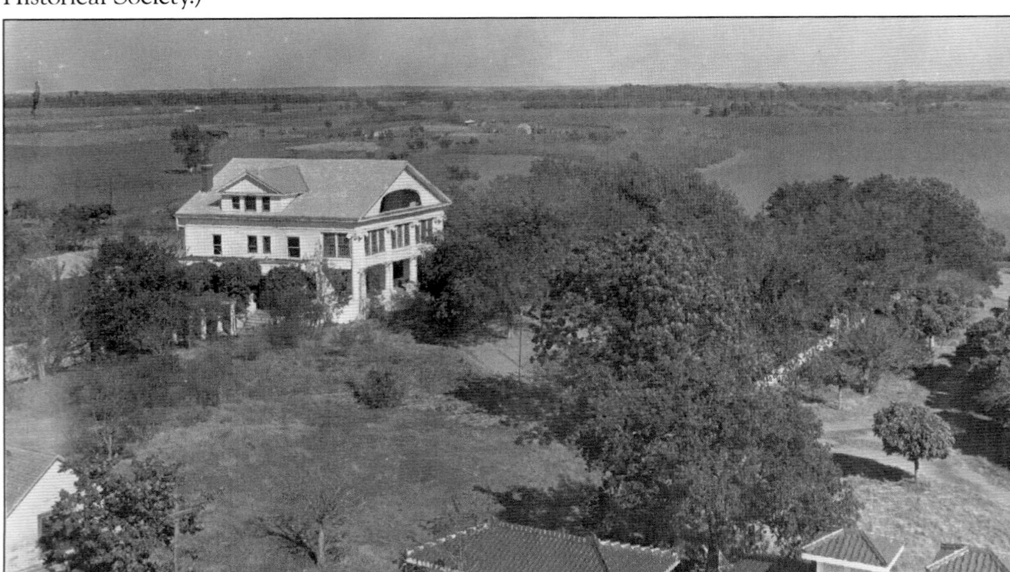

The first cinemas appeared as early as 1896, but going to the movies would not become part of America's landscape until the early 1900s. Cinemas like the WigWam Theatre in Sulphur, Oklahoma, pictured here in the summer around 1912, were typical silent movie houses of the time. (Courtesy of the Oklahoma Historical Society.)

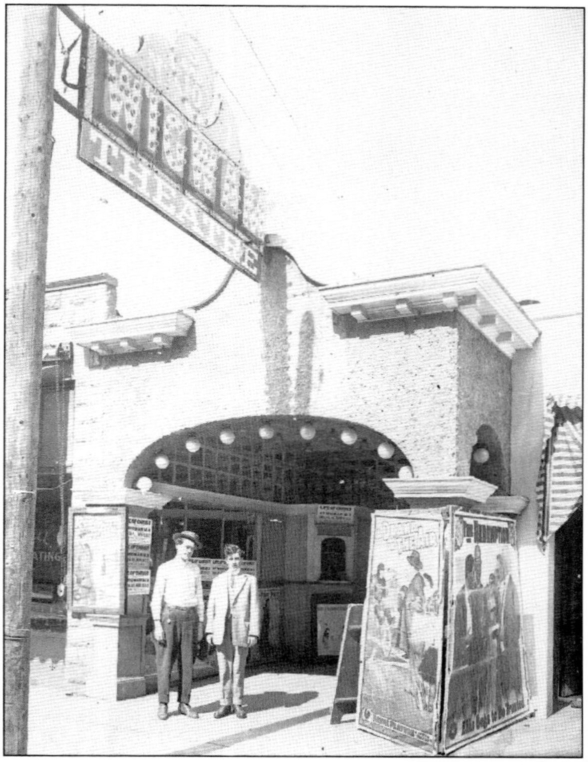

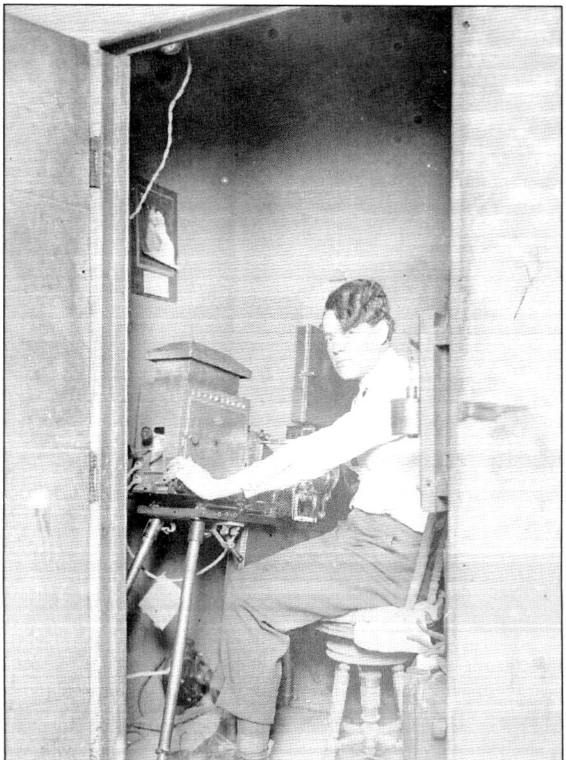

Projector rooms from early theatres were often configured like this c. 1912 image of the WigWam Theatre in Sulphur, Oklahoma. However, some theatres were open-air venues, due to lack of interior air conditioning. The WigWam's projector room, pictured here, is very small, and the heat and dangers from its projector put the projectionist and theatre at risk. (Courtesy of the Oklahoma Historical Society.)

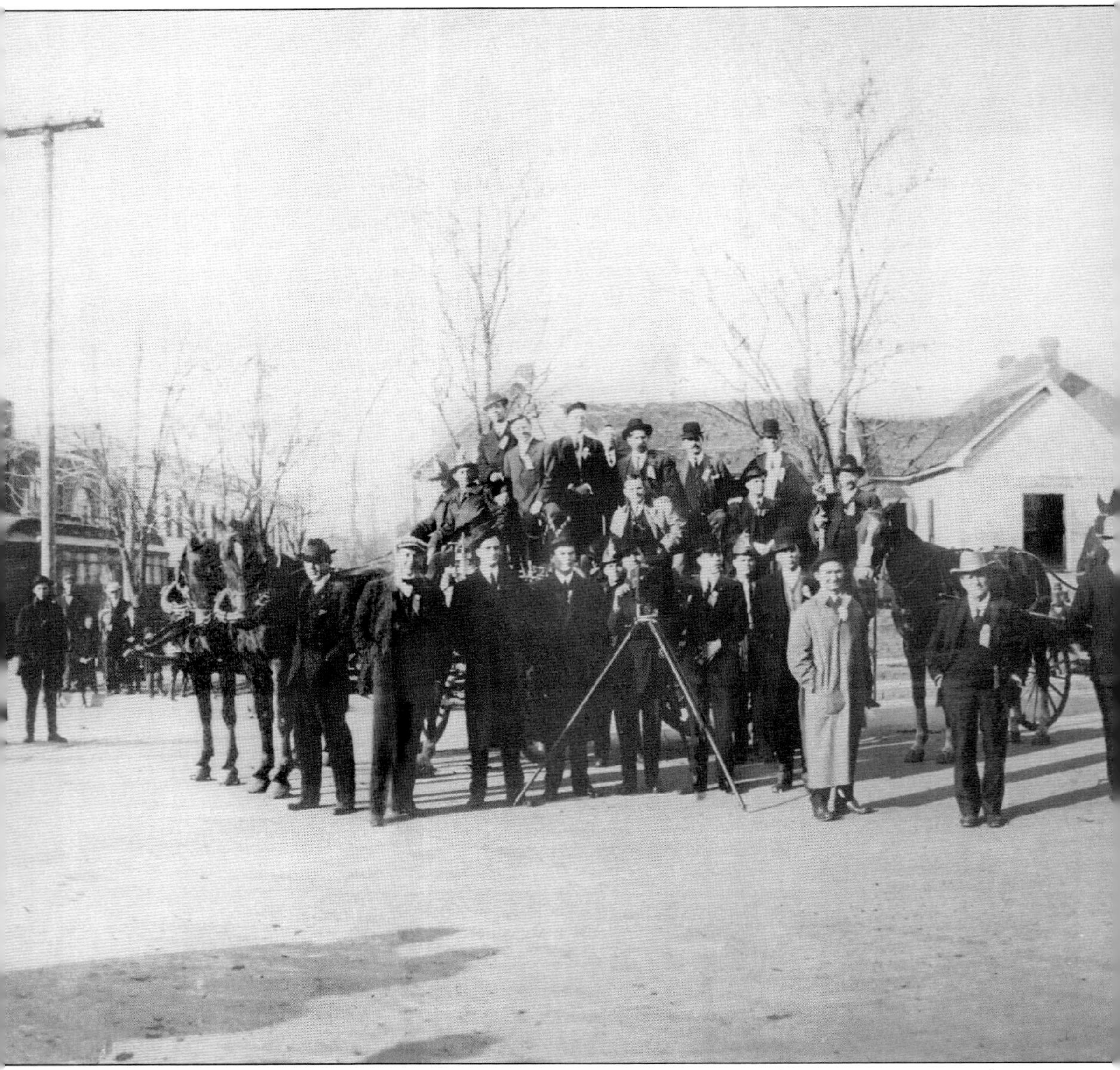

On February 11, 1913, this photograph of Oklahoma's first and founding convention members of the National Motion Picture Exhibitors League was taken on the northeast corner of California and Walker Avenues. An early trolley car is seen passing in front of the Oklahoma City Auditorium (later the Trianon Ballroom) and Oddfellows buildings. Firefighters from Oklahoma City's Station

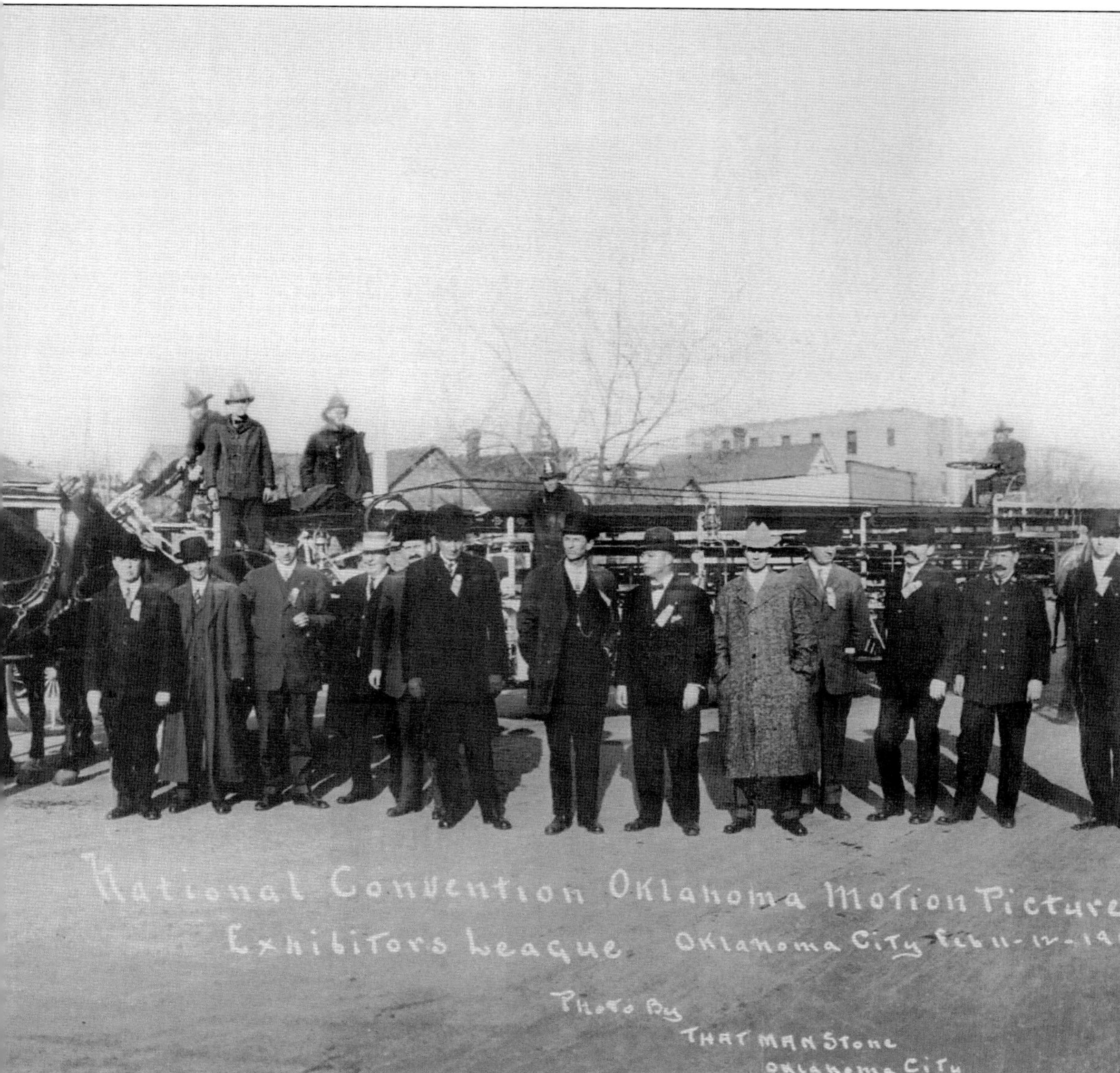

No. 1 stand on their horse-drawn fire equipment along the back row. From left to right, along the front row is Carl Gregg of Tulsa (12th man) and John A. Steinson of McAlester (20th man), both newly elected as national and first vice presidents. The meeting was held at the then-two-year-old Skirvin Hotel. (Courtesy of George Verstraete; First Rate Company.)

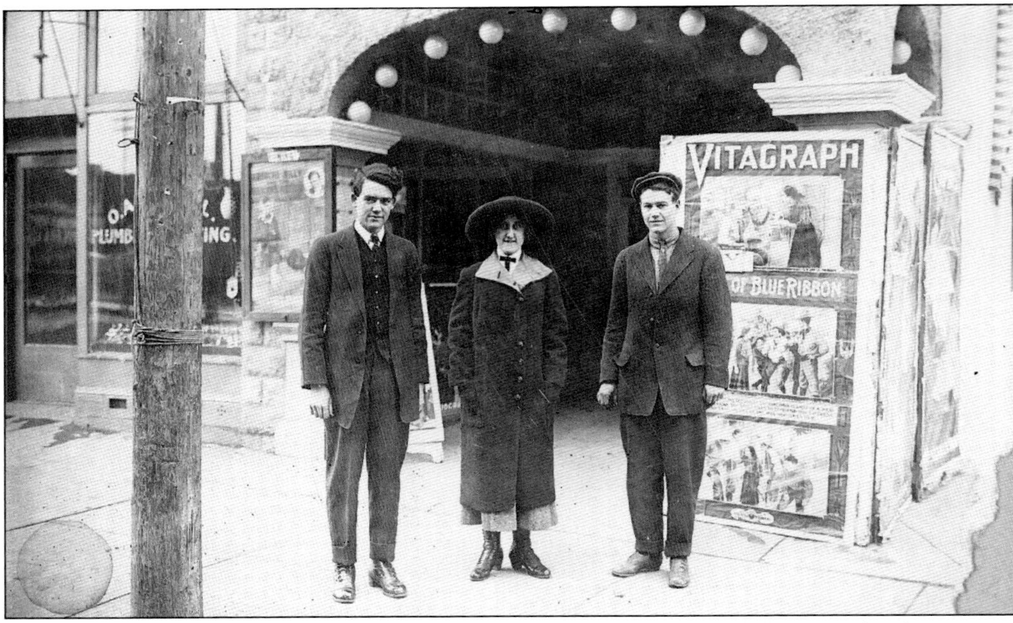

Unfortunately, the commonly used film stock developed by Eastman Kodak was made of nitrate and was extremely flammable, essentially the same chemically as guncotton. This is what probably led the WigWam, pictured here during the winter, to burn to the ground on April 14, 1918, engulfing an entire city block along with it. (Courtesy of the Oklahoma Historical Society.)

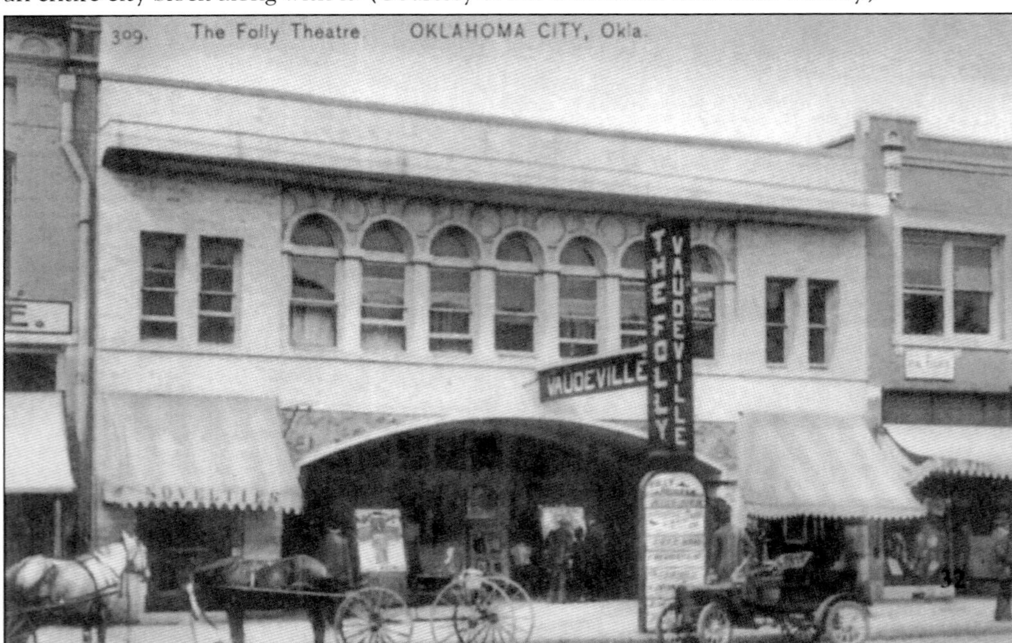

On Sunday, September 20, 1908, the Folly Theatre, pictured here, opened at 125 West Grand Avenue. The theatre experienced at least three fires over the course of 35 years. On October 14, 1947, another fire resulting in $6,000 in damages revealed previous unsafe fire conditions within the structure, forcing building superintendent Walter E. Nelson to condemn the structure. The theatre was demolished that same year. (Courtesy of Doug Loudenback.)

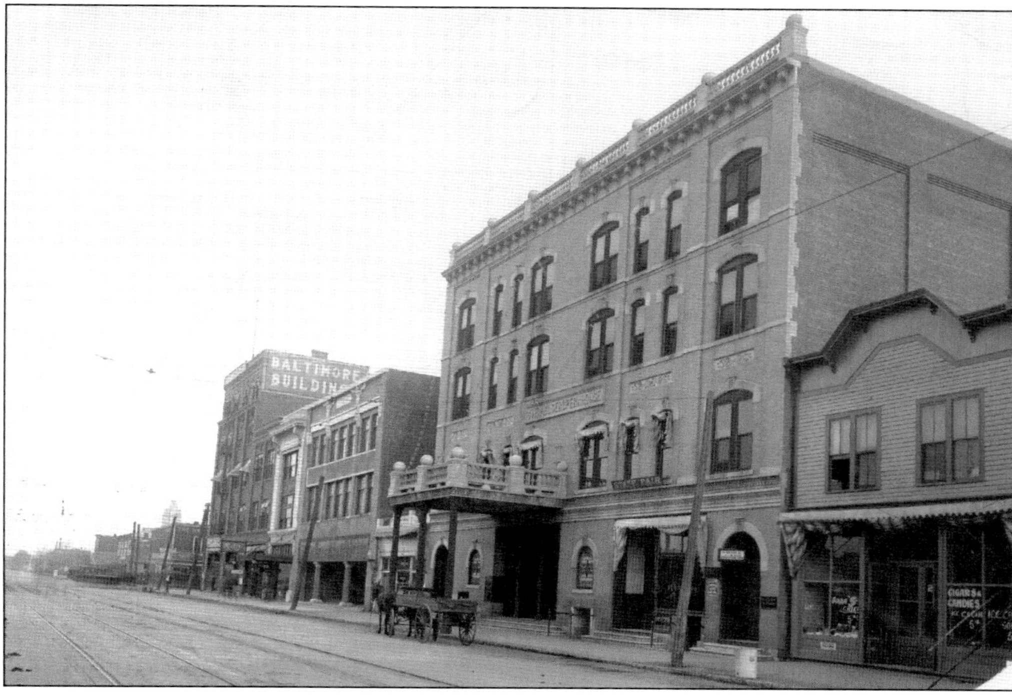

The Overholser Opera House, constructed in 1903 at 217 West Grand Avenue, became one of Oklahoma City's first theatres. The opulent theatre hosted numerous stage and musical performances, including notables such as Sarah Bernhardt and Lillian Russell, until it converted to the Orpheum Theater in 1928 after acquisition by Warner Brothers. (Above, courtesy of the Oklahoma Historical Society; below, courtesy of Doug Loudenback.)

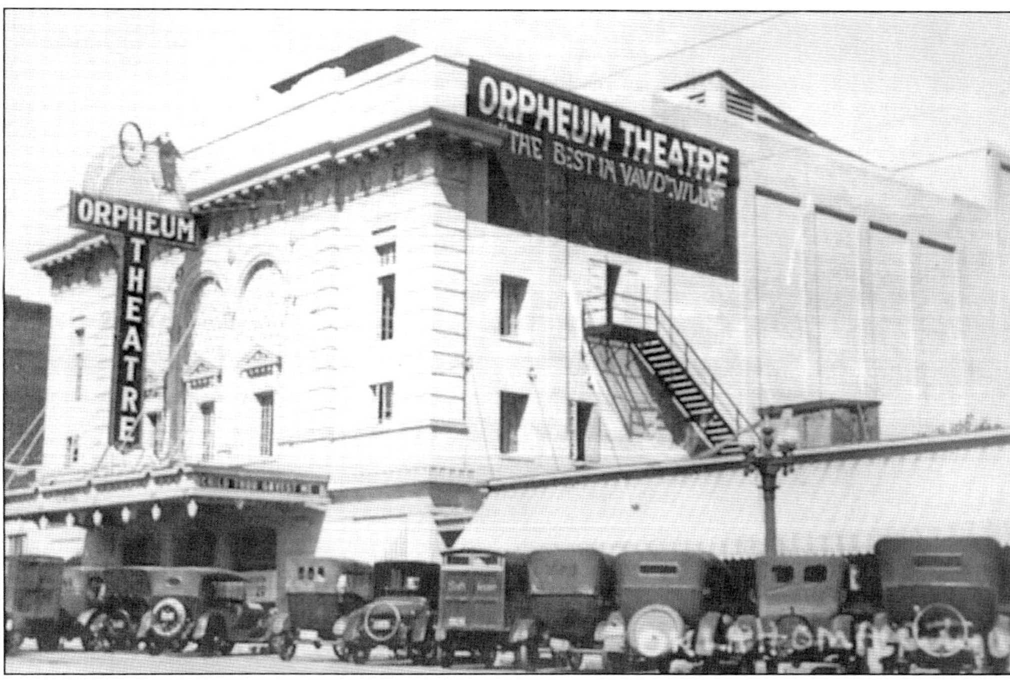

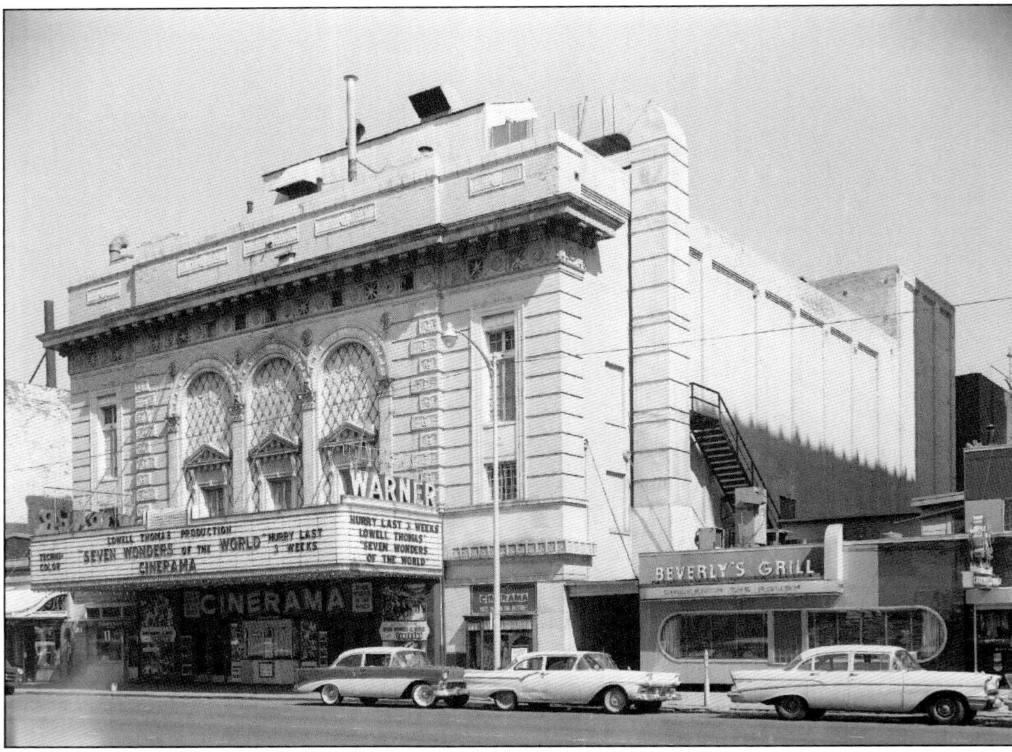

Some time around 1930, the Orpheum Theatre was renamed Warner Theatre, seen above, and became Oklahoma City's only vaudeville and screening house. In its 1931 opening week, the duo of George Burns and Gracie Allen played the Warner along with other acts from an RKO franchise. On Monday, May 21, 1956, Cinerama was introduced to the Warner, a process where three projectors operated simultaneously, showing the motion picture on a curved 60-foot-by-24-foot screen, making the image appear six times larger than normal, as seen below. The opening-night price was $10 per ticket. However, low box office attendance over the next seven months forced theatre owners to remove the Cinerama and resume normal first-run showings in January 1957. The theater closed in 1964 and was integrated into the adjacent Center City parking garage structure. (Both, courtesy of the Oklahoma Historical Society.)

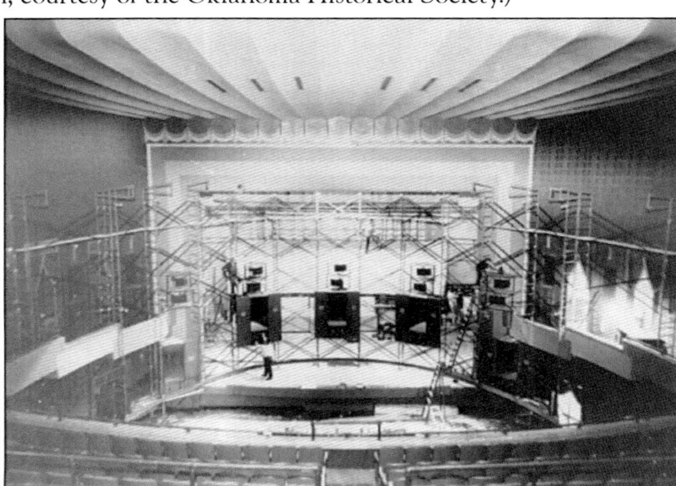

On the 100 block of West Main Street, the former Cooper Theatre was renamed Criterion (right) after the large New York house of the same name in December 1921. The 1,900-seat theater reopened in April after more than half a million dollars in elaborate renovations (below), including massive $25,000 art glass panels, a crystal chandelier, walls of velvet, deep cushioned seats, French doors, a tea room, two orchestra pits, and a massive organ with 3,500 pipes on which the *William Tell Overture* was played on opening night. The theater also introduced silent reels accompanied by live music. The Criterion formed the Dramatic Art Club to promote Oklahoma City talent and was hailed by the *Oklahoman* as "a symphony in brick and stone." The theater published the *Criterion Courier*, a 36-page tabloid available to patrons only. The magazine was extensively decorated with half-tones, engravings, and a full-color cover. In 1954, the theater became the first to break the city's Jim Crow barrier and integrate African Americans among its patrons. The theater operated until 1963 and then briefly again as a burlesque show house until 1967. The Urban Renewal Authority purchased the Criterion in May 1972 and razed it in February 1973. (Both, courtesy of the Oklahoma Historical Society.)

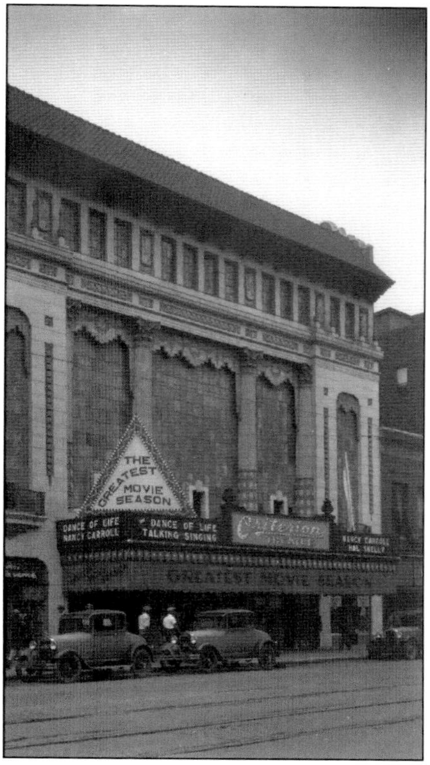

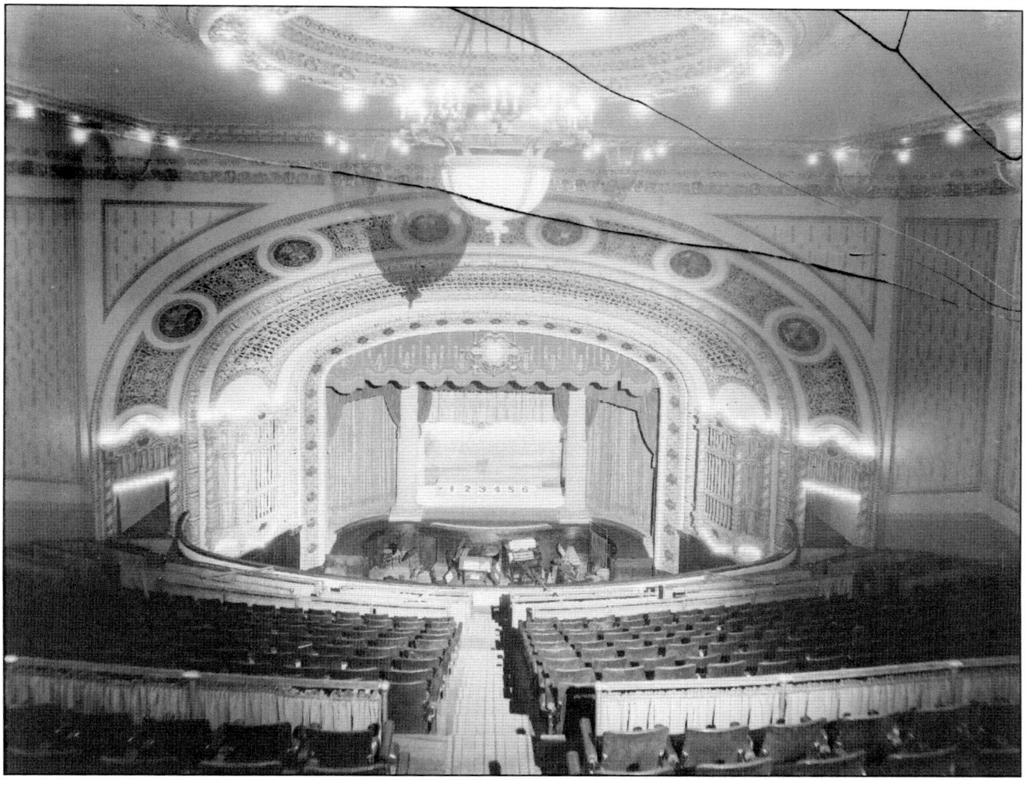

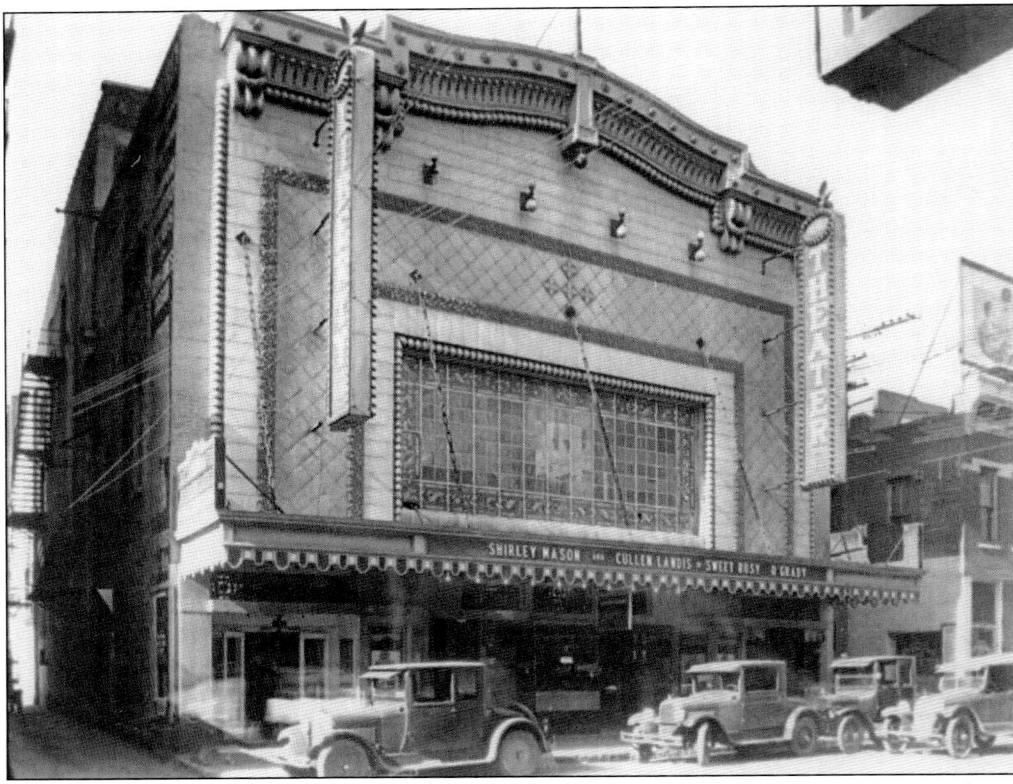

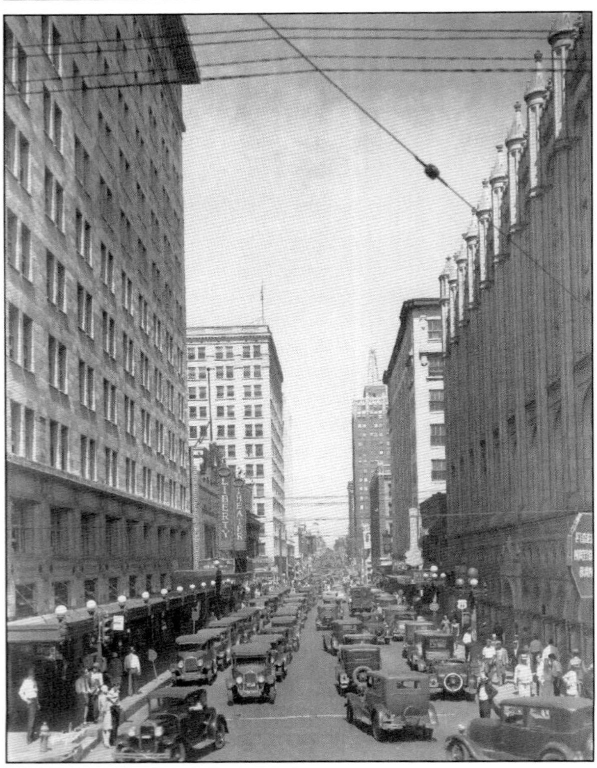

The Liberty Theater (above and left) opened in 1915 at 19 North Robinson Avenue and featured both stage and screen performances. In 1916, the theater was plagued with a bitter stagehands strike, and in 1918, its orchestra walked out. The theater was managed by Warner for many years until a four-year legal battle over lease and purchase rights ended in 1950 and it was sold to the Cooper Foundation, which also owned the Criterion Theatre. Liberty was renamed Harber and in April 1959 was renovated and renamed Cooper Theater. It featured a wall-to-wall Cinemiracle screen arrangement. The theater was closed in 1975 and acquired by the Urban Renewal Authority. (Above, courtesy of Doug Loudenback; left, courtesy of the Oklahoma Historical Society.)

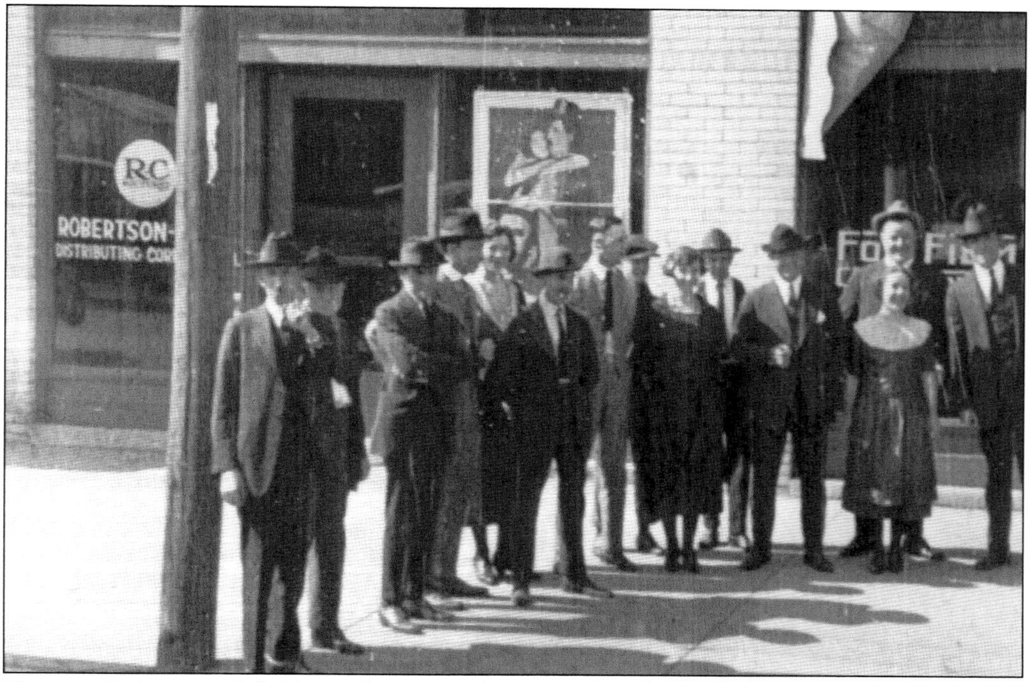

Here, the Robertson-Cole film exchange, an American distributor of silent British films, occupies 7–15 South Walker Avenue in 1921. Robertson-Cole remained here from 1920 to 1922, when a corporate reorganization changed the name to Film Booking Offices of America (FBO). The FBO film exchange then relocated to 127 South Hudson Avenue. The building in this image stood on the corner of Walker and Grand Avenues. It was razed by the Urban Renewal Authority on February 1, 1973. (Courtesy of Robert Allison via RetroMetroOKC.org.)

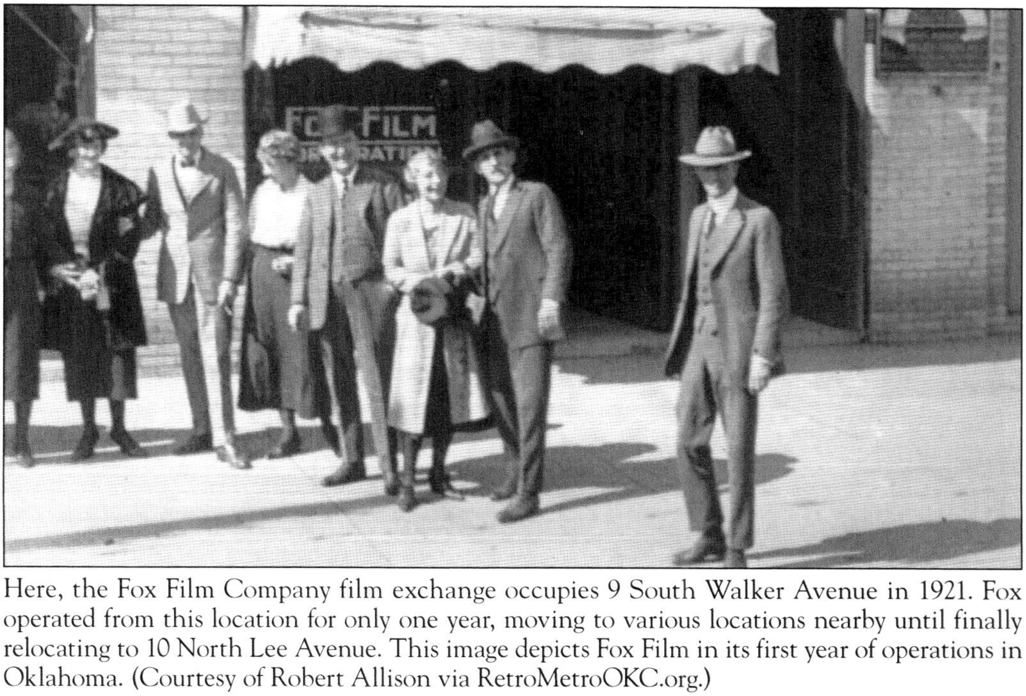

Here, the Fox Film Company film exchange occupies 9 South Walker Avenue in 1921. Fox operated from this location for only one year, moving to various locations nearby until finally relocating to 10 North Lee Avenue. This image depicts Fox Film in its first year of operations in Oklahoma. (Courtesy of Robert Allison via RetroMetroOKC.org.)

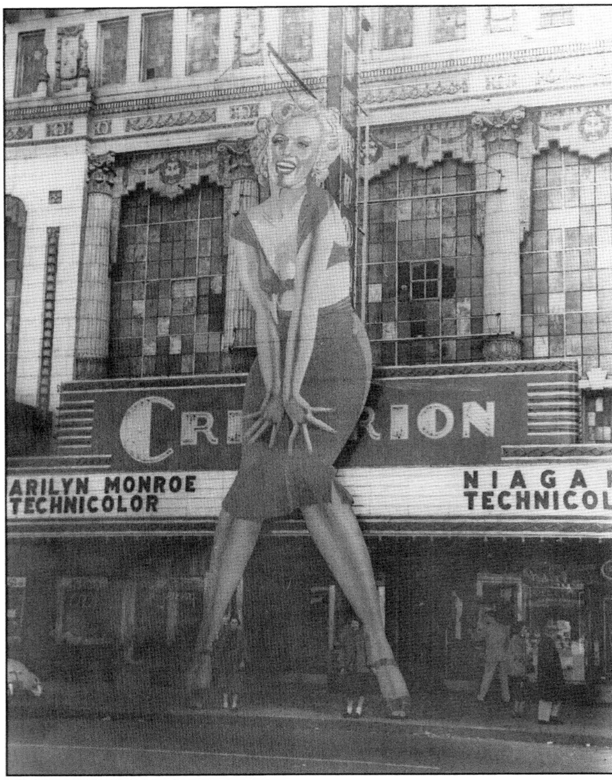

On February 17, 1953, the image at left captured a three-story Marilyn Monroe display promoting her film *Niagara* along the front facade of the Criterion Theatre on the 100 block of West Main Street. Below, Anthony Quinn stands in front of the Midwest Theater at 16 North Harvey Avenue on July 15, 1947, preparing for the premiere of *Black Gold* by Allied Artists. The film centers on an Oklahoma racehorse named Black Gold that won the 1924 Kentucky Derby. Gov. Roy Turner was instrumental in bringing the film's premiere to Oklahoma City. Two other stars were present at the event. Elyse Knox and Katherine Demille, Quinn's leading ladies, were also present. (Left, courtesy of Doug Loudenback; below, courtesy of the Oklahoma Historical Society.)

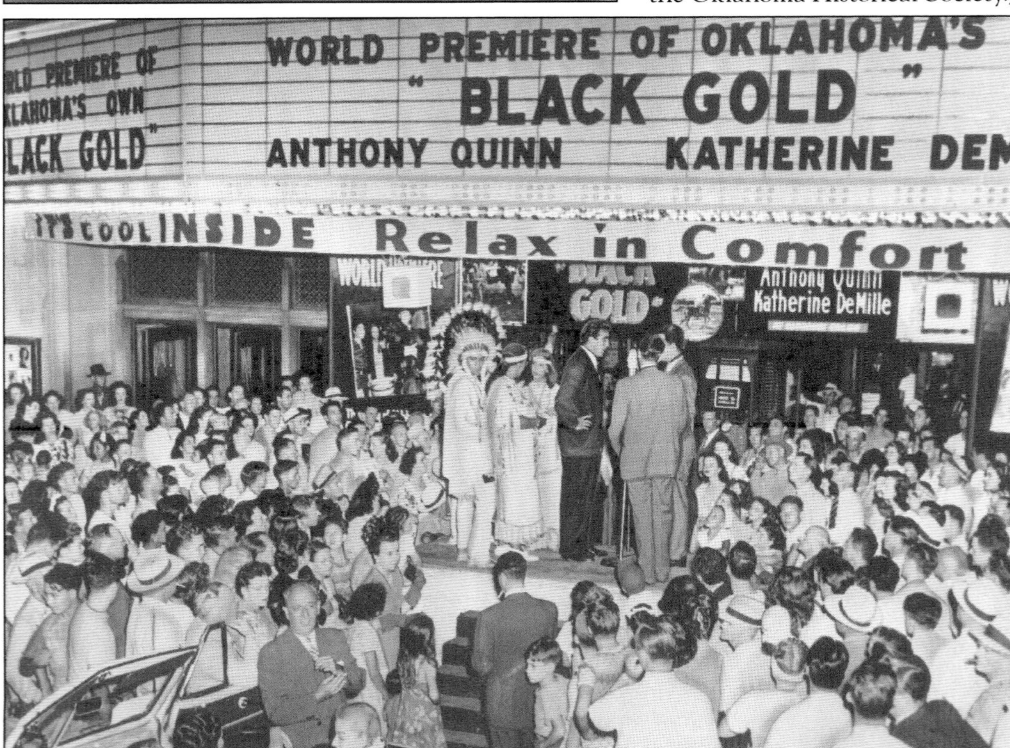

Two

Birth by Fire

As film exchanges sprang up across the cityscape, so too did an inherent and deadly threat. Filmmakers shot their films on a transparent flexible plasticized cellulose nitrate film base. A known drawback was that it was extremely flammable, with the nitrate being similar chemically to guncotton. Nitrate stock remained in use until around 1952.

Projection booth fires were most common at the beginning of the century, when film was exposed to heat passing through the gate. Nitrate film contained oxygen, feeding the flames and consuming the room quickly. Such fires were impossible to extinguish in time. These types of incidents resulted in fires where audiences were killed by smoke, flames, or resulting stampedes.

Film exchanges were also vulnerable. On Monday, February 11, 1929, thousands of feet of stored film ignited in a storeroom at the Mid-West Film Exchange at 119 South Hudson Avenue, resulting in more than $100,000 in damages. As soon as the blaze erupted, staff from the adjacent Tiffany-Stahl and Warner Brothers film exchanges immediately crated their stock in fireproof shipping containers.

On Saturday, August 12, 1933, a series of violent explosions at Allied Film Exchange's 704 West Grand Avenue offices damaged three other buildings and gutted the exchange. Four thousand rolls of film ignited and blew out the front windows, and a second blast tore through the rear walls. Flames flung across the street ignited a three-story building at 10 South Lee Avenue. Damage also occurred to the Majestic Pictures Film Exchange at 706 and Columbia Pictures at 702 West Grand Avenue. Fourteen fire trucks arrived with their crews to stifle the blaze. Less than three years later, another fire broke out in Allied's offices due to smoldering film.

Realizing the inherent threat exchanges posed early on to the large number of timber-constructed buildings, city leaders passed stringent building codes for fireproof buildings and film vaults by emergency resolution on September 22, 1920. The first consolidated film exchange building constructed under the new codes was the Vitagraph at 123 South Hudson Avenue, which opened on December 22, 1920, and housed approximately 15 film exchanges. A second and larger exchange was constructed at 523 South Robinson Avenue in 1926, but demand for larger spaces and migration to the 600–700 blocks of West Grand Avenue resulted in a third and final exchange at 700 West Grand Avenue later that same year. Patrons and personnel affectionately dubbed the grouping of exchanges and ancillary businesses along Grand Avenue "Film Row."

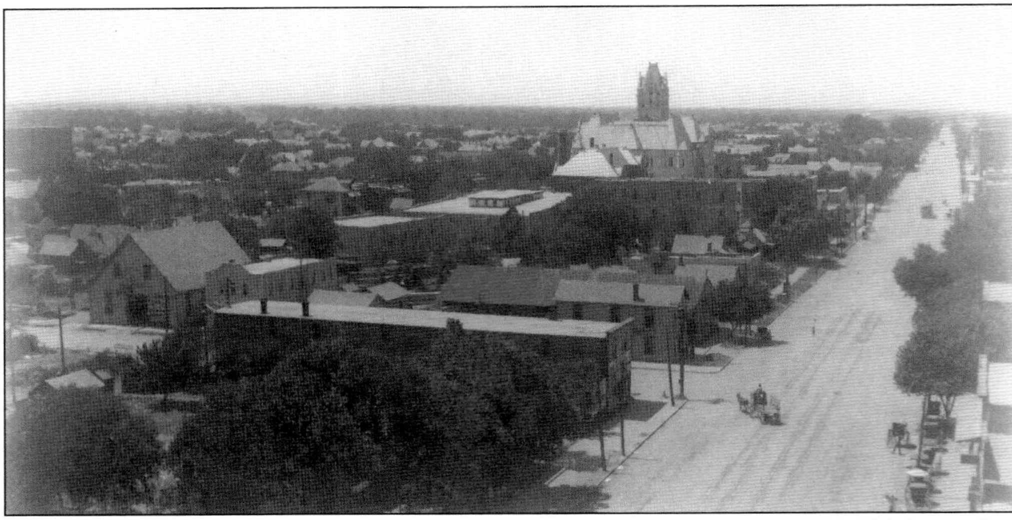

This early view looks to the southwest from Hudson Avenue and Main Street in Oklahoma City. The tower-like structure is the old Oklahoma County Courthouse. Beyond the courthouse, the street running from east to west is Grand Avenue, the future home of Film Row. This area was on the very outskirts of the city, where stored flammable film stock would not jeopardize the tightly clustered buildings of downtown. (Courtesy of Robert Allison via RetroMetroOKC.org.)

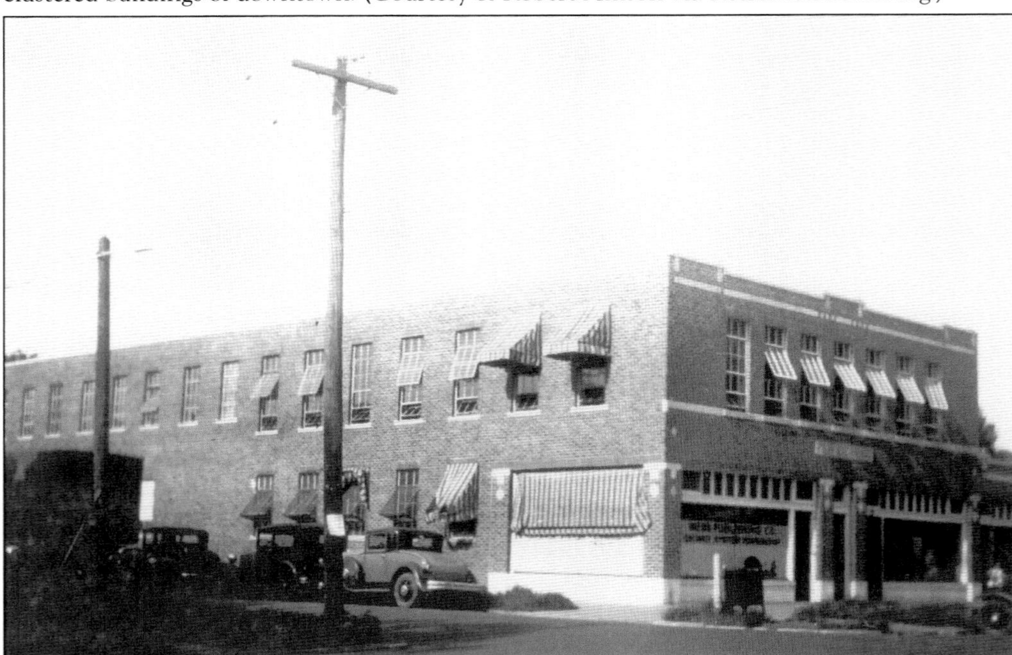

This is the earliest known image of the Film Exchange building constructed at 700 West Grand Avenue in 1926. In 1927, the Liberty Specialty Film Distributing Corporation, the first exchange on Film Row, moved into the building. This was followed by approximately 16 others over the next five years, one being Columbia Pictures, which would remain for 42 years in the 702 West Grand Avenue space. The second door from the left corner of the building would eventually lead to a second-floor screening room. In this image, the building housed the Webb Publishing Company for a short time. (Courtesy of George Verstraete; First Rate Company.)

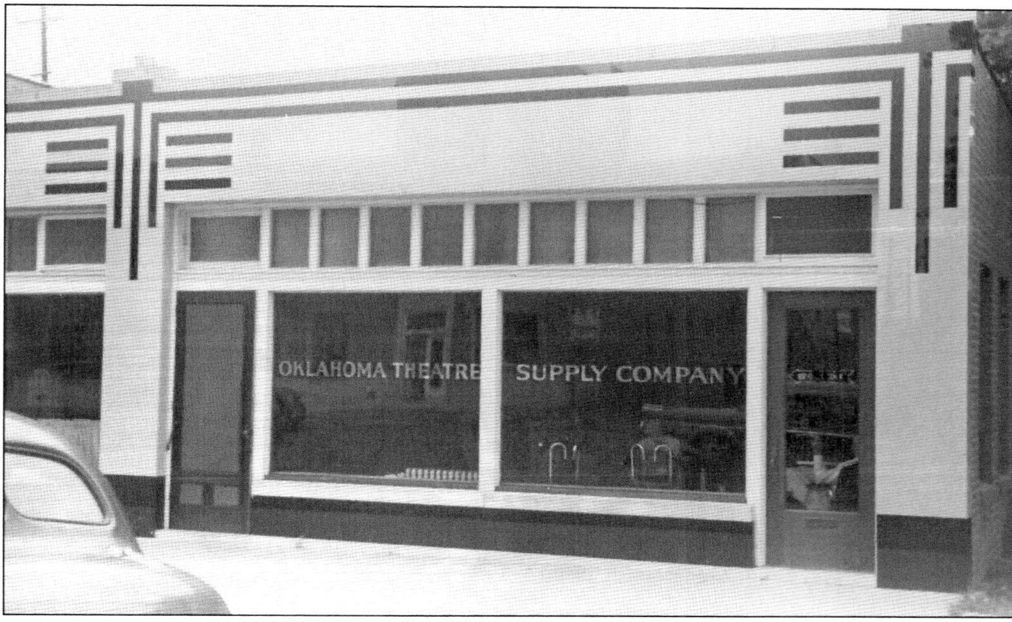

In 1936, the Oklahoma Theatre Supply Company, owned by J. Eldon and Maxine Peek, operated from the 708 West Grand Avenue space of the Film Exchange building. The company offered everything a projection room or theatre would need, including concession equipment and ancillary items. The Theatre Supply stayed in 708 West Grand Avenue until it relocated to 628 West Grand Avenue in 1946. (Courtesy of the J. Eldon and Maxine Peek Estate.)

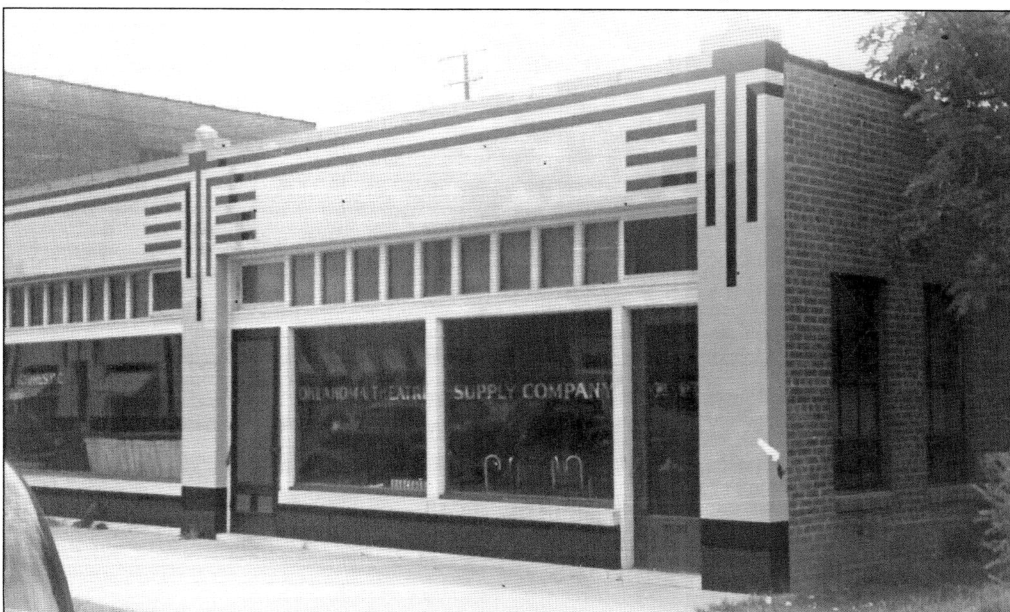

In this early image showing a different angle of the Oklahoma Theatre Supply Company at West Grand Avenue, the Radio Keith Orpheum Distributing Corporation (RKO Pictures) offices can be seen next door on West Grand Avenue. The RKO Pictures film exchange operated from this space until 1950. Multiple other exchanges operated in the space afterwards. (Courtesy of the J. Eldon and Maxine Peek Estate.)

HARMON CONSTRUCTION COMPANY

GENERAL CONTRACTORS

PHONE 3-5511
P. O. BOX 1414

OKLAHOMA CITY, OKLAHOMA

February 3, 1936

Herskowitz Estate,
c/o Mr. P. H. Weathers, Architect,
512 Herskowitz Building,
Oklahoma City, Oklahoma.

Gentlemen:

We hereby propose to furnish all labor and materials necessary to erect and complete the newly proposed building for Vitagraph, Incorporated, to be located at the southeast corner of West Grand and South Lee Streets, on Lots 15 and 16, Block 7, Main Street Addition, Oklahoma City, Oklahoma, as per plans, specifications and addendum as prepared by Mr. P. H. Weathers, Architect, Oklahoma City, Oklahoma, for the sum of:

Thirty five thousand eight hund eighty seven—DOLLARS ($35,887.00).

ALTERNATE NO. 1: For the omission of the air conditioning tower, including the footings, slab, structural steel, etc., and replacing of the solid slab with bar joists and high rib slab as specified for balance of roof, the above to make ~~an addition or~~ deduction of

DOLLARS ($524.00).

ALTERNATE NO. 2: For the omission of Venetian Blinds as specified, deduct from the base bid the sum of:

DOLLARS ($231.00).

ALTERNATE NO. 3: For using refrigerated air conditioning in lieu of the washed air system as originally specified, this alternate includes the omission of the air conditioning room as deducted in Alternate #1, the addition of approximately sixteen (16) feet of pipe tunnel, enlarging exterior wall opening to the basement, ~~add or~~ deduct the sum of: This alternate based on proposition submitted by the Renz Engineering Company:

DOLLARS ($411.00).

Note: We have figured Venetian Blinds on all openings on North Elevation, two (2) openings on East Elevation, two (2) openings on West Elevation.

Respectfully submitted,

Harmon Construction Company

By Allan Harmon

AH;s

The Harmon Construction letter above, dated February 3, 1936, proposes to the Herskowitz estate, in care of Patrick Henry Weathers, the construction of a new Vitagraph Pictures Film Exchange office at 630 West Grand Avenue for the sum of $35,887. The new exchange would have air-conditioning, an addition that may have been included to protect the stored film stocks. Patrick Henry Weathers was a prominent architect who specialized in courthouses and schools across the nation. (Courtesy of Robert Mulzet.)

R K O DISTRIBUTING CORPORATION

706 W. GRAND AVENUE, OKLAHOMA CITY, OKLA.

RKO Radio Pictures

June 29, 1936

Mr. J. O. Rohde
Vitagraph, Inc.,
630 West Grand
Oklahoma City, Oklahoma

Dear Mr. Rohde:

We understand that you are interested in erecting a building to be used as a Motion Picture Exchange Building in Oklahoma City. This company is now considering proposals for leasing a building of this nature to be used as Exchange quarters in this city.

We will require approximately 5,000 square feet of floor space and we are now submitting proposals for such a building to our Home Office for consideration. You are no doubt familiar with the city building code regarding construction of film exchange buildings and such a building must necessarily conform to the building code.

Our particular requirements for such a building would include an adequate heating and washed air cooling system to be installed in the basement provided for the purpose; five film vaults; standard size, to be equipped with racks and such other equipment as provided by the fire regulations; a sprinkler system which we understand must protect film shipping rooms, inspection room, vaults, ~~and poster room~~; adequate toilet facilities, including a ladies lounge; a supply room, approximately 8' x 12'; a separate enclosed office to be used as a private office, approximately 14' x 14'; a separate private office which shall not adjoin the office mentioned above, about 10' x 12'; a railing and booking counter in the general office with provisions for a passage way from the front door of the office to the poster department.

We believe that the items listed above represent the major construction work.

In submitting your proposals, we ask that same be based on a ten year lease period effective from April 1, 1937.

We ask that you advise us if you are insterested in submitting a proposal for this building upon receipt of this letter. At the same time, advise us as to the approximate date that you will be able to submit a definite proposal.

Yours very truly

RBW:L

R. B. Williams, Branch Manager

On June 29, 1936, branch manager R.B. Williams of Radio Keith Orpheum Distributing Corporation (RKO Pictures) sent the above letter to J.O. Rohde about leasing the soon-to-be-built Vitagraph exchange building at 630 West Grand Avenue. Specific requests of the building included 5,000 square feet of floor space, five film vaults, and film shipping rooms. (Courtesy of Robert Mulzet.)

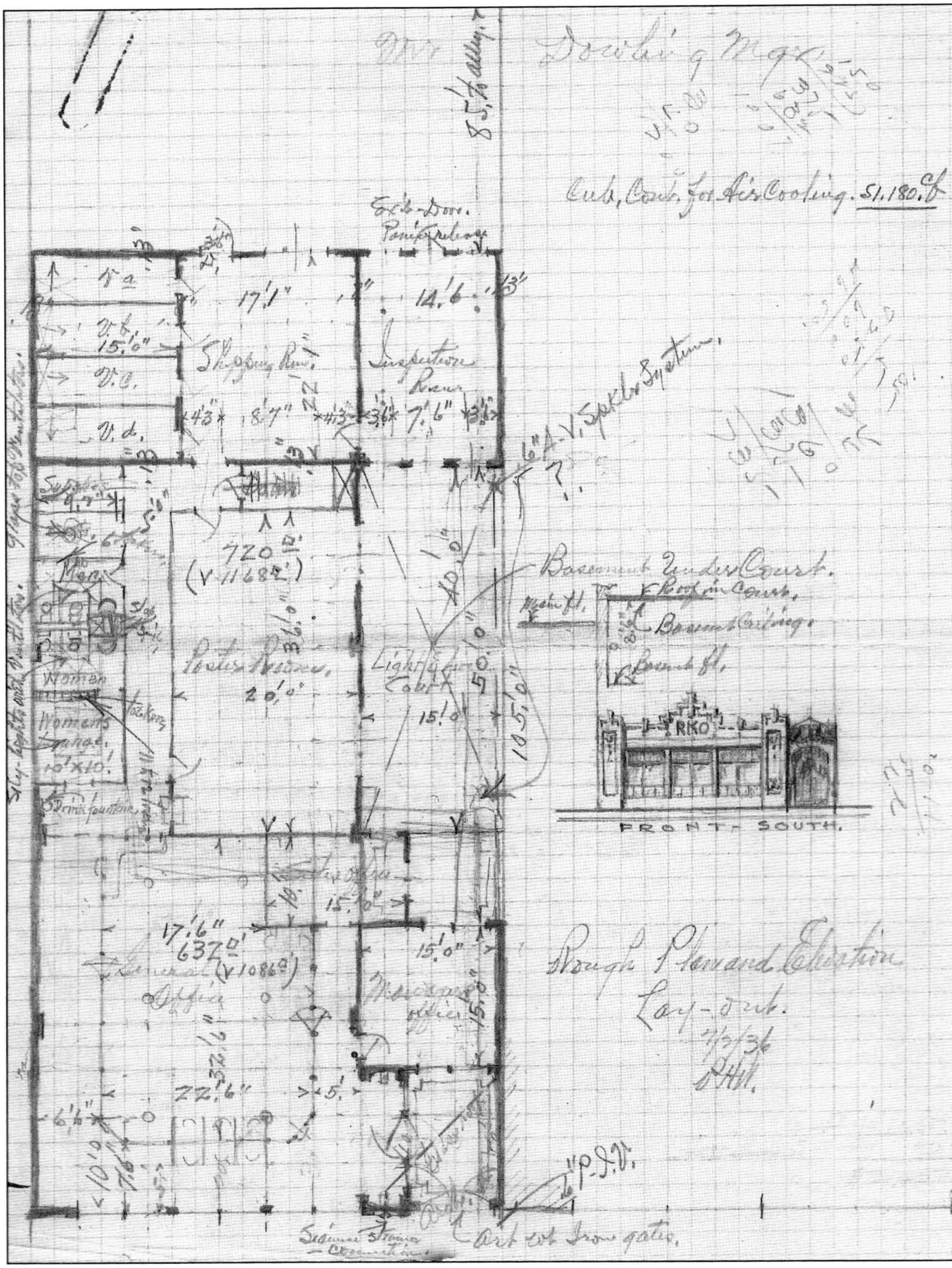

On July 3, 1936, prominent architect Patrick Henry Weathers sketched the layout and facade envisioned for the 630 West Grand Avenue film exchange building. Included in the sketch are film vaults, a ladies' lounge, general office space, a poster room, and basement dimensions. The sketch P.H. Weathers provided of the facade was both dramatic and artistic, a signature of his popular public buildings. (Courtesy of Robert Mulzet.)

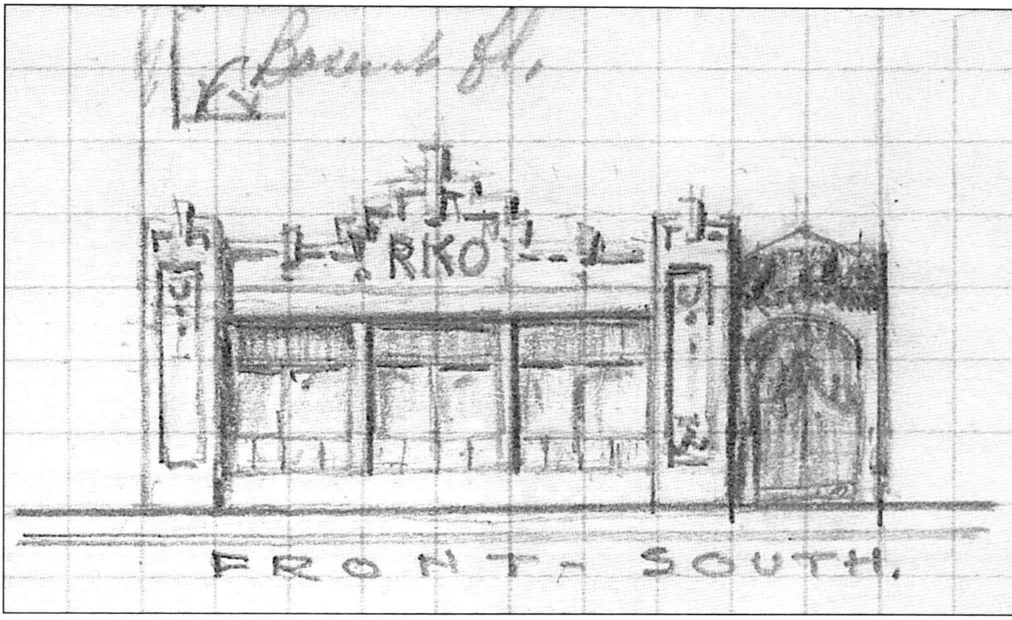

The above image is a close-up of the P.H. Weathers sketch of 630 West Grand Avenue's facade. Below is a 1946 image of the building, nearly 10 years after construction. The building's unique design is the most elaborate and identifiable of all other buildings along Film Row. In this particular image, Warner Brothers Film Exchange occupies the building. It is unclear if RKO ever occupied the building, as Oklahoma City records show the company remained in its 706 West Grand Avenue space from 1930 to 1950. Warner Brothers took possession of 630 West Grand Avenue in 1937 and remained for many years. (Sketch courtesy of Robert Mulzet; photograph courtesy of Warner Brothers Entertainment and the USC Cinematic Arts Library.)

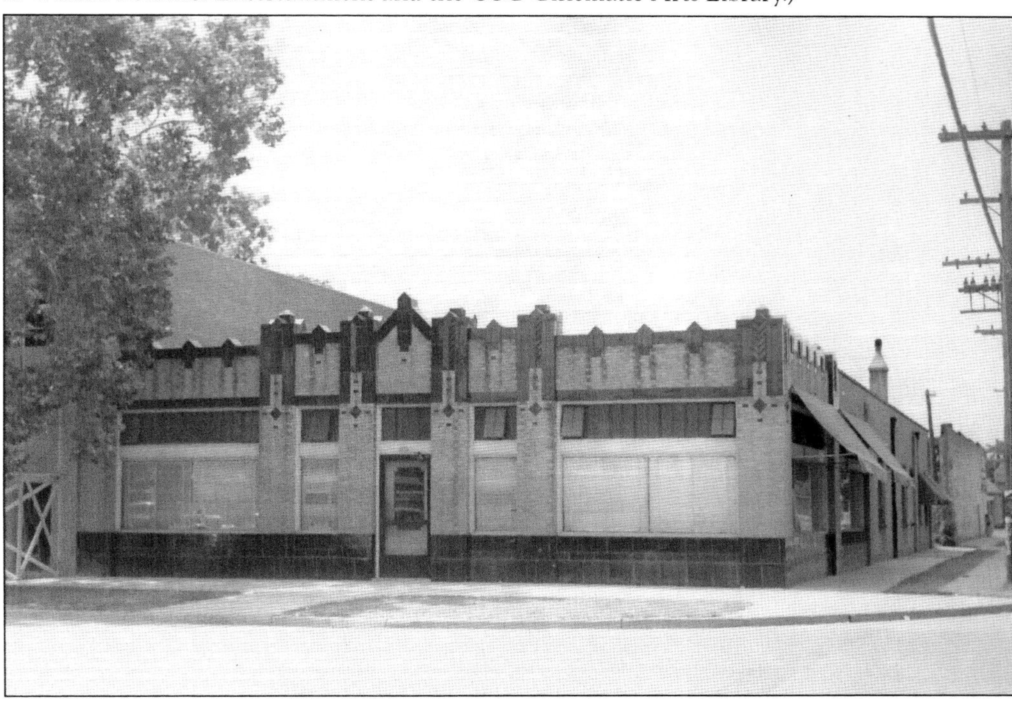

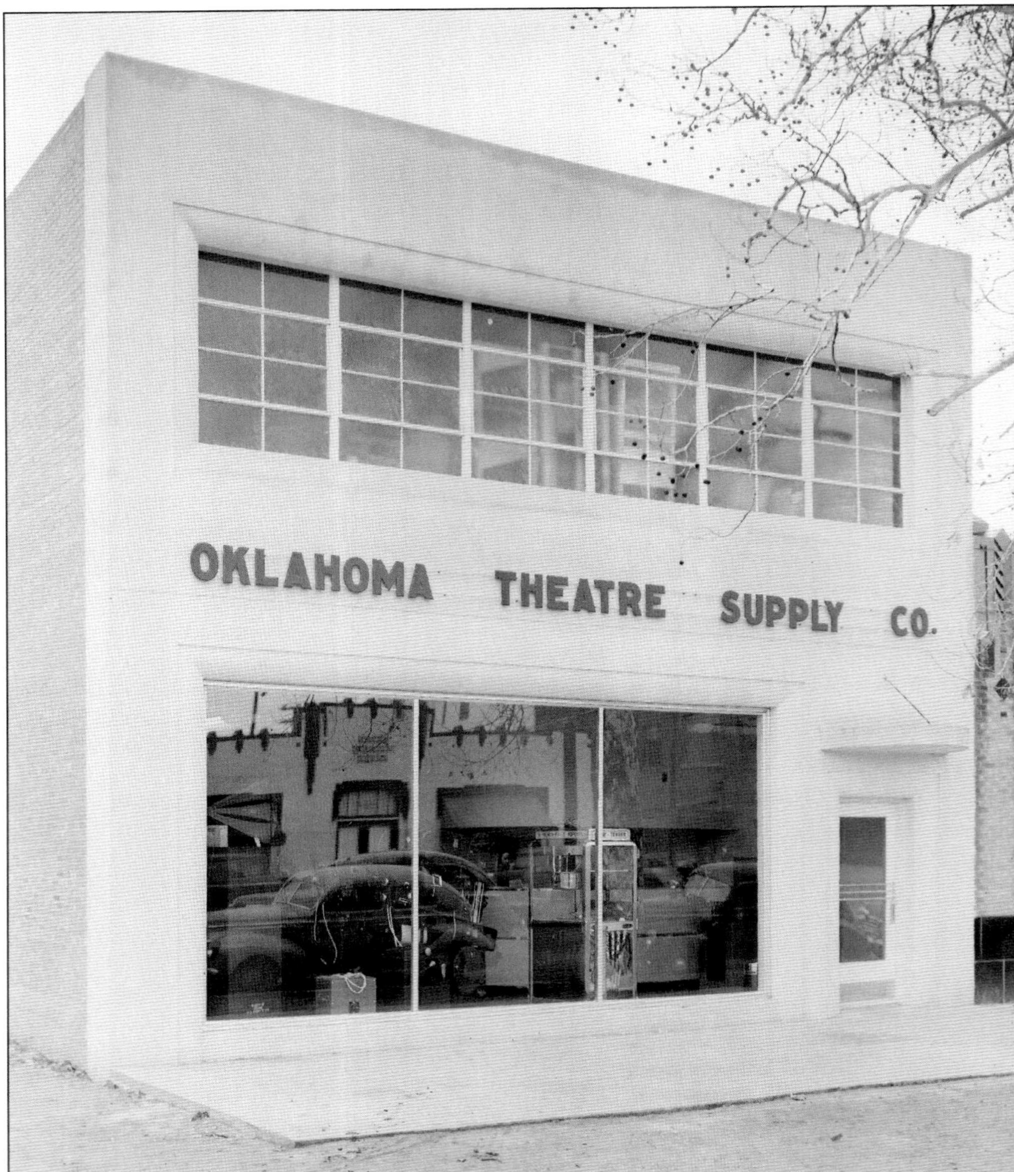

This image is of the Oklahoma Theatre Supply Company shortly after it completed construction at 628 West Grand Avenue in 1946. Owners Maxine and Eldon Peek designed and constructed the new building "as a wedding gift to themselves," as Maxine said. The Oklahoma Theatre Supply was responsible for most of the Midwest's upgrade of silent theatres to sound and installation of drive-in theatre sound systems and speakers. The Peeks were honored at one point with a silver-plated drive-in speaker for the installation of one million speakers and displayed it proudly in their showroom. An arson fire in the adjacent Glass Bar seriously threatened the Oklahoma Theatre Supply Company on Christmas Eve 1988, while firefighters battled the three-alarm blaze. Smoke and water damage was the only casualty for the supply. The company served as the most senior supplier of theatre needs and concession equipment until it closed in 2004. It remained the longest operating company with a direct connection to Film Row in Oklahoma City. (Courtesy of the J. Eldon and Maxine Peek Estate.)

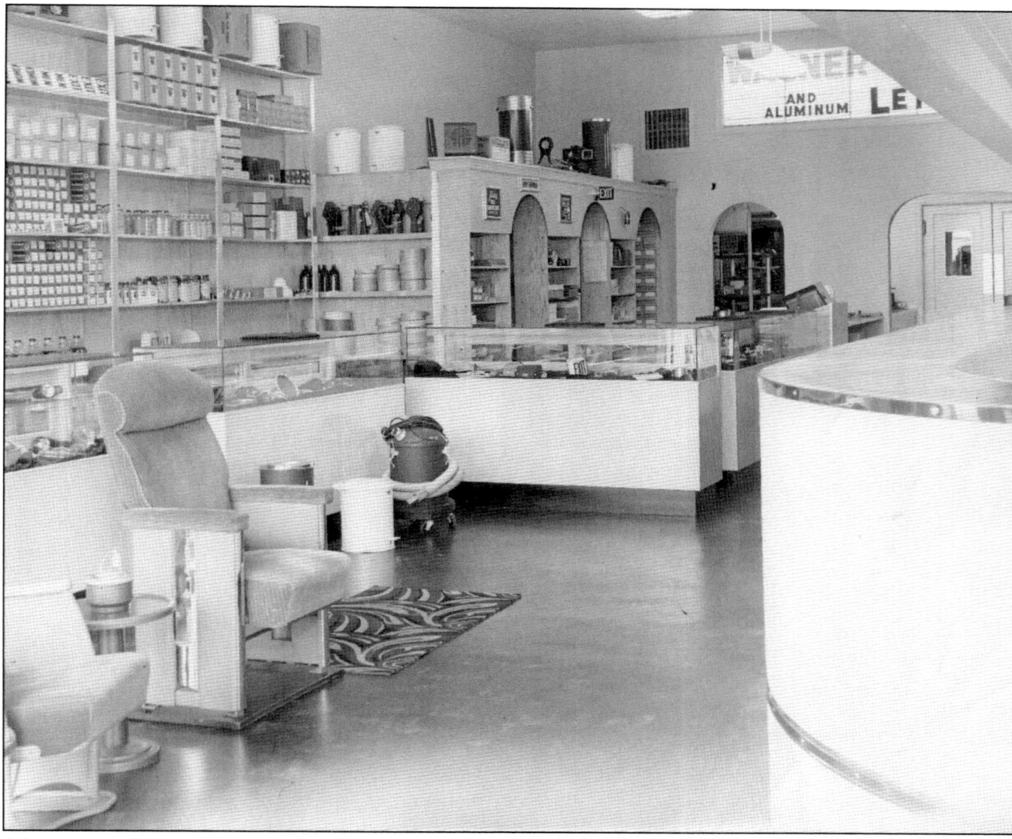

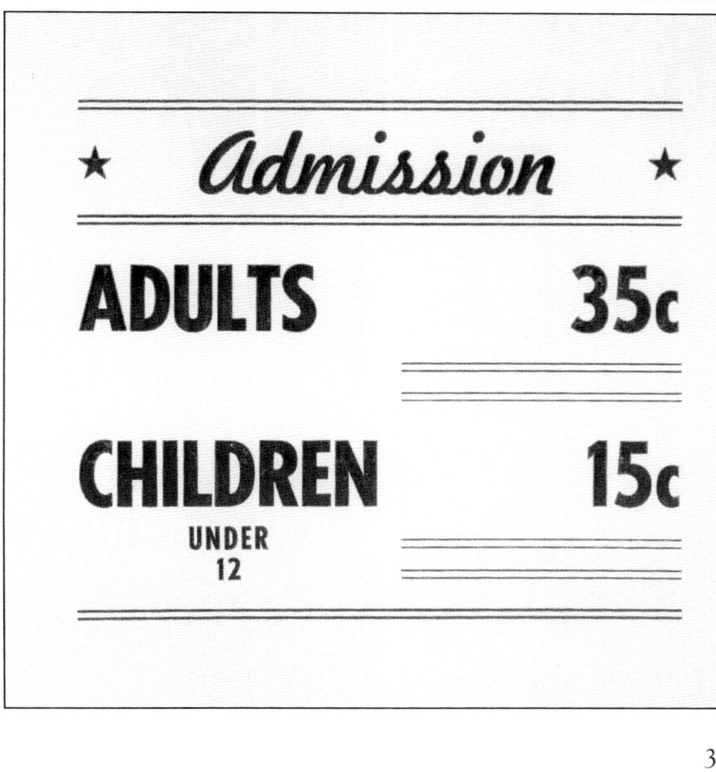

This view of the Oklahoma Theatre Supply Company's showroom at 628 West Grand Avenue is from around 1950. The company provided cases of projector lenses, theatre seating, carpeting, tickets, signage, and more throughout its 74-year history. An example at right shows an admission price sign. Towards 2004, the company resorted to sales of popcorn and ancillary supplies for schools due to theatre supply and economic changes. (Both, courtesy of the J. Eldon and Maxine Peek Estate.)

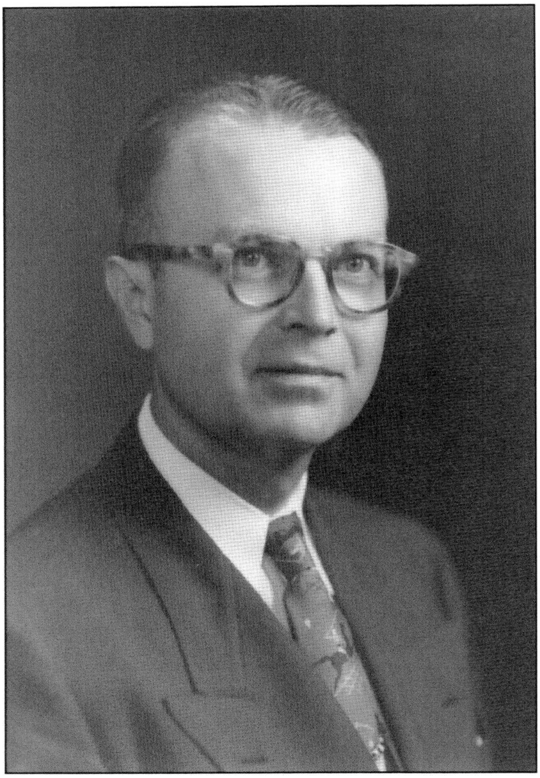

Seen in these c. 1947 images are J. Eldon and Maxine Peek, husband and wife and owners of the Oklahoma Theatre Supply Company. Eldon, an engineering graduate of Oklahoma State University, started the company by installing projectors and concession machines. After his death in March 1988, Maxine continued the business with help from her granddaughter. The Peeks operated the Oklahoma Theatre Supply and the Missouri Theatre Supply Companies from 1930 until Maxine closed in July 2004 at the age of 92 and after 74 years of operation. The Oklahoma Theatre Supply was the last company to close its doors from the bygone era of Film Row. (Both, courtesy of the J. Eldon and Maxine Peek Estate.)

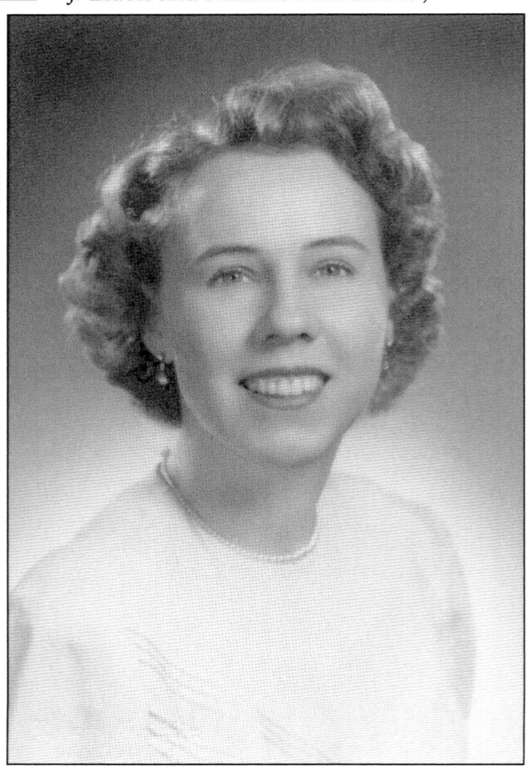

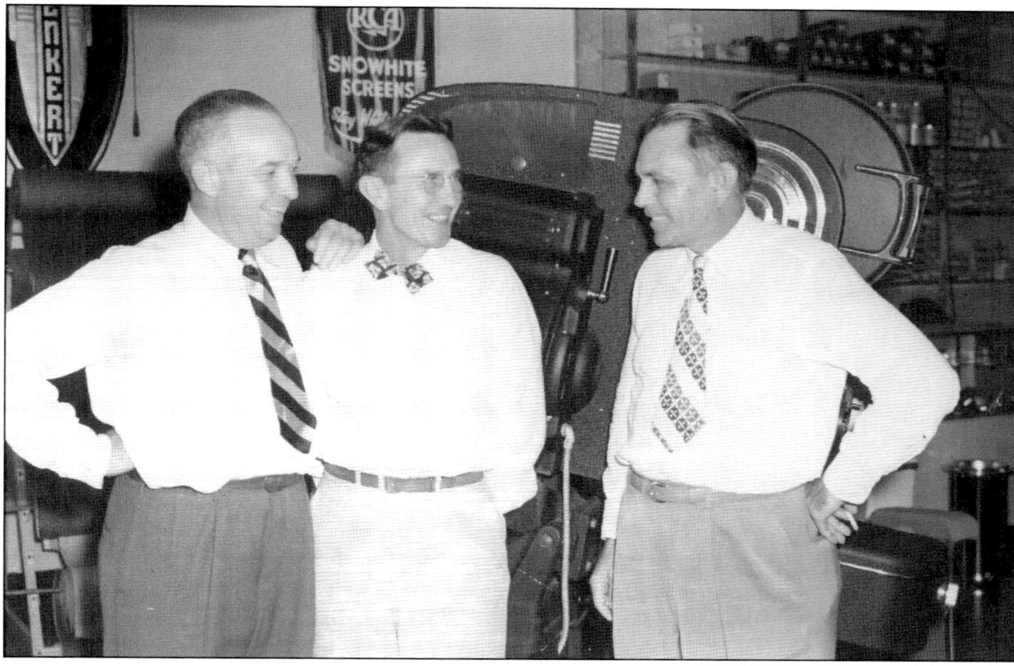

In this c. 1948 image of the Oklahoma Theatre Supply Company showroom at 628 West Grand Avenue, three men stand in front of a projector and are surrounded by cases of projector lenses, boxes of carbon rods, concession equipment, and other ancillary theater needs. Owner Maxine Peek stated that the supply company "kept an entire projector room in stock as we would often replace one every few months or so due to flash fires. Those were exciting times." (Courtesy of the J. Eldon and Maxine Peek Estate.)

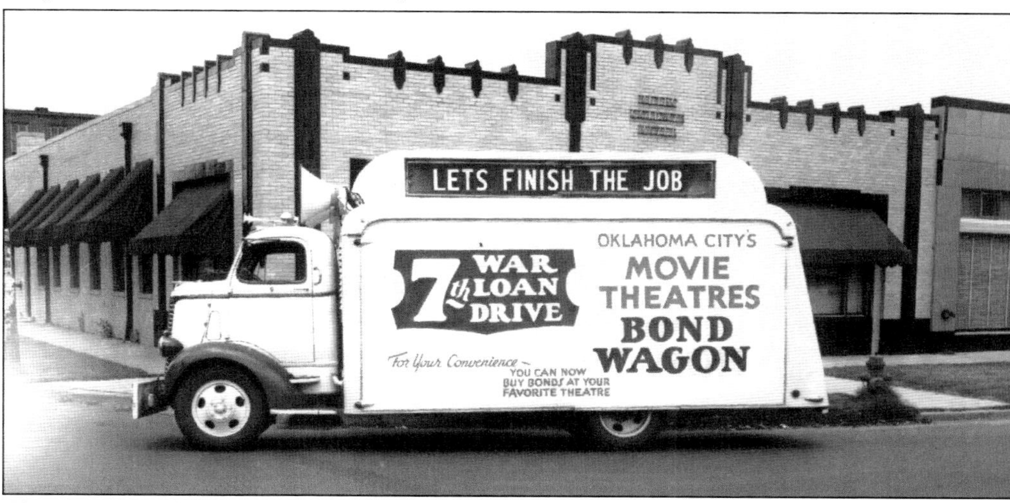

The Metro-Goldwyn-Mayer (MGM) film exchange, built in 1936, sits at 629 West Grand Avenue in this image. On June 29, 1945, this photograph captured a Griffith Theatres marketing truck promoting the purchase of war bonds on the northeast corner of Lee and Grand Avenues. Behind the truck is the MGM building. The name Metro-Goldwyn-Mayer appears in raised metal letters on the facade. This building also housed one of Film Row's four known screening rooms. The design of this building was duplicated in the Film Row of Seattle, Washington, and it still stands today. (Courtesy of the Oklahoma Historical Society.)

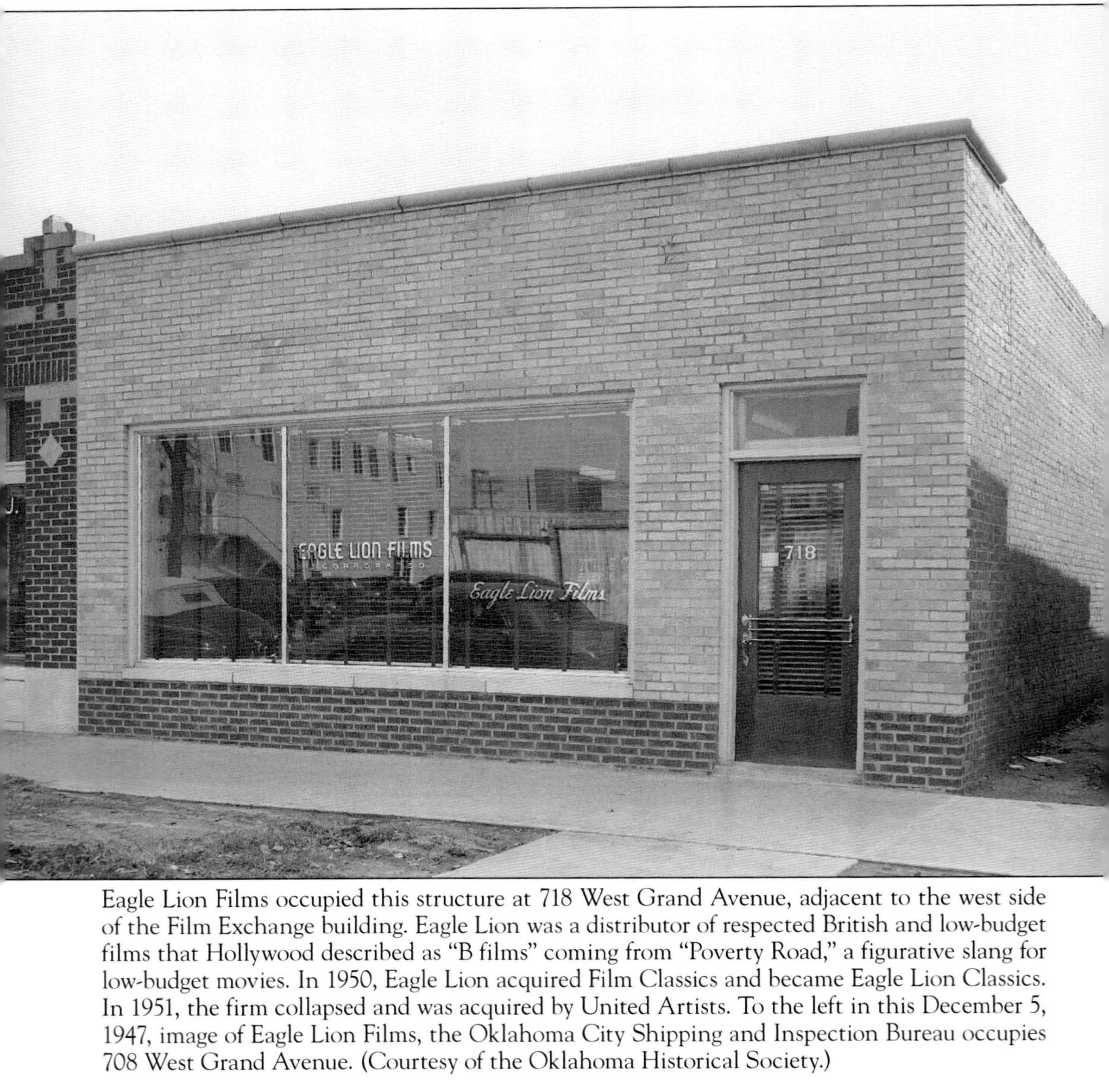

Eagle Lion Films occupied this structure at 718 West Grand Avenue, adjacent to the west side of the Film Exchange building. Eagle Lion was a distributor of respected British and low-budget films that Hollywood described as "B films" coming from "Poverty Road," a figurative slang for low-budget movies. In 1950, Eagle Lion acquired Film Classics and became Eagle Lion Classics. In 1951, the firm collapsed and was acquired by United Artists. To the left in this December 5, 1947, image of Eagle Lion Films, the Oklahoma City Shipping and Inspection Bureau occupies 708 West Grand Avenue. (Courtesy of the Oklahoma Historical Society.)

At right is Eagle Lion Films branch manager C.A. York, of whom very little is known. Below he stands feigning disgust during a gimmick sales marketing campaign. The "crapper award" pictured here was a ruse to garner more theatre ticket sales from June 4 to December 2, 1948. Bill Heineman refers to William J. Heineman, vice president of sales for Eagle Lion Films until its collapse. (Both, courtesy of the Oklahoma Historical Society.)

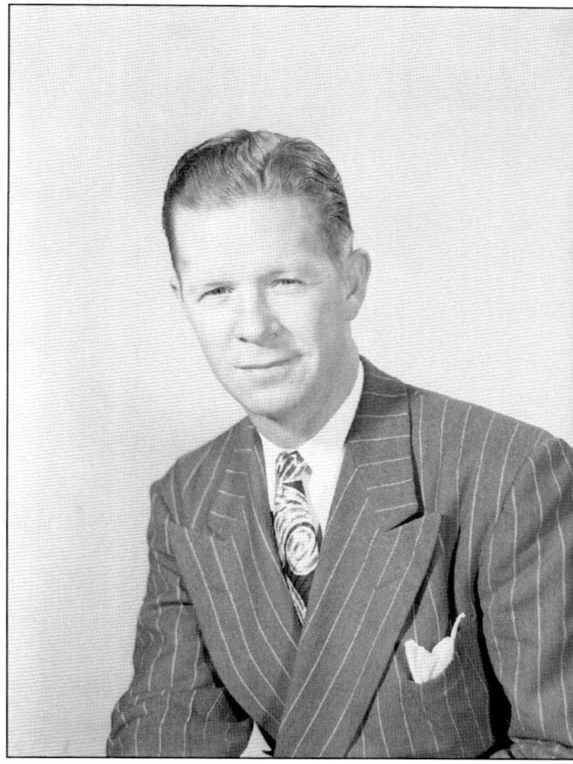

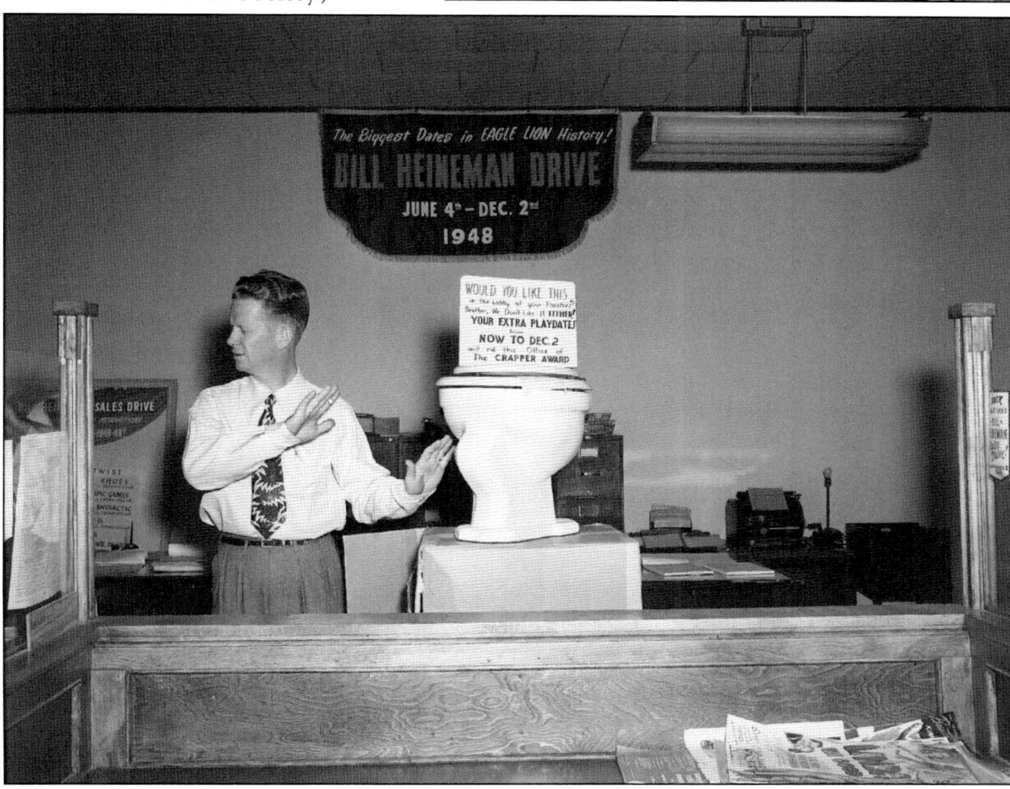

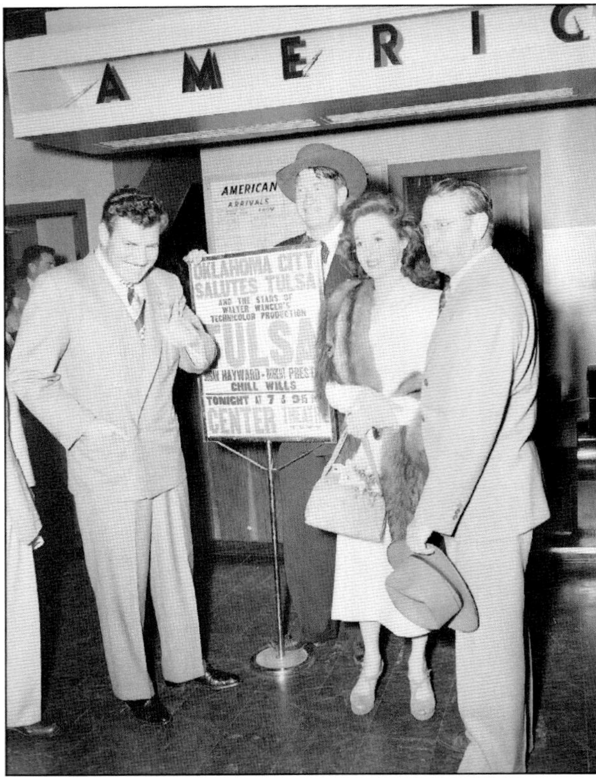

Stars from the Eagle Lion film *Tulsa* gather around a lobby placard about the film in Oklahoma City on Thursday, April 14, 1949. On the right stands actor and *Tulsa* leading man Robert Preston. Comedian and costar Chill Wills is center with lead actress Susan Hayward. The film premiered in Tulsa on Wednesday after a gala parade of oil equipment and the film's stars. The actors arrived in Oklahoma City via airplane Thursday afternoon for the red-carpet downtown gala that evening at Center Theater. The cast, joined by their spouses, await events below. From left to right are Chill Wills (holding his hat); his wife, Hattie Wills; Susan Hayward; Catherine Preston; and her husband, Robert Preston. Hayward's husband and fellow actor Jess Barker stands to the far right. (Both, courtesy of the Oklahoma Historical Society.)

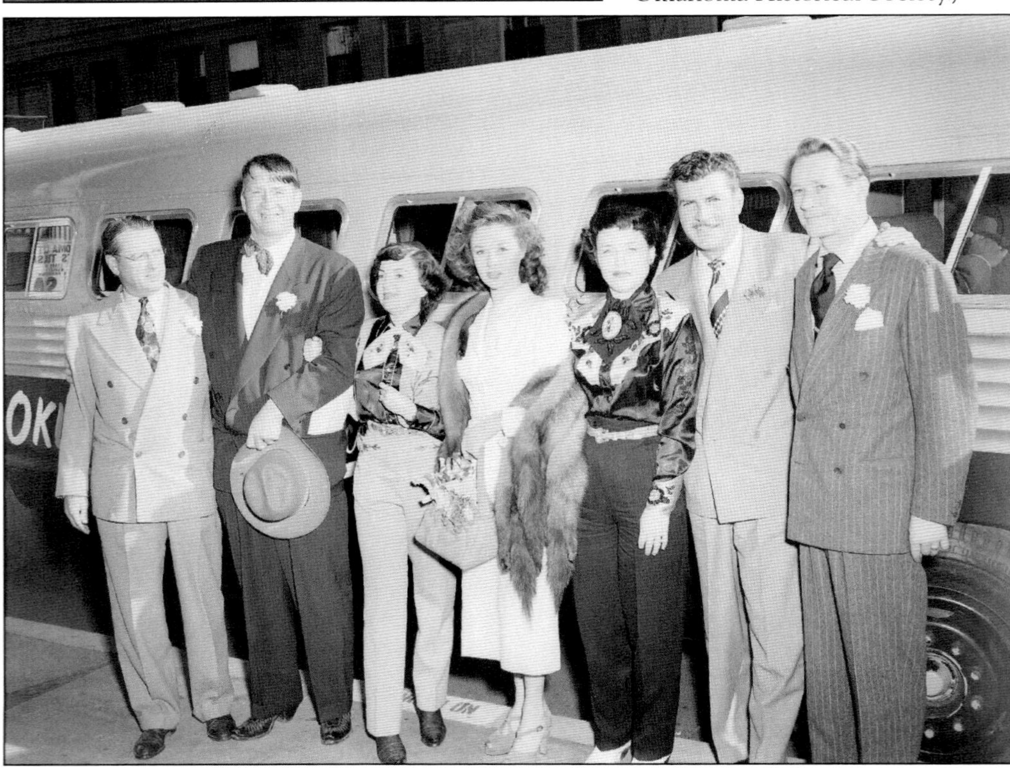

In this April 14, 1949, image, actor Chill Wills poses with majorette Marion Giblet, who led 60 members of the Central Red Skirts drum and bugle corps down a 60-foot red carpet from the Skirvin Tower at 101 Park Avenue past 500 onlookers to the Skirvin Hotel across Broadway Avenue. The *Tulsa* film dignitaries and more than 100 business and social leaders followed. The small parade followed the 9:00 p.m. Centre Theatre Oklahoma City premiere of the film. Unidentified dinner guests enjoy post–*Tulsa* premiere activities in the Skirvin Hotel's Venetian Room below. (Both, courtesy of the Oklahoma Historical Society.)

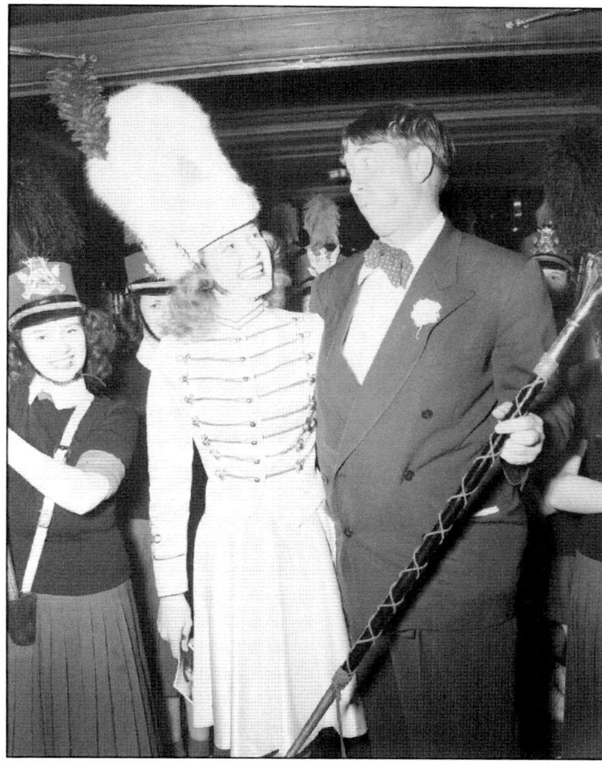

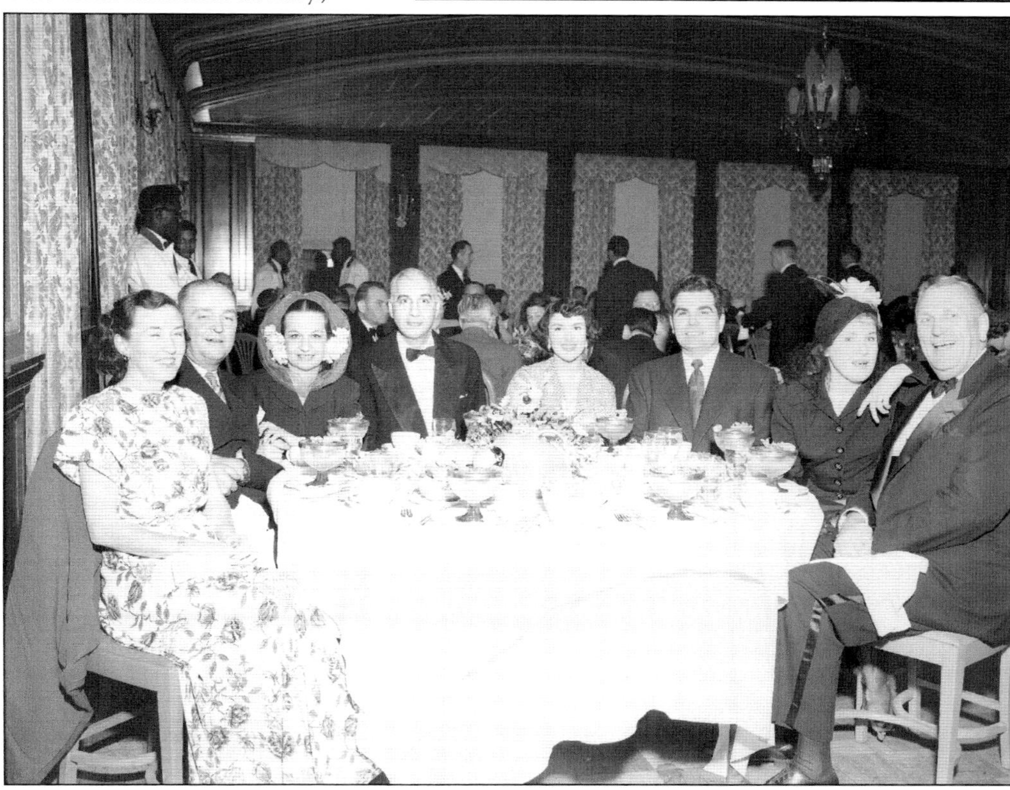

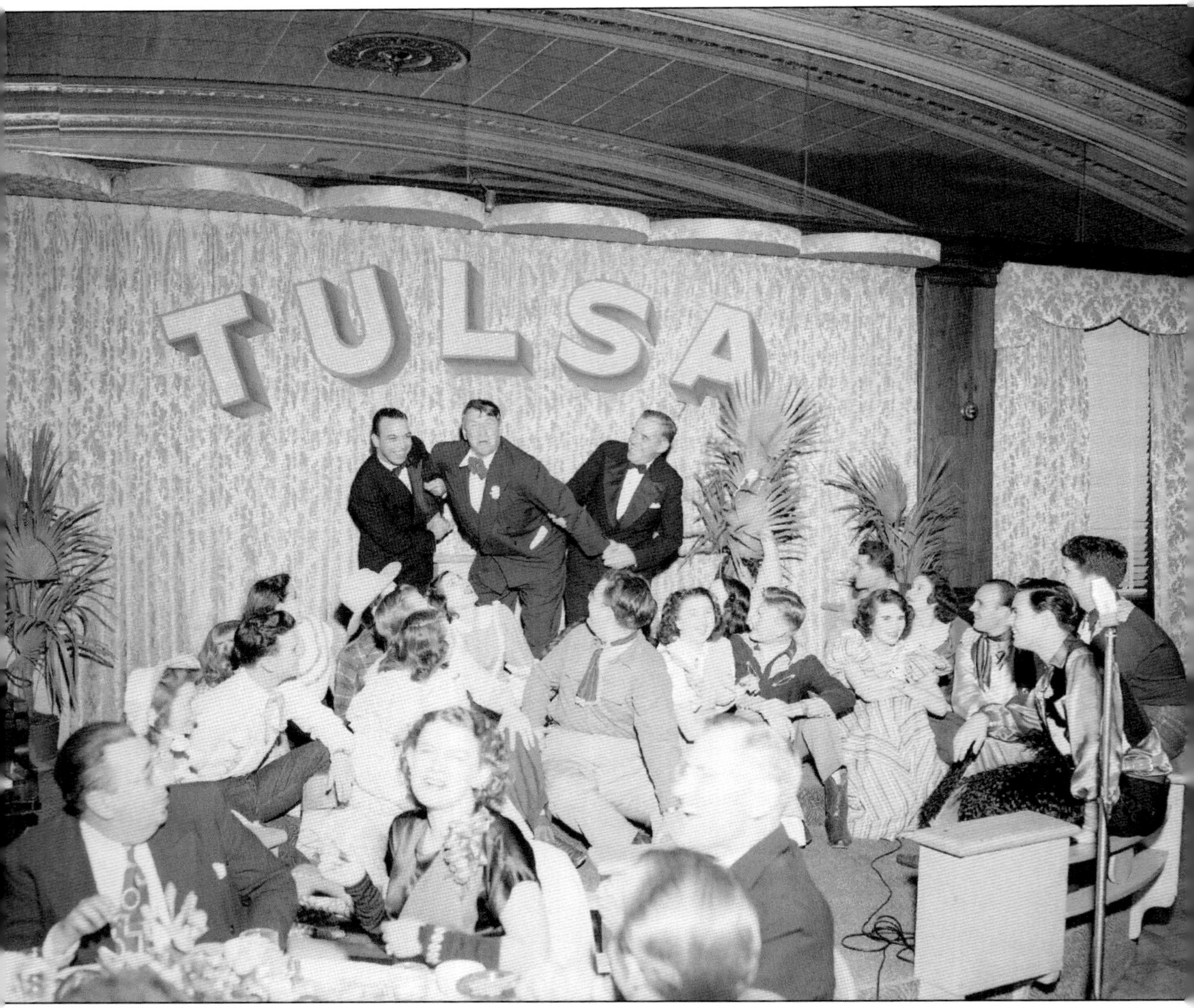

During the post-premiere dinner for *Tulsa* in the Skirvin Hotel's Venetian Room on the evening of April 14, 1949, Chill Wills regaled the audience of his run in with Tulsa, Oklahoma, police on the previous evening. Because Wills was wearing an unpressed suit due to his second being unavailable, Tulsa police officers thought him to be a gatecrasher during premiere activities and tossed him out. According to Wills, he went looking for his wife after stomping around town all day. "I felt like I owned the town. I thought everyone knew me. But when I started down those steps, this officer caught hold of my arm. . . . After a little scuffle he really put one on me—that's when I knew it wasn't a gag. The whole thing kind of caught me with my yard goods down." Wills swung his arm and declared during the Oklahoma City dinner that he hoped "they don't twist my arm here, too!" The name of the film appears behind him. (Courtesy of the Oklahoma Historical Society.)

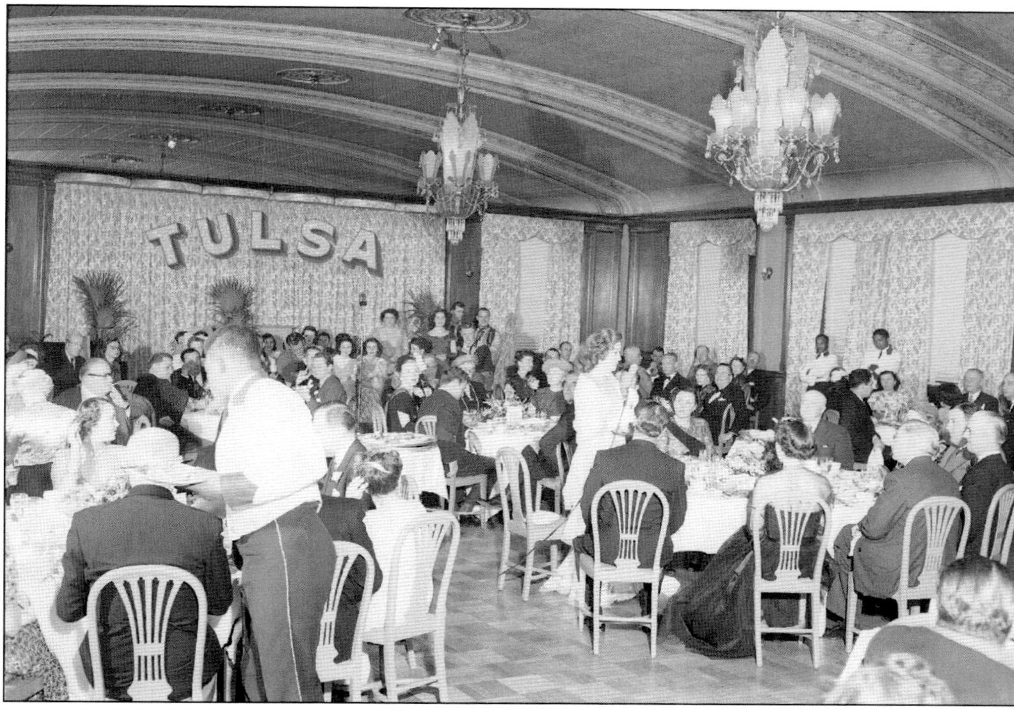

In the April 14, 1949, image above, starlet Susan Hayward stands with a microphone between costar Chill Wills, Oklahoma governor Roy Turner, and wife Jessica Turner. Hayward probably speaks of Oklahoma's support in producing the film *Tulsa*. Oklahoma landscapes are featured in nearly all of the film's outdoor scenes, for which director Stuart "Stoops" Heisler was nominated for an Academy Award in cinematography. The popular and vivid process of Technicolor, adding to the film's popularity, captured scenes in and around the city of Tulsa and Oklahoma's broad vistas. Sitting directly behind her is Robert Preston. Below, an Oklahoma chorus entertains dinner guests with the name of the film appearing behind them. (Both, courtesy of the Oklahoma Historical Society.)

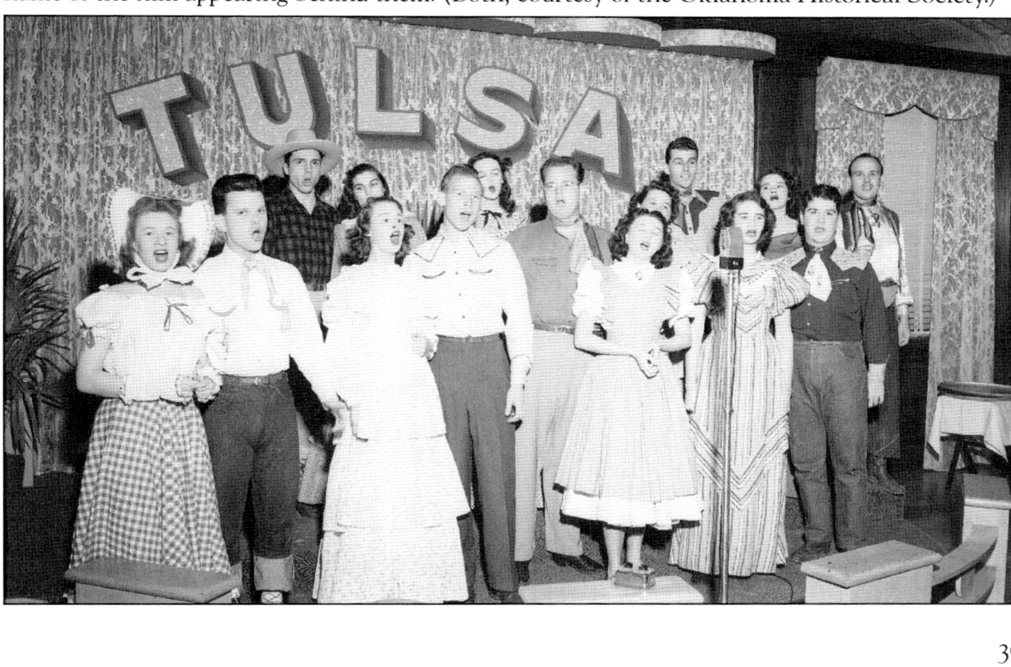

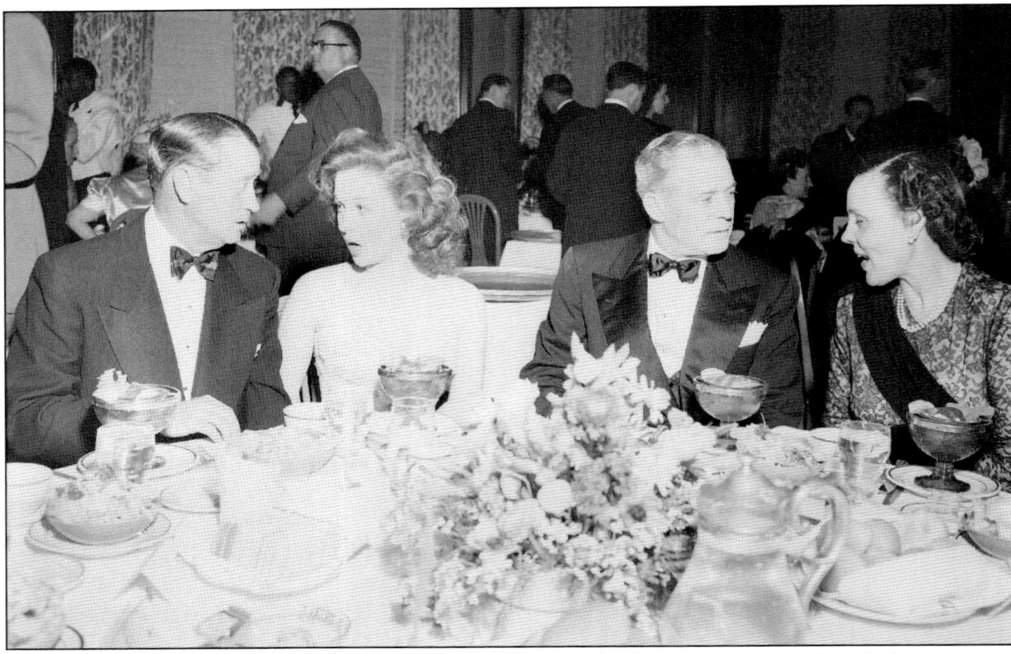

During the April 14, 1949, post–*Tulsa* premiere dinner, the film's cast mingled with dinner guests in the Skirvin Hotel's Venetian Room. From left to right, costar Chill Wills chats with leading lady Susan Hayward, while Oklahoma governor Roy Turner and his wife, Jessica Turner, sit next to them during pre-dinner appetizers. *Tulsa* utilized Governor Turner's cattle ranch for many of the film's outdoor scenes. Below, Susan Hayward poses with oilman and former Oklahoma governor turned senator Robert S. Kerr. Hayward's husband, Jess Barker, poses with Grayce Kerr, the senator's wife. Robert S. Kerr was one of Oklahoma's most influential leaders and businessmen. (Both, courtesy of the Oklahoma Historical Society.)

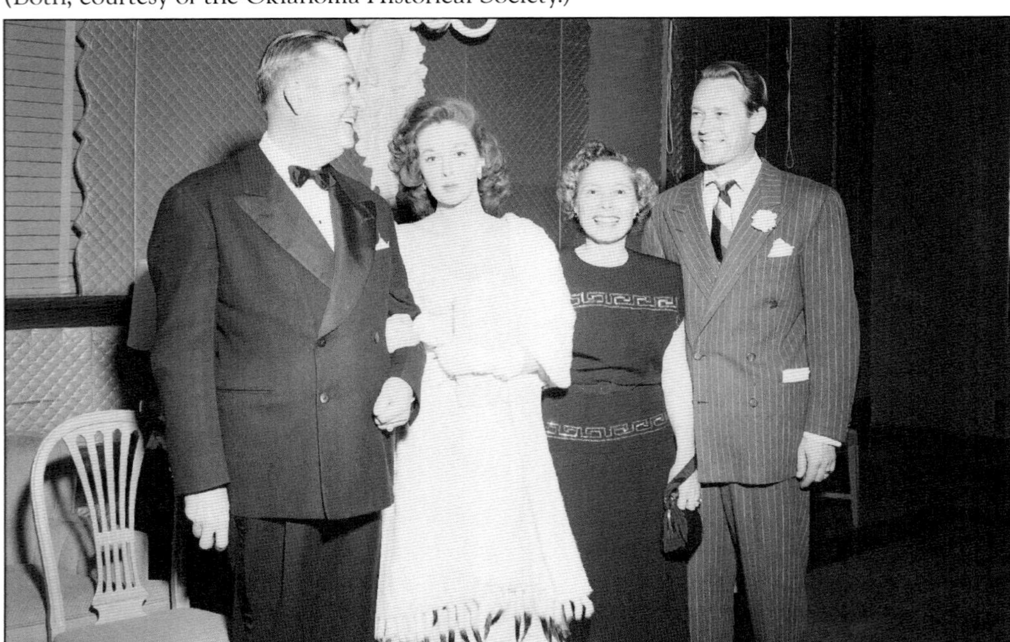

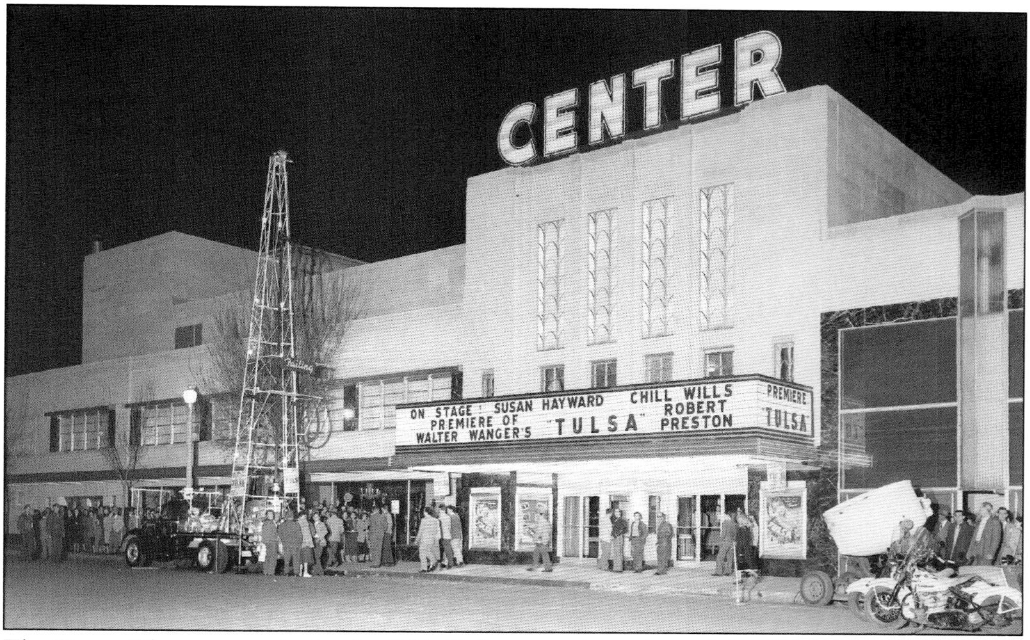

The Center Theater, seen in the April 14, 1949, image above, hosted the Oklahoma City premiere of *Tulsa*, an Eagle Lion film starring Susan Hayward, Robert Preston, and Chill Wills. A faux oil derrick stands outside the theater entrance with a huge spotlight to the right. The *Tulsa* cast, Gov. Roy Turner, Sen. Robert S. Kerr, and 100 Oklahoma City business and social leaders were among the approximately 200 guests of the film's premiere. Below, two unidentified people pose with a large promotional display in the theater's lobby. The Center Theater opened on Christmas Day, 1947. After many years of vacancy starting in the 1970s, the theater and an adjacent structure became home to the Oklahoma City Art Museum's Donald W. Reynolds Visual Arts Center in 2002. Now the Noble Theater, it hosts numerous events and special screenings of foreign, independent, and classic films each week, occasionally with a film's cast or crew present. (Both, courtesy of the Oklahoma Historical Society.)

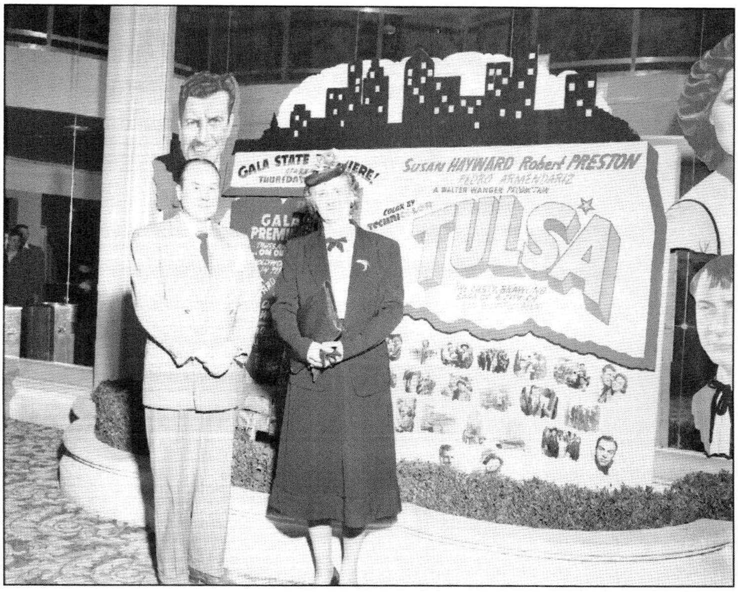

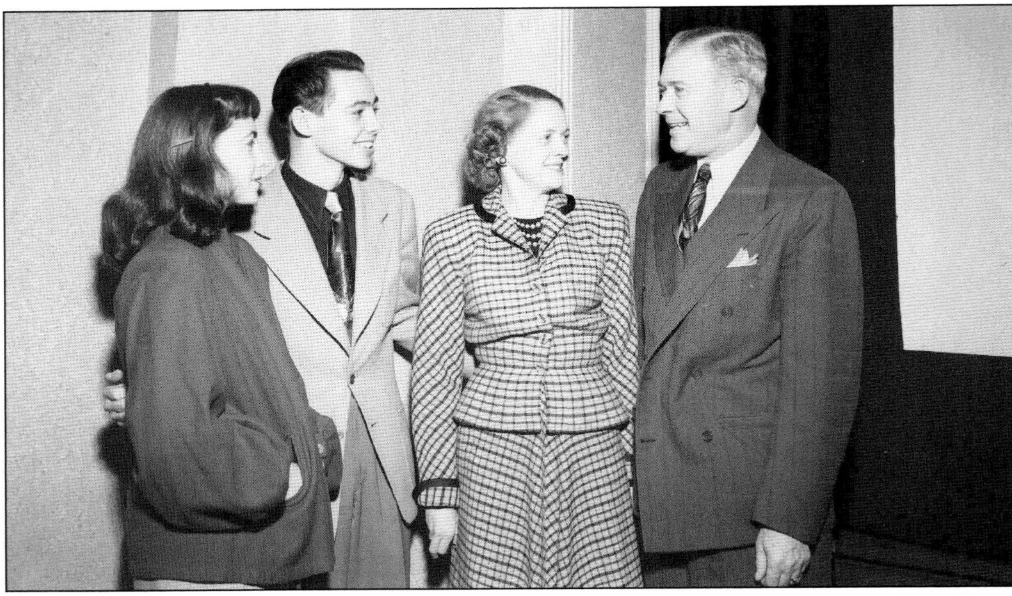

Roy Joseph Turner, Oklahoma's 13th governor, poses with his wife, Jessica E. Turner, and his adopted twin children, Roy and Betty Turner, in front of the 20th Century Fox screening room movie screen at 10 North Lee Avenue. Governor Turner was an advocate for Oklahoma filmmaking. In 1948, he encouraged shooting scenes on his cattle ranch to producers of the motion picture *Tulsa*, which premiered in Oklahoma City and Tulsa in April 1949. (Courtesy of the Oklahoma Historical Society.)

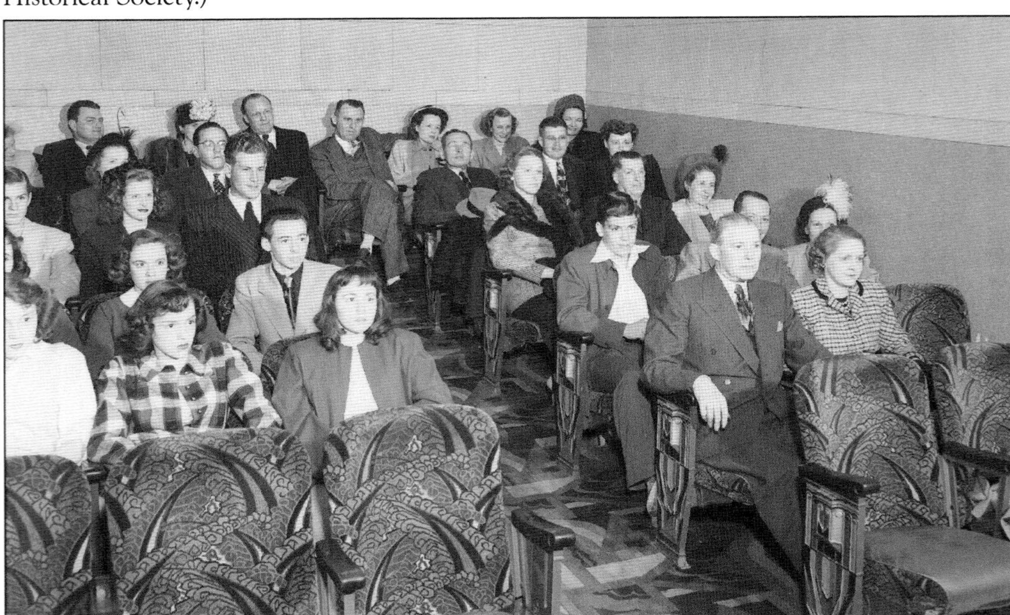

This c. 1949 image shows the 20th Century Fox screening room at 10 North Lee Avenue in Oklahoma City. Sitting in the front row at far right is Oklahoma's 13th governor, Roy Joseph Turner, and his wife, Jessica E. Turner. Their adopted twin children sit to the left. In the front row is Betty Turner, and behind her is brother Roy W. Turner. This 38-seat screening room was among the most active of the four known rooms along Film Row. (Courtesy of the Oklahoma Historical Society.)

Two unidentified men pose in the Odom Drive-In Theatre projection room at 9900 South Shields Avenue in this July 9, 1947, image. They stand with two Super Simplex E-7 projectors with front shutters. These projectors pre-date Cinemascope, an anamorphic lens series used between 1953 and 1967 that allowed the motion pictures to be widescreen. The Odom would later become 77 Drive-In. (Courtesy of the Oklahoma Historical Society.)

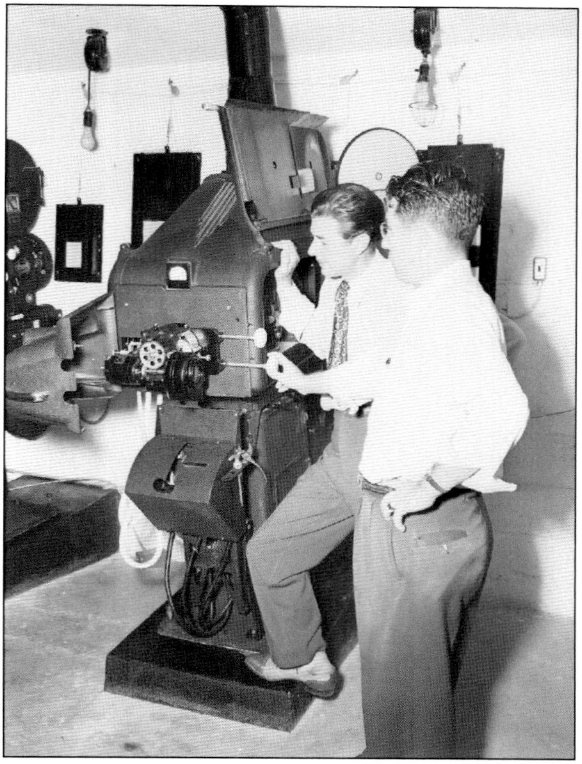

The lamps appearing on the rear of these two Super Simplex E-7 projectors are Peerless Type 15 Magnarc lamps. The arcs used 36 volts DC at 38 amps. This could also be supplied with a rectifier or motor-generator. Carbon rods brought together in the casing produced the intense illumination needed to project the image onto the large screen sometimes hundreds of feet away. (Courtesy of the Oklahoma Historical Society.)

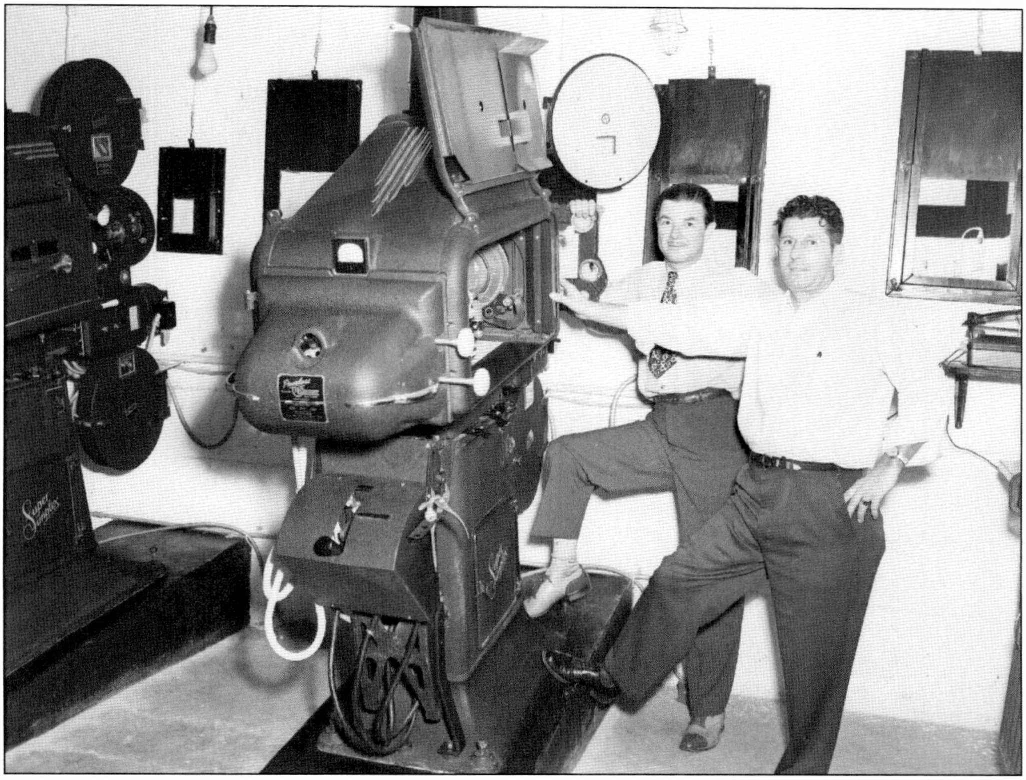

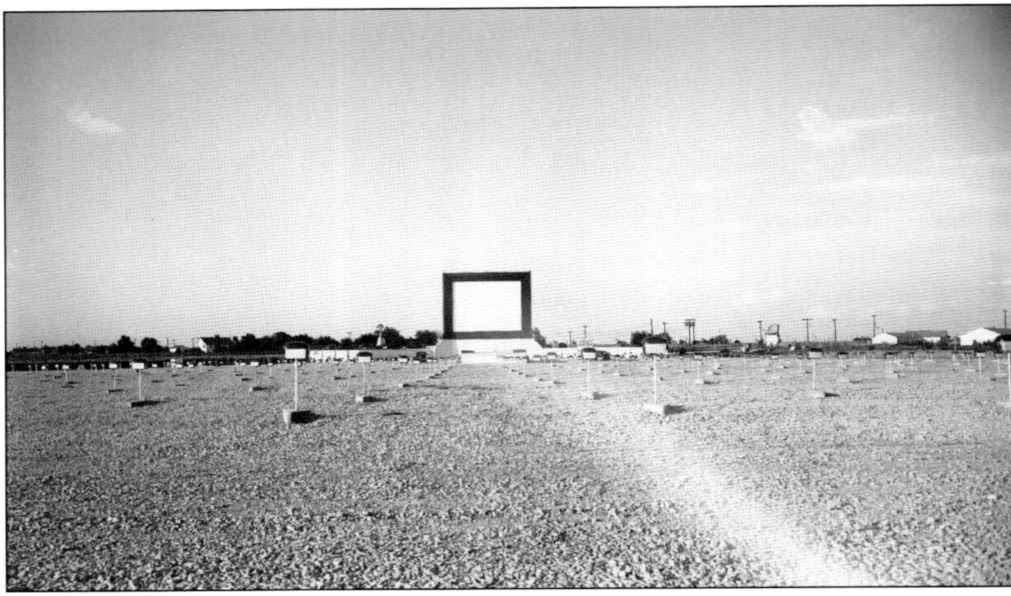

The round cans seen in the image below along the front of these Super Simplex E-7 projectors are the film magazines. In the days of nitrate film, it was required that all film reels be encased in metal cans at all times. The ever-present danger of fire produced highly toxic smoke, and nitrate film was impossible to extinguish, as it even burns underwater. Above, the Odom Drive-In Theatre is home to this projector room. Note the oil wells in the distant background along the right. (Both, courtesy of the Oklahoma Historical Society.)

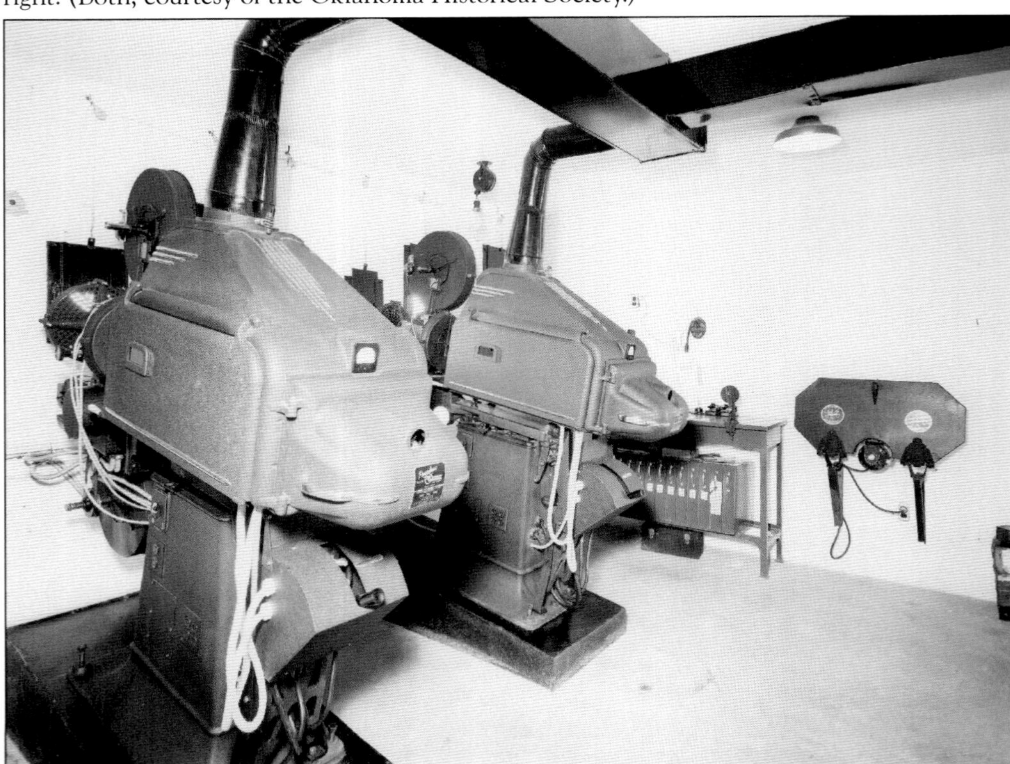

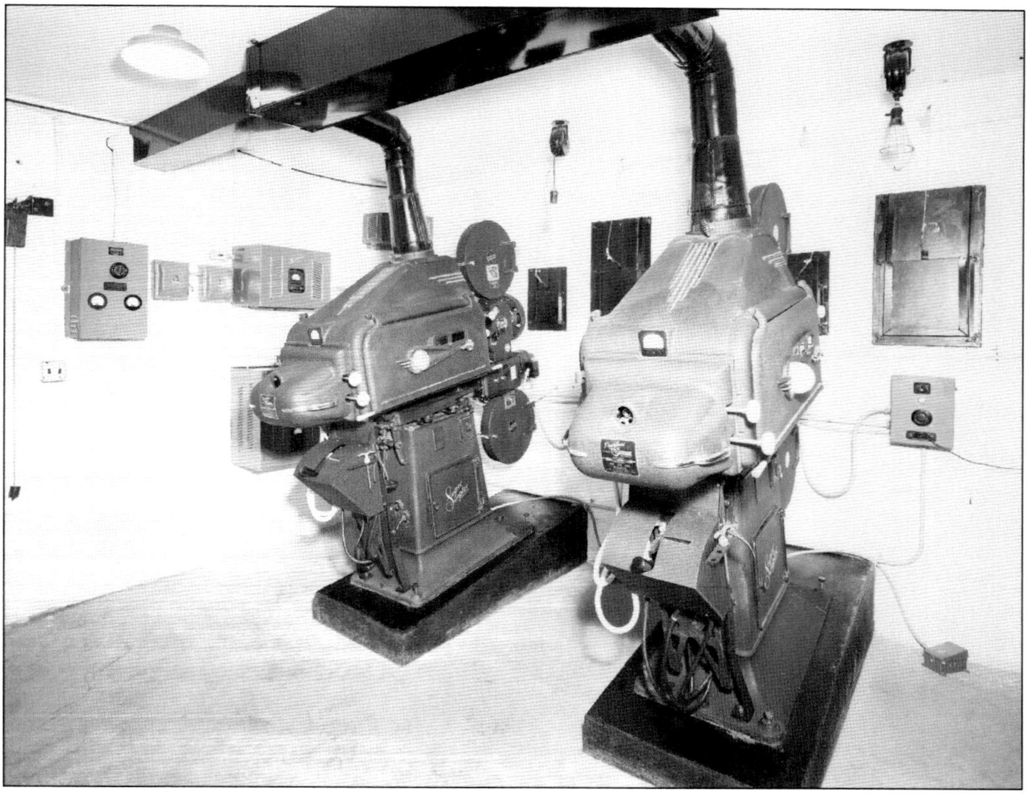

Fire shutters over the projection portholes in front of these Super Simplex E-7 projectors were attached to chains or lines that ran the length of the projection booth. In the event of a film fire, the operator could quickly lower all the doors, usually from a master toggle, which would shutter all the portholes at once to limit smoke billowing into the auditorium. The stacks above the projectors were used as chimneys for heat, carbon rod smoke, and the venting of potential smoke from a fire to reduce risk to audiences in enclosed auditoriums. Many projectionists from this era suffered upper respiratory problems later in their lives from the inhalation of carbon rod smoke. (Courtesy of the Oklahoma Historical Society.)

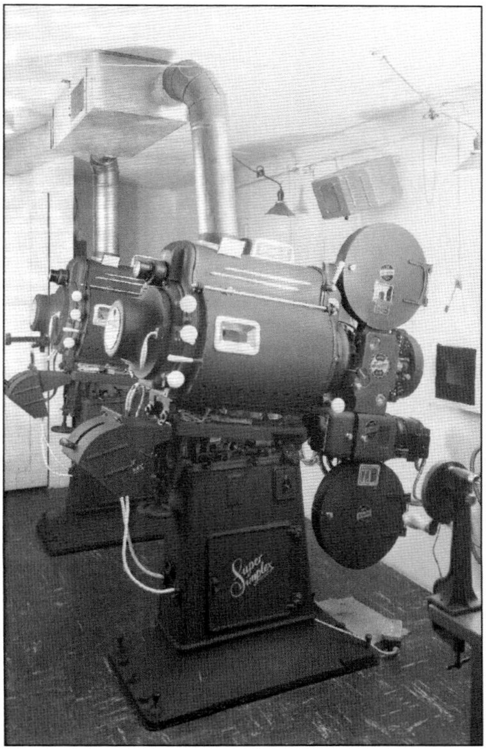

This c. 1947 image shows another pair of Super Simplex E-7 projectors configured for an unknown indoor theater. Although the body style is different from the previous projectors, they still use Peerless Type 15 Magnarc lamps. Note the manual film rewinder in the foreground for rewinding reels of film. (Courtesy of the Oklahoma Historical Society.)

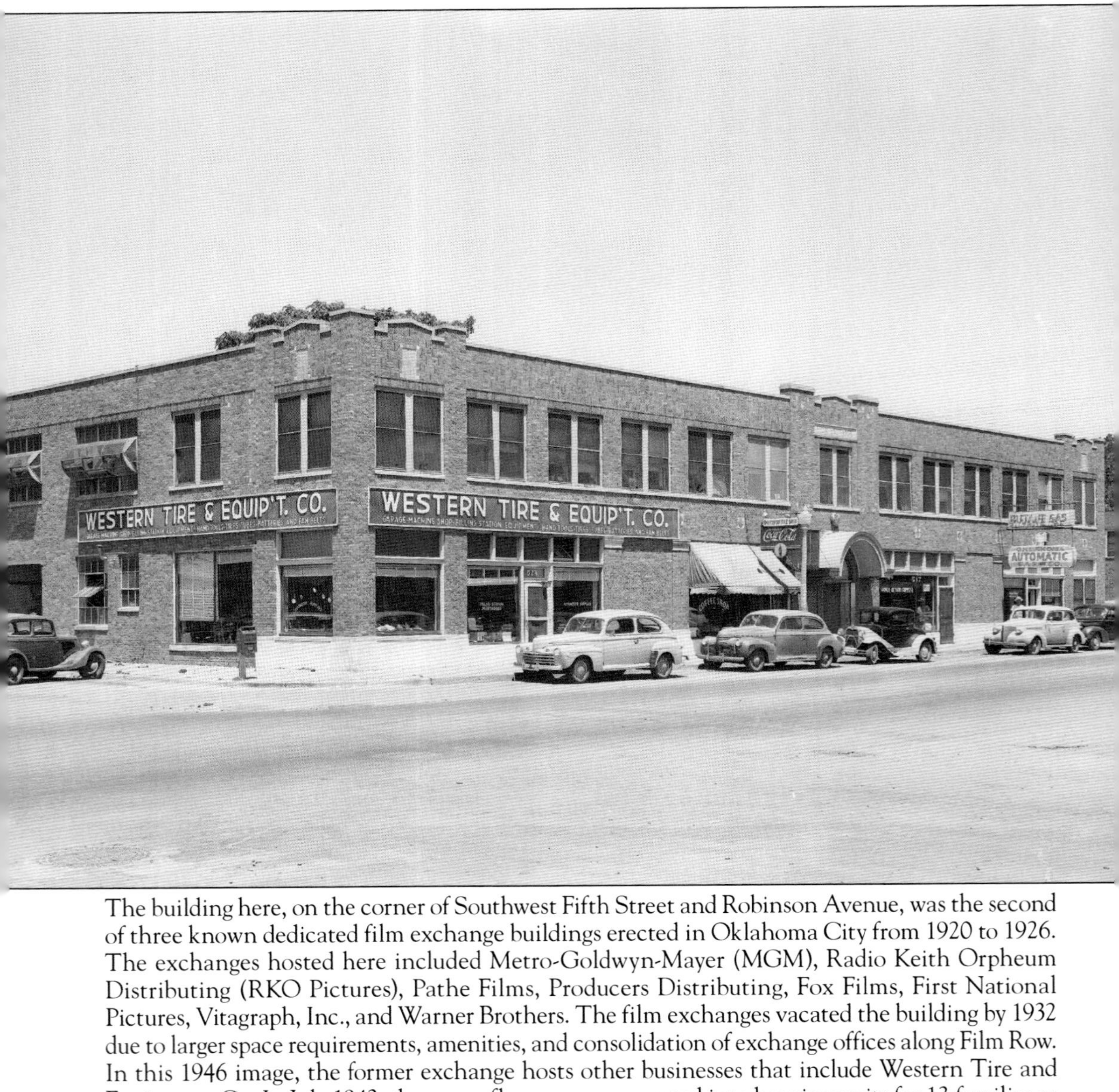

The building here, on the corner of Southwest Fifth Street and Robinson Avenue, was the second of three known dedicated film exchange buildings erected in Oklahoma City from 1920 to 1926. The exchanges hosted here included Metro-Goldwyn-Mayer (MGM), Radio Keith Orpheum Distributing (RKO Pictures), Pathe Films, Producers Distributing, Fox Films, First National Pictures, Vitagraph, Inc., and Warner Brothers. The film exchanges vacated the building by 1932 due to larger space requirements, amenities, and consolidation of exchange offices along Film Row. In this 1946 image, the former exchange hosts other businesses that include Western Tire and Equipment Co. In July 1943, the upper floors were converted into housing units for 13 families as a federal housing project, which included nine four-room and four three-room apartments. From 1968 to around 1984, the Oklahoma City Rescue Mission provided services from this location with the motto "soup, soap, and salvation." It remained vacant for many years until acquired by the Asset Group in Oklahoma City in 2009. A citywide revitalization of downtown called Project 180 and Maps 3, at the time of this writing, threatens to demolish the building. (Courtesy of the Oklahoma Historical Society.)

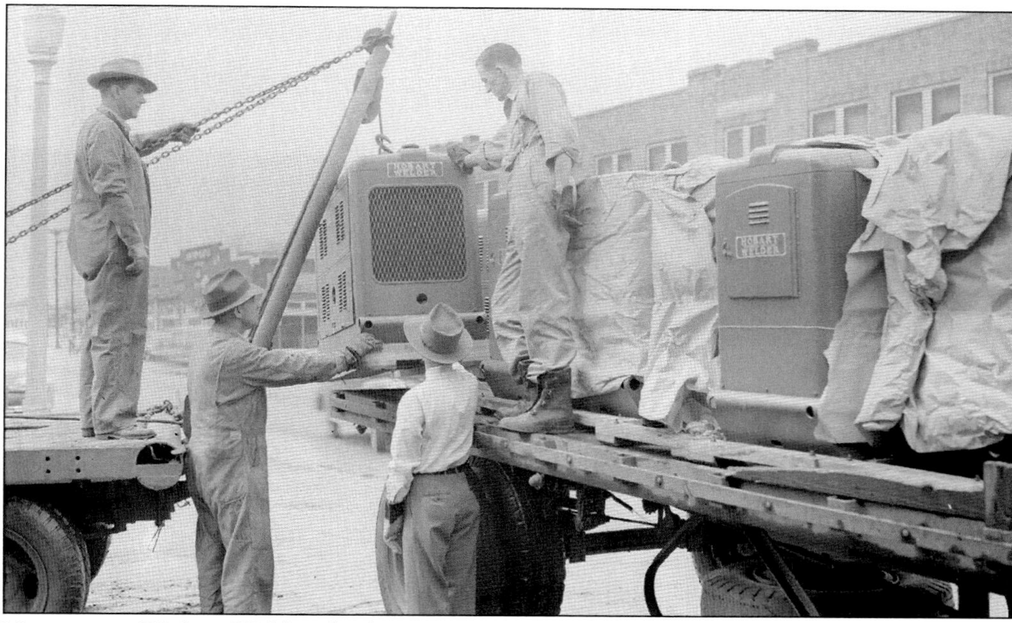

Here, men of Hobart Welding load generators and portable equipment on a flatbed truck across the street from the Film Exchange building on the northeast corner of Southwest Fifth Street and Robinson Avenue in Oklahoma City. The lentil with the words Film Exchange over the building's main entrance is just visible above the center generator. This view is of the building's southeast corner in 1946. (Courtesy of the Oklahoma Historical Society.)

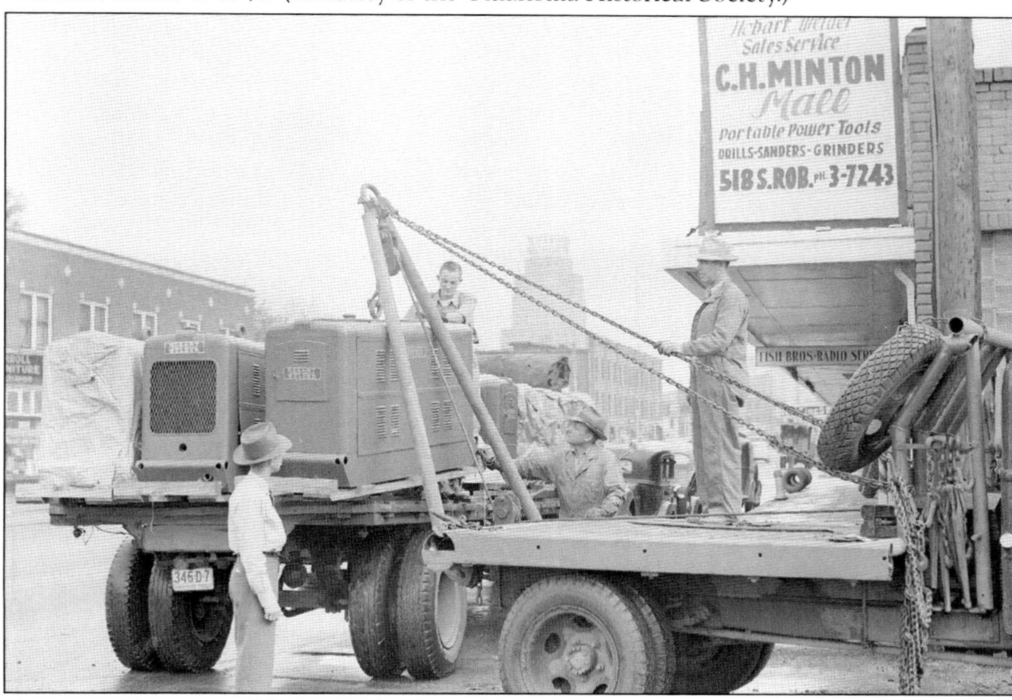

Here is another view of the men of Hobart Welding loading generators and portable equipment across the street from the Film Exchange building. This view is of the building's northeast corner in 1946. (Courtesy of the Oklahoma Historical Society.)

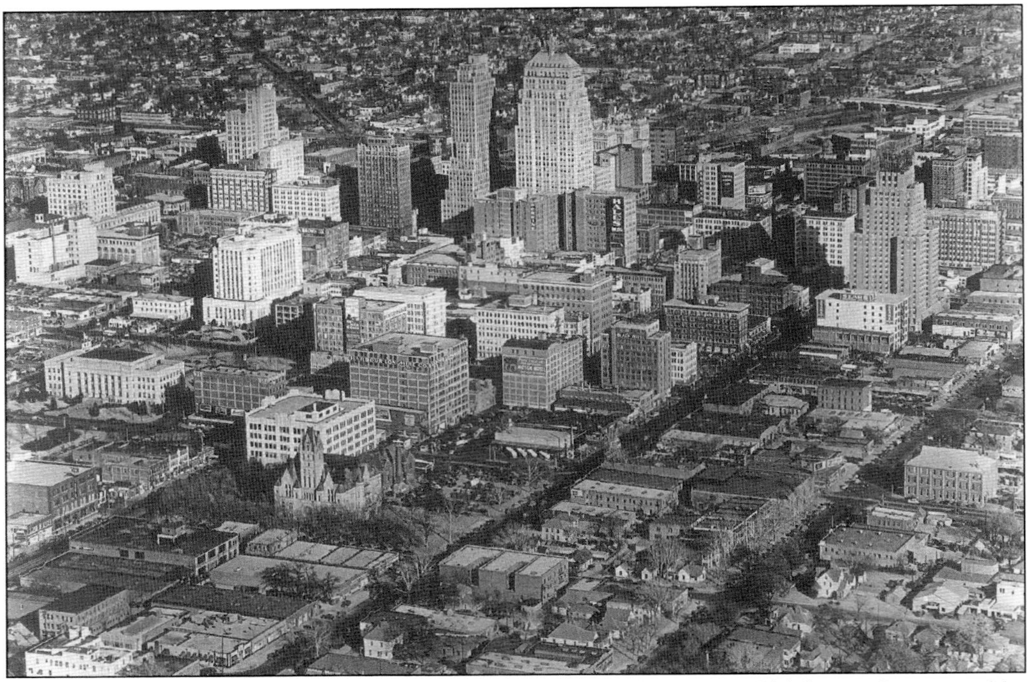

In this rare c. 1947 photograph, the southwest portion of downtown Oklahoma City is visible. The blown-up view below shows Film Row along Grand Avenue. In the lower left is Paramount Pictures, whose name adorns the south-facing facade in large letters. To the left of its front entrance is another door that leads to its screening room, operated by Russell Godwin. Across the street is the Film Exchange building, with Warner Brothers, Oklahoma Theatre Supply, and National Screen Services to the east. On the northeast corner of this intersection sits Metro-Goldwyn-Mayer (MGM) and "Poverty Row" to the east. Behind MGM is 20th Century Fox. Across from Fox are Griffith Theatres' home offices. Numerous exchanges were operating along this portion of Grand, Main, and California Avenues at this time. This photograph captures many of the structures that urban renewal would raze to the ground in later years. (Both, courtesy of George Verstraete; First Rate Company.)

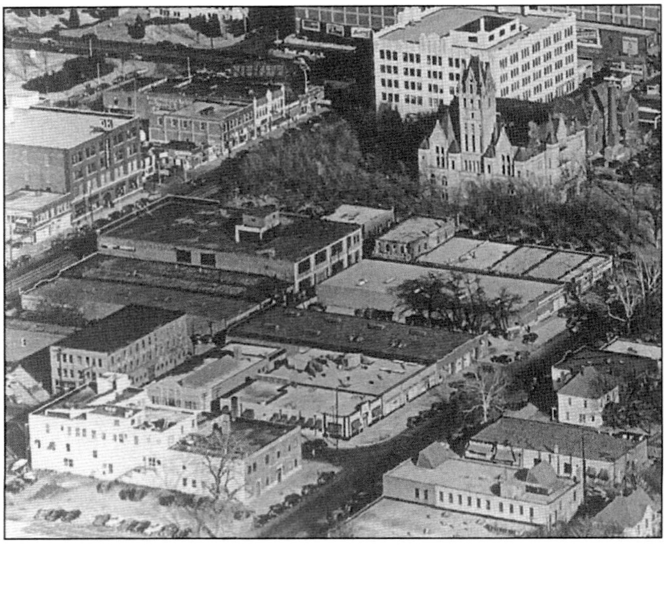

Three

Paramount Times

Paramount Pictures appears to have first arrived in Oklahoma City as the Famous Players-Lasky Corporation in 1926 at 514 West Grand Avenue, although Paramount Publix owned and operated theaters in Oklahoma as early as 1915. In 1931, after settling on the name Paramount Pictures, the exchange found its more permanent address at 701 West Grand Avenue. It stayed there until 1956 when a final move took it to the Commerce Exchange Building at 130 West Grand Avenue in Oklahoma City.

Branch manager Carl Howard Weaver Sr. guided the Paramount Pictures exchange through its golden years of operation along Film Row from the late 1930s until the mid-1950s. During Paramount's tenure, numerous motion picture stars and starlets along with their production teams often toured Oklahoma City on promotional press junkets for their films or to aid in charitable events.

Paramount Pictures, like other area exchanges, did the promoting, renting, and shipping of their films to theaters within their area and exhibitors from across Oklahoma and surrounding states. Paramount-owned theaters ran Paramount Picture films exclusively and provided them with many marketing tools produced in the exchange offices.

The exchange also offered one of four known screening rooms along Film Row. Russell Godwin operated the miniature cinema, although Paramount owned the equipment. Godwin served as manager, projectionist, usher, and janitor while also working for famed Oklahoma City filmmaker and cinematographer Arthur Ramsey. Paramount's cinema could only seat 50 patrons, although the normal compliment was around 20 and as few as one or two. For 50¢ a reel, exhibitors and booking agents would screen films for box office appeal. Viewings were also available to newspaper critics about a week before a movie's release to public theaters. Russell Godwin eventually moved away from Oklahoma when offered a lucrative job with RKO Pictures. Video Independent Theatres acquired Paramount's building during the 1950s and incorporated the building into its structure until its own departure from Film Row in 1983.

Very few photographs exist of Film Row's bygone years or of its operations except in the numerous photographs salvaged many years ago by former employee Roger Rice of Paramount's neighbor, Griffith Theatres at 11 North Lee Avenue. Like most collections, these photographs had very little information, if any, inscribed on them. After months of research through numerous trade journals, archives, and eyewitness accounts, these images finally reveal many of their secrets and share the story of Oklahoma City's Paramount Pictures Film Exchange and its people.

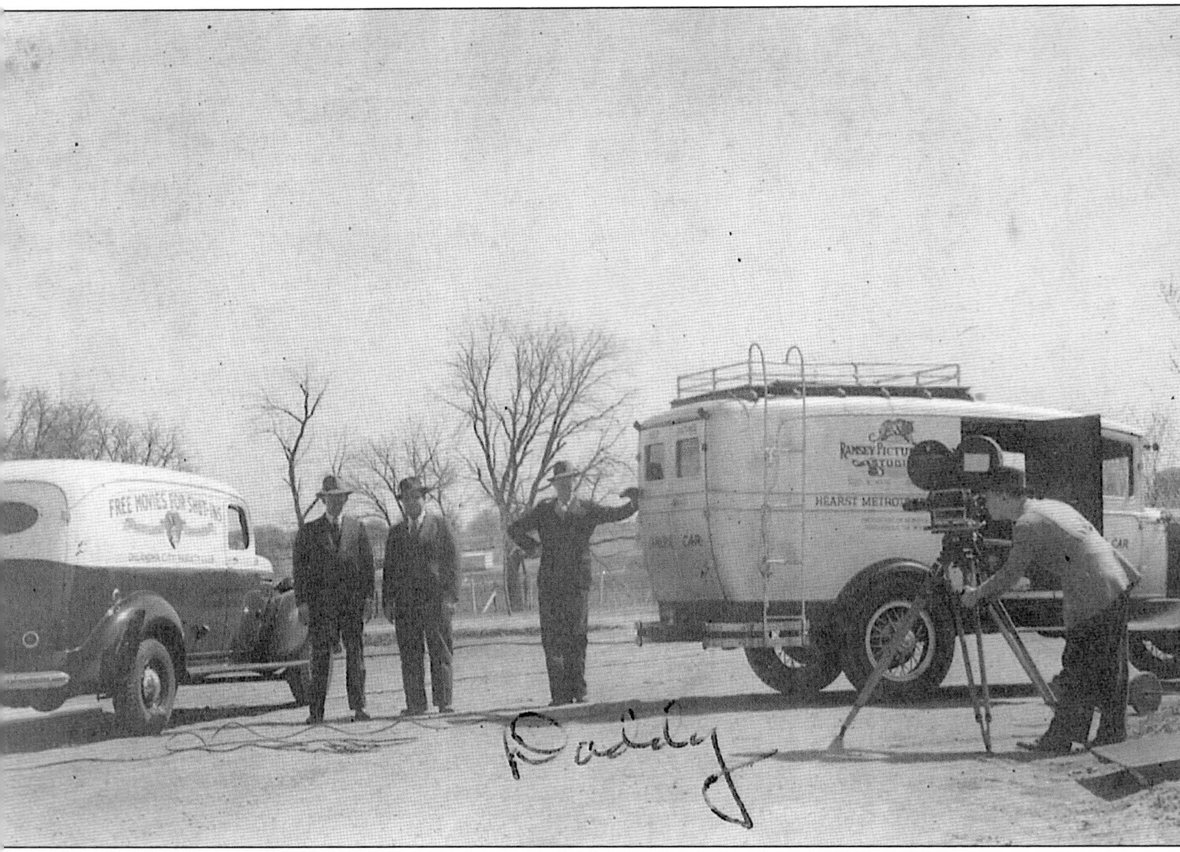

This c. 1940 image is of famed Oklahoma filmmaker Arthur Ramsey and his associates filming an unknown scene adjacent to a sound and movie truck purchased by the Variety Club of Oklahoma City around May 1940. The Variety Club paid the wages of the truck's driver and used the vehicle as a means to bring films donated by film exchanges to patients of the Crippled Children's Hospital, Norman Sanatorium, orphanages, and other shut-ins unable to venture out. The truck's signage reads "Free Movies For Shut-Ins; Oklahoma City Variety Club." The truck on the right is Ramsey's camera truck. Ramsey is operating his motion picture camera, while his colleague Russell Godwin leans on the truck nearby observing. Godwin was the one-man operator of the Paramount Pictures Film Exchange screening room at 701 West Grand Avenue. (Courtesy of Fred Godwin.)

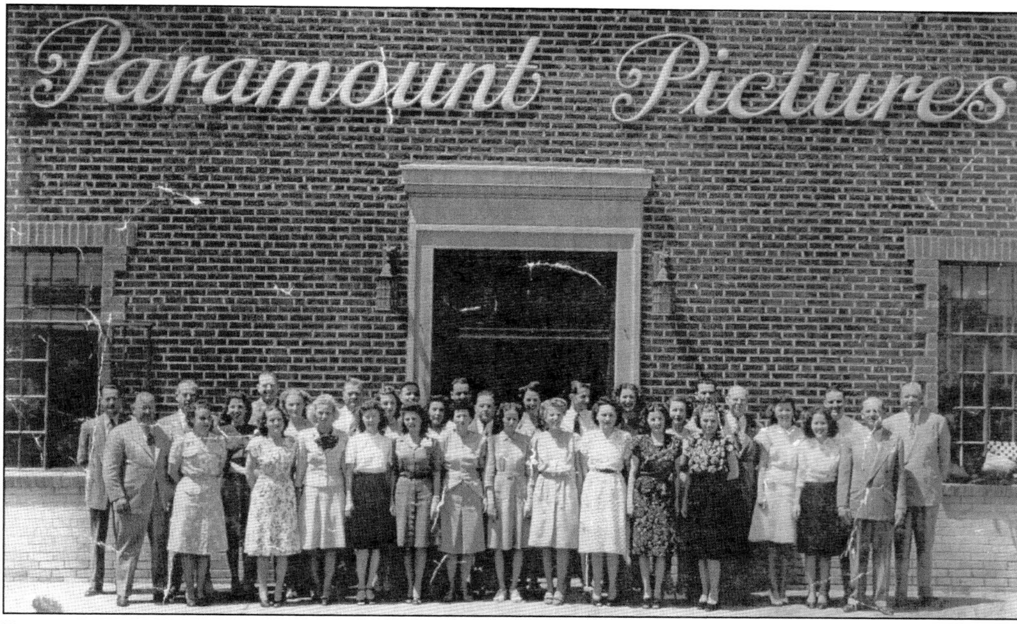

Paramount Pictures Film Exchange management and staff pose in front of their 701 West Grand Avenue offices in 1943. Just to the left (not shown) is the entrance to Paramount's screening room, one of four that operated along Film Row. Paramount's assistant distribution chief for the western United States, Duke Clark, stands at the far right with branch manager Carl H. Weaver. (Courtesy of the author's private collection.)

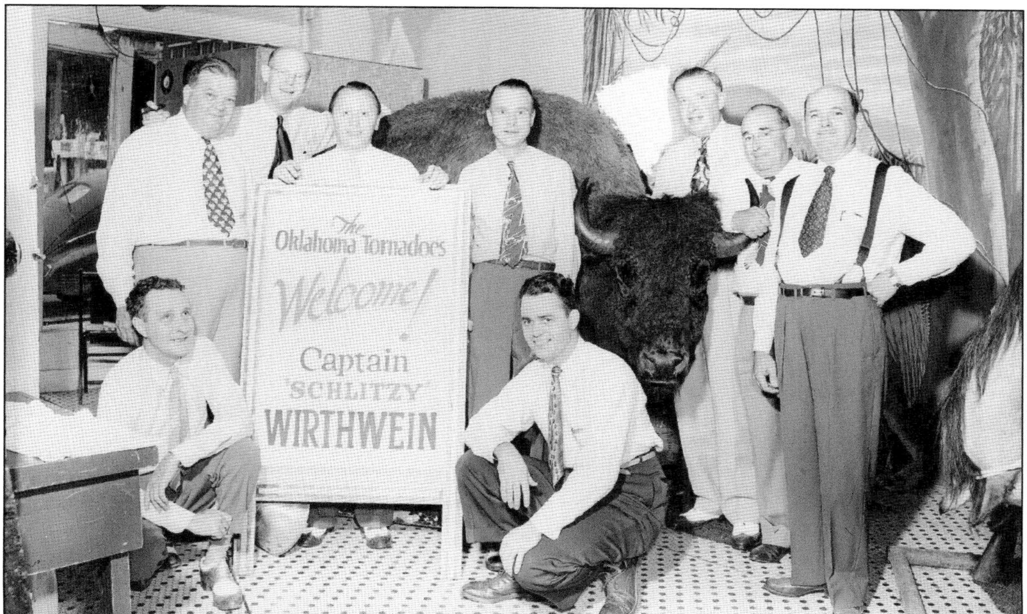

In this c. 1945 image, Paramount Pictures Film Exchange booking agents, management, and possibly art department personnel pose in the art department space with a sign welcoming home World War II veteran Captain Wirthwein, who may have been involved with the Oklahoma Tornadoes, a Texas-based Cajun music group. The man pictured far right is Paramount Pictures Film Exchange branch manager Carl H. Weaver. (Courtesy of the Oklahoma Historical Society.)

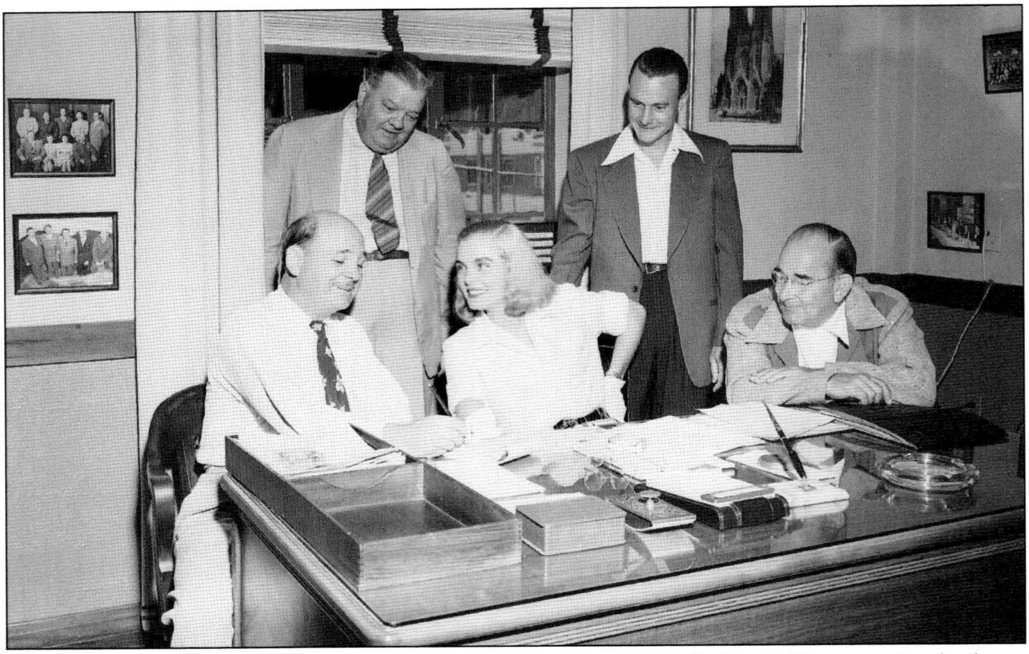

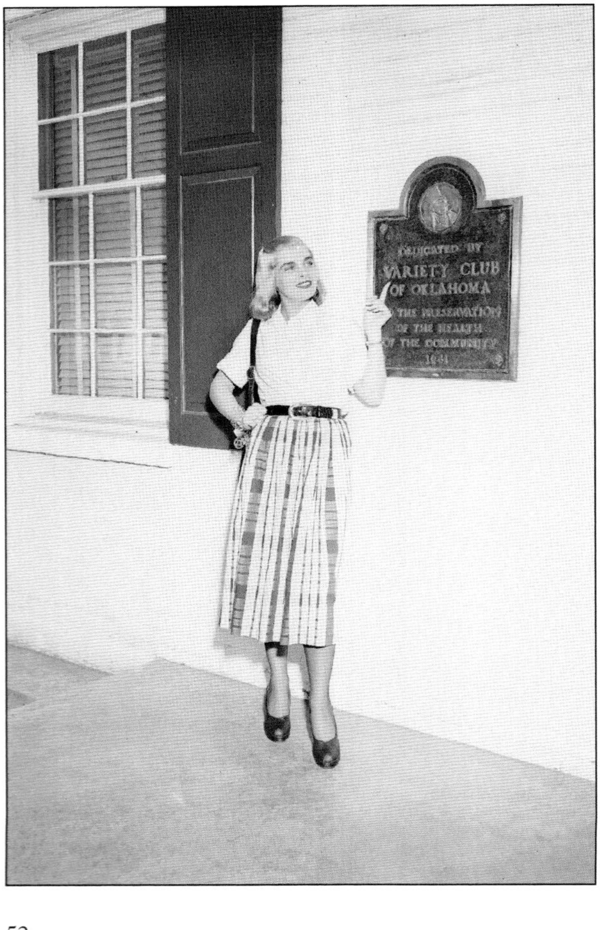

On July 28, 1947, actress Lizabeth Scott sits with the Paramount Pictures Film Exchange management team in the branch manager's office, running through details promoting her latest film, *Desert Fury*, at the Criterion Theatre later in the day. Sitting to the right of her is Paramount branch manager Carl H. Weaver. (Courtesy of the Oklahoma Historical Society.)

Film exchanges were often involved with fundraising efforts in Oklahoma City and sometimes recruited visiting actors. Here, actress Lizabeth Scott visits the Oklahoma City Variety Club Health Center for tuberculosis treatment of underprivileged children and adults at 500 South Walker Avenue during her time promoting the film *Desert Fury* on July 28, 1947. (Courtesy of the Oklahoma Historical Society.)

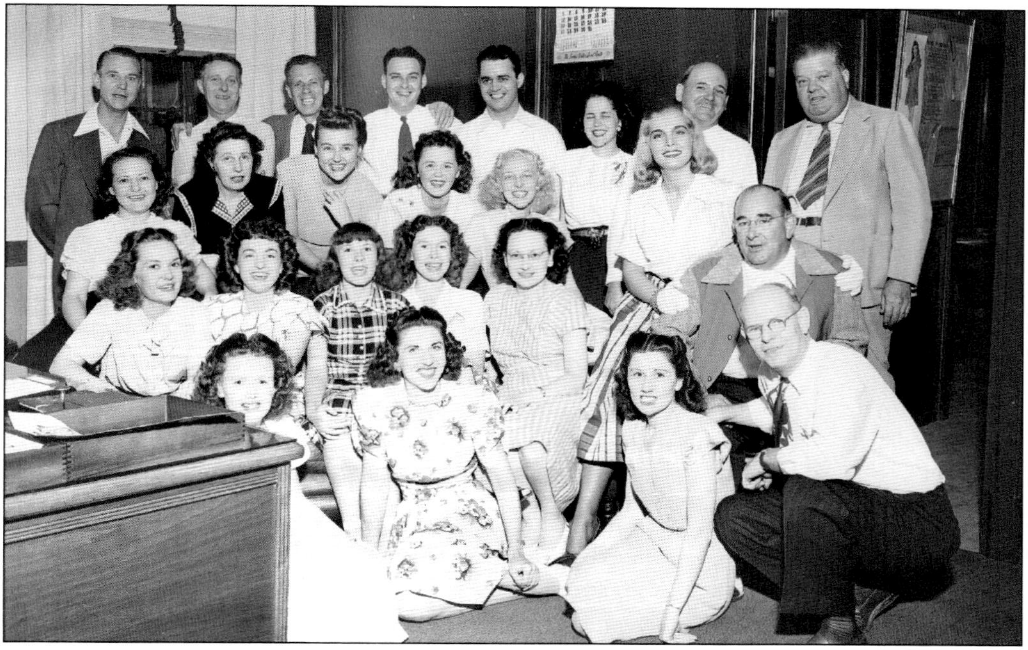

Here, actress Lizabeth Scott poses with Paramount Pictures Film Exchange employees in the branch manager's office as she prepares to depart on her Oklahoma City tour for *Desert Fury*. Lizabeth Scott sits on the right wearing white gloves. Behind her stands branch manager Carl H. Weaver. (Courtesy of the Oklahoma Historical Society.)

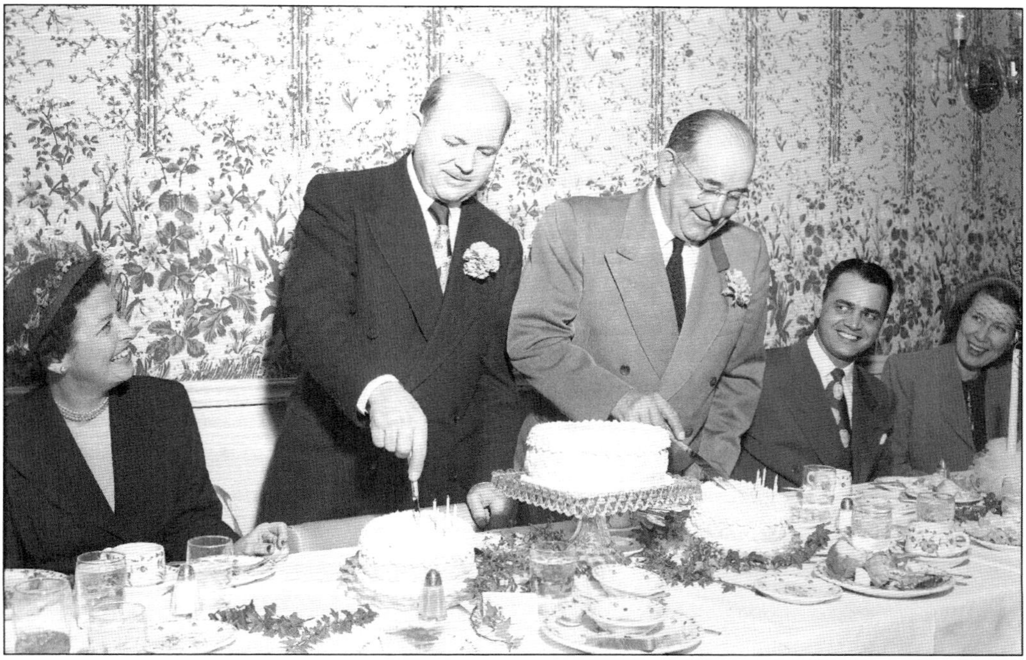

In 1948, Paramount Pictures Film Exchange employees and their spouses gathered for their 10th business anniversary in Oklahoma City. Seen are Paramount branch manager Carl H. "Buck" Weaver (left) and his business partner Sam (last name unknown) cutting their anniversary cakes. (Courtesy of the Oklahoma Historical Society.)

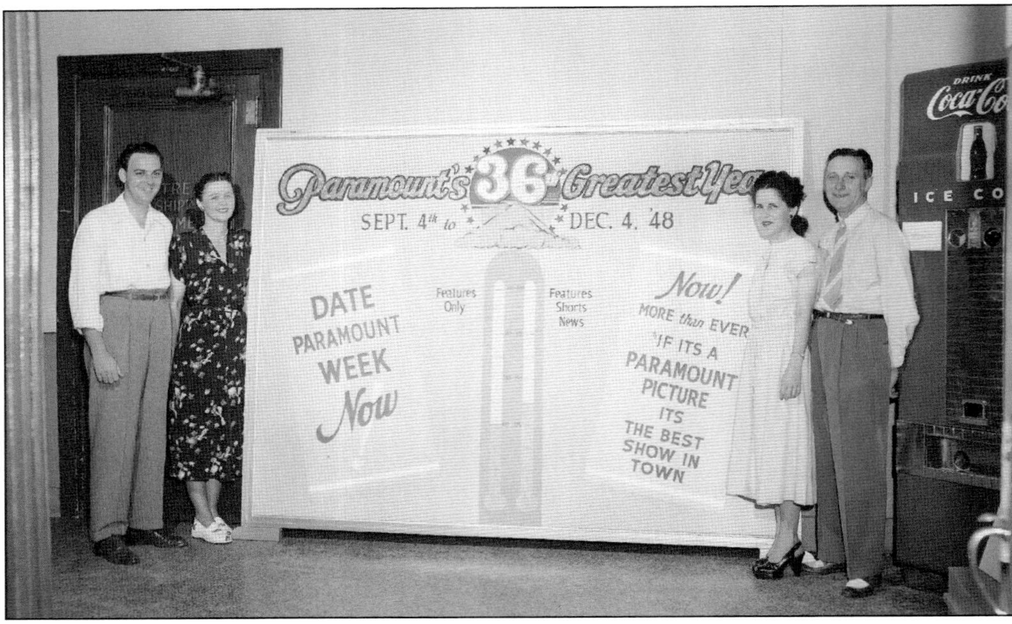

In this c. 1949 image, Paramount Pictures Film Exchange bookers display a comparison of features versus features, shorts, and news showings. These numbers helped booking agents serve their exhibitors better. This particular image captures the figures for the last months of 1948. (Courtesy of the Oklahoma Historical Society.)

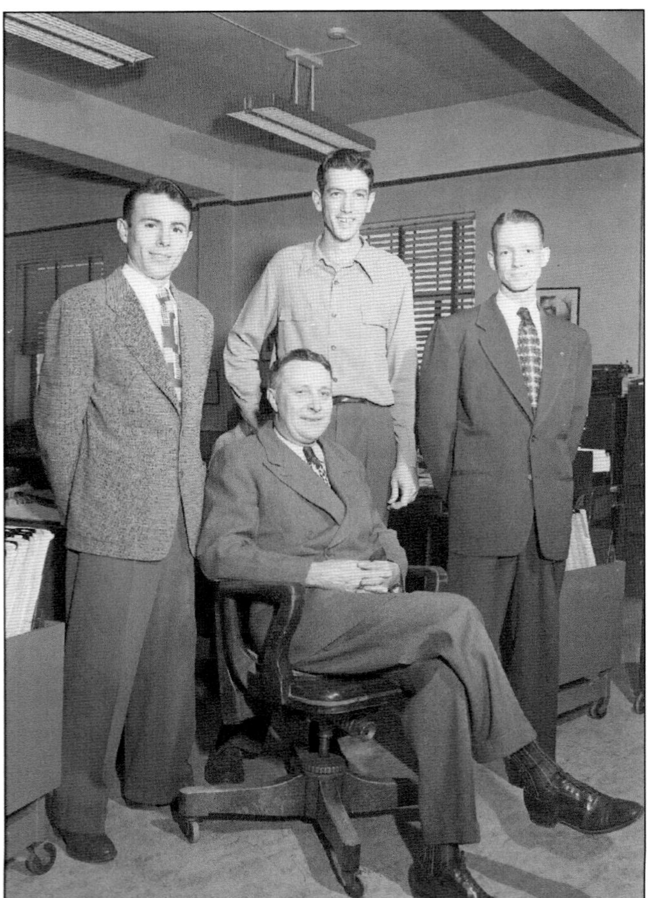

In this c. 1949 image, four unidentified film-booking agents for Paramount Pictures Film Exchange pose in their 701 West Grand Avenue offices. Movie theatre owners would visit the exchange to screen upcoming or new movies, and agents would assist them in determining what pricing and film packages would be best for their venue. (Courtesy of the Oklahoma Historical Society.)

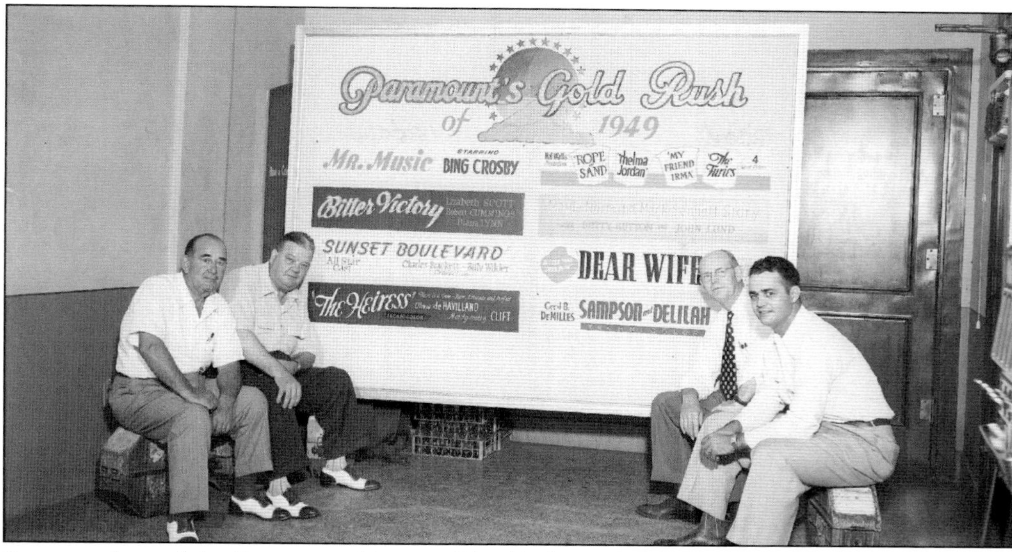

Four members of the Paramount Pictures Film Exchange management team share a marketing display promoting upcoming films for 1949. These promotional displays were for use in selected theatre lobbies or in the 701 West Grand Avenue film exchange office. (Courtesy of the Oklahoma Historical Society.)

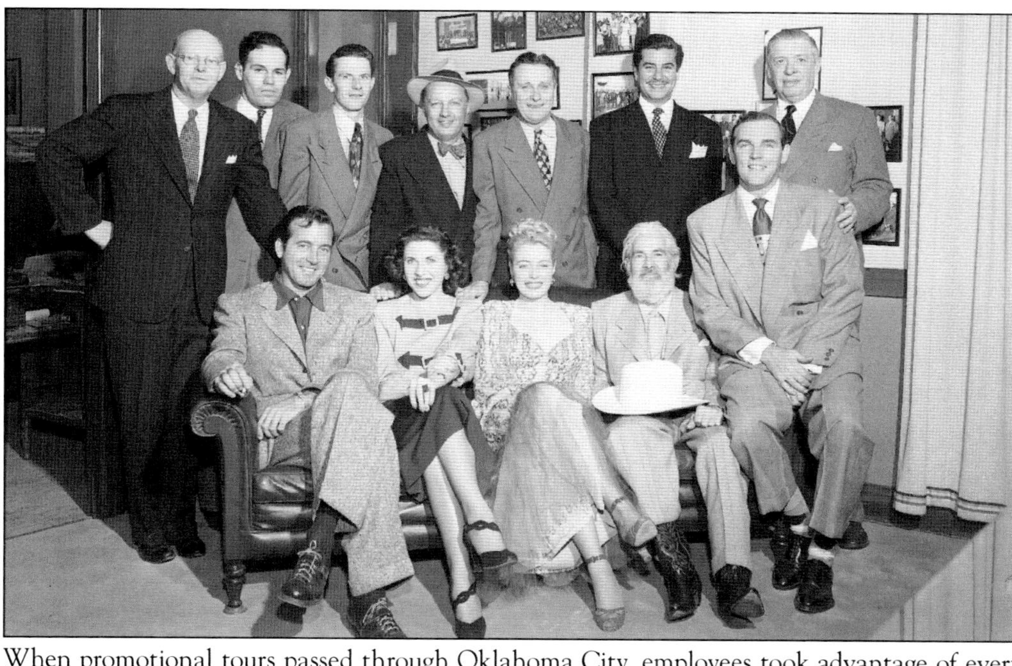

When promotional tours passed through Oklahoma City, employees took advantage of every chance to preserve the moment. Here, cast and crew from the movie *El Paso* pose with Paramount exchange booking agents at 701 West Grand Avenue prior to the film's local premiere at the Criterion Theatre on March 27, 1949. Film producer Bill Thomas stands fourth from the left. Actor Eduardo Noriega stands second from the right with Duke Clark, Paramount distribution chief for the western United States, at far right. Actor John Payne, the film's hero, sits on the left next to blonde heroine actress Mary Beth Hughes, western character actor George "Gabby" Hayes, and actor Paul Hogan (right). (Courtesy of the Oklahoma Historical Society.)

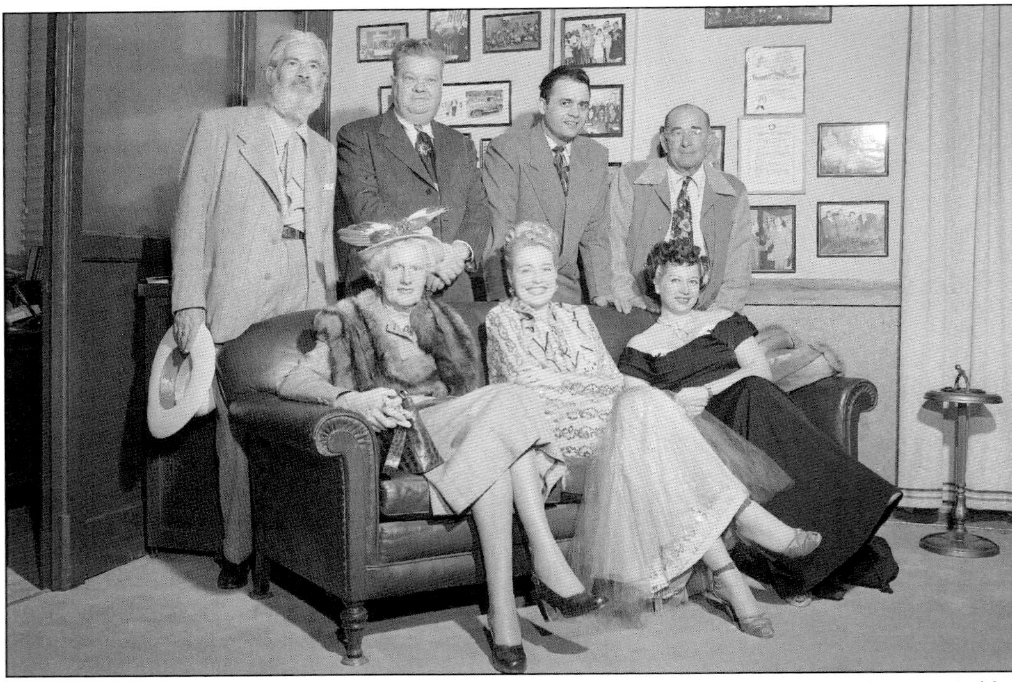

Paramount's film exchange management poses to the right of western character actor George "Gabby" Hayes (standing) and his wife, Olivia (sitting in front). To the right of her are actresses Mary Beth Hughes, the film's heroine (center), and Helen Forrest. (Courtesy of the Oklahoma Historical Society.)

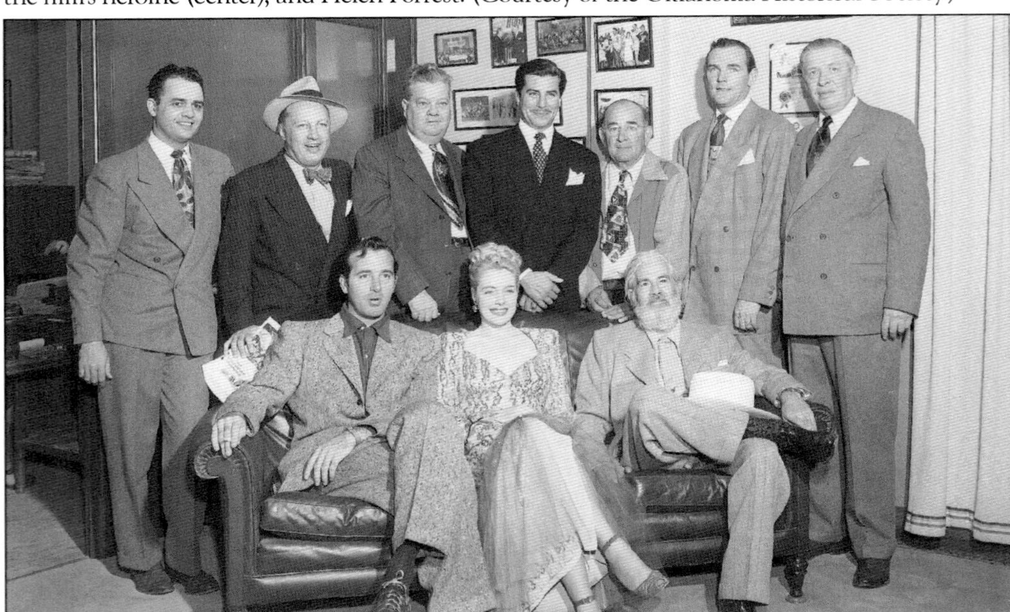

Here, Paramount management poses again in branch manager Carl Weaver's office with *El Paso* film producer Bill Thomas (standing second from left), actor Eduardo Noriega (standing center), actor Paul Hogan (second from right), and distribution chief Duke Clark (far right). Sitting from left to right are actor John Payne, actress Mary Beth Hughes, and actor George "Gabby" Hayes. (Courtesy of the Oklahoma Historical Society.)

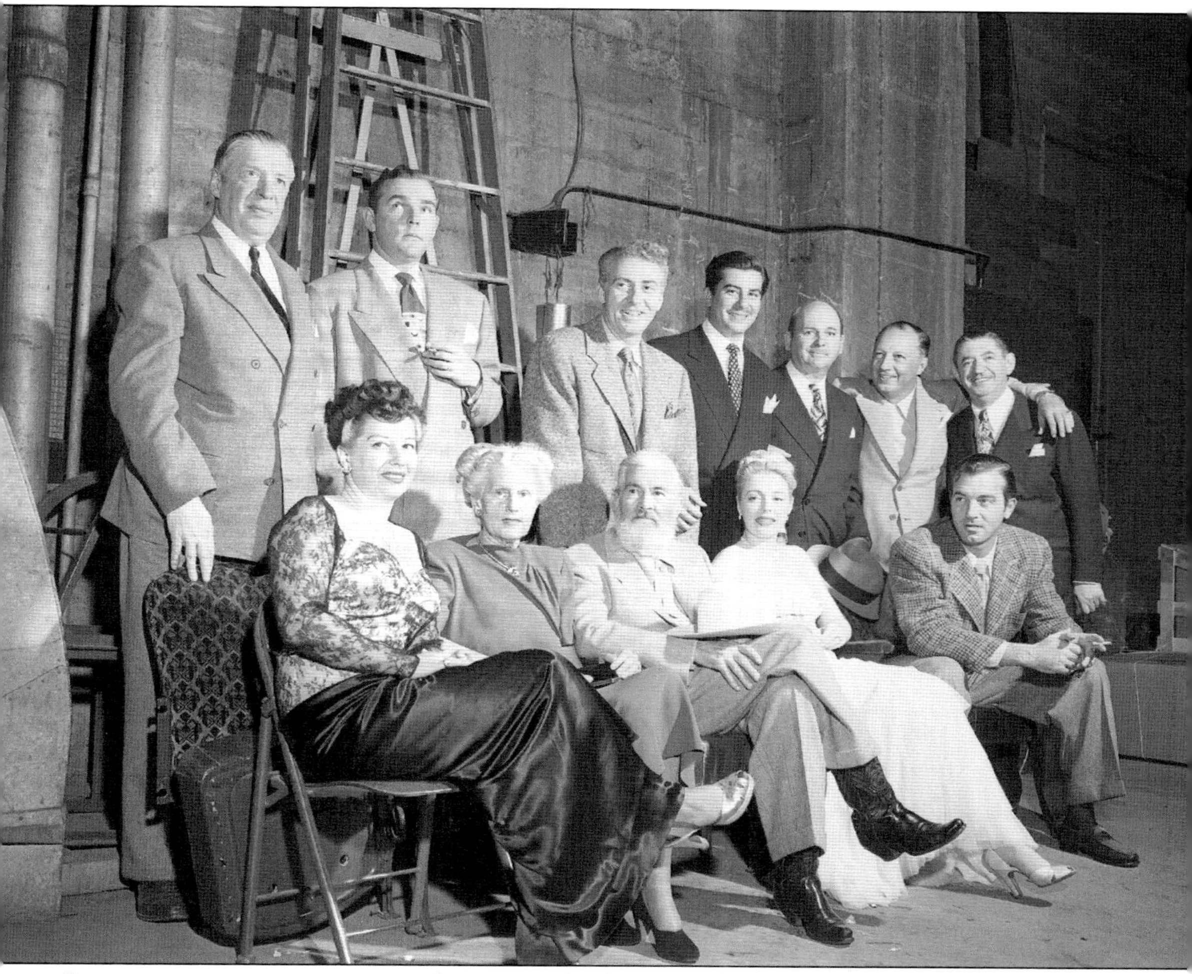

Paramount management poses one last time at the Criterion Theatre premier on March 28, 1949, with the complete touring cast and crew from the movie *El Paso*. Along the back row stand, from left to right, Paramount distribution chief for the western United States Duke Clark, actors Paul Hogan, Frank Faylen, and Eduardo Noriega, branch manager Carl H. Weaver, producer Bill Thomas, and composer Harry Revel. Sitting from left to right are actress Helen Forrest, Olivia Hayes, character actor George "Gabby" Hayes, heroine Mary Beth Hughes, and hero John Payne. (Courtesy of the Oklahoma Historical Society.)

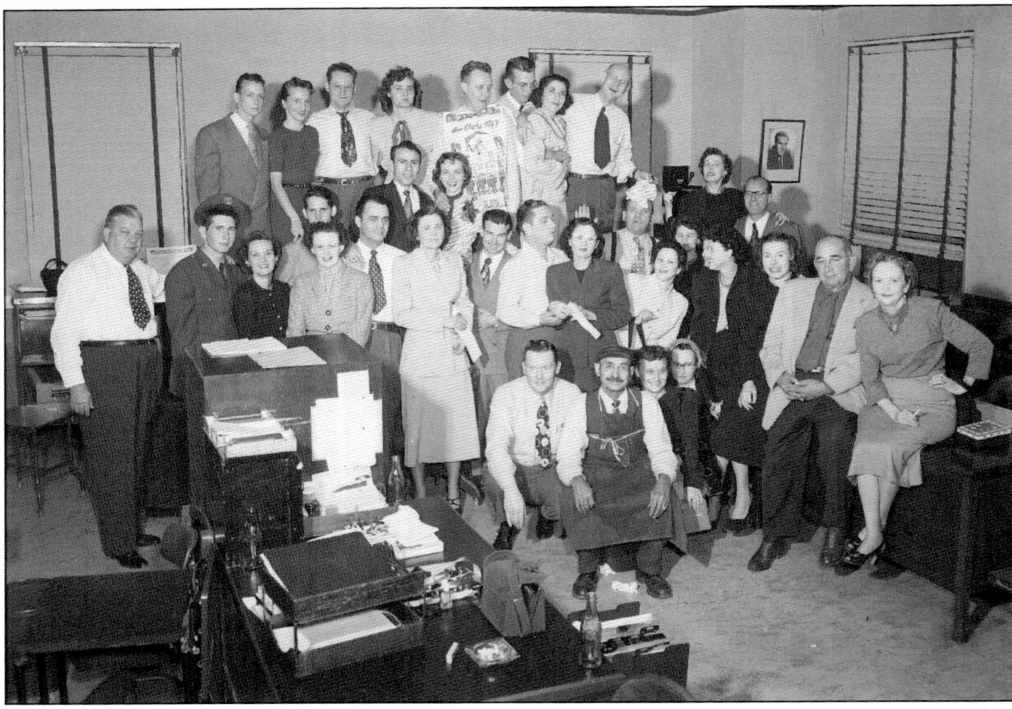

Paramount Pictures Film Exchange employees pose during birthday celebrations for one of their film booking managers. Branch manager Carl H. "Buck" Weaver stands among the crowd toward the right with a playful employee's apron upon his head. Below, a group of employees and a visiting serviceman gather in the branch manager's office for another quick snapshot of the moment in this c. 1949 image. (Both, courtesy of the Oklahoma Historical Society.)

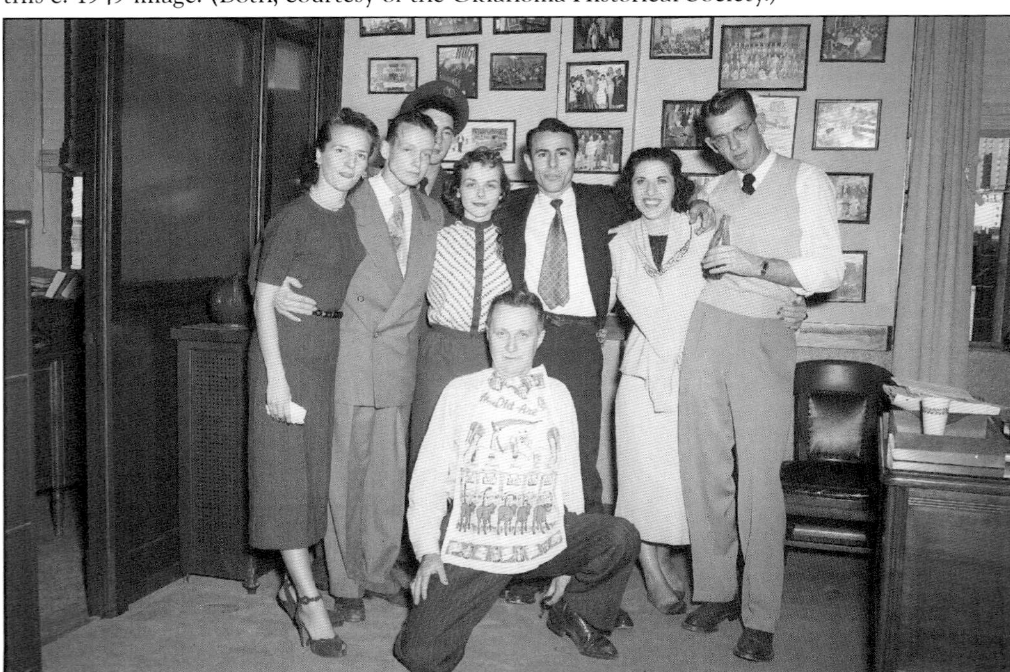

On May 23, 1949, a custom leather saddle was signed by visiting actors to Oklahoma City and was later given away to a young man in Georgia as a prize. Here, Paramount Pictures branch manager Carl H. "Buck" Weaver stands in his office with actors Dick Foote and William Demarest (right) as they playfully pretend to ride an imaginary horse with the saddle. Foote was in Oklahoma City promoting his film *Streets of Laredo*. (Courtesy of the Oklahoma Historical Society.)

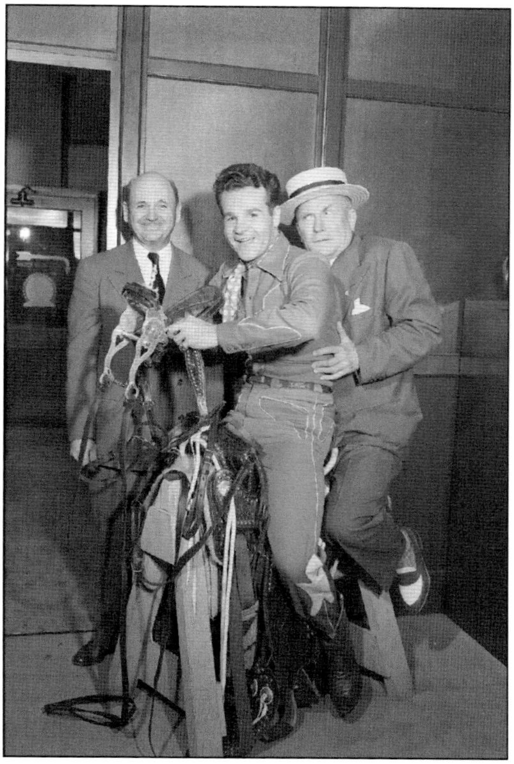

Actor Dick Foote, in western wear, poses with fellow actors and Paramount Pictures Film Exchange management during his promotional tour for *Streets of Laredo*. This May 23, 1949, image was taken in Carl Weaver's Paramount office. Weaver stands with actor William Demarest along the right while from left to right sit actresses Nan Leslie, Gail Russell, and Corine Calves, whose signatures also appeared on the prize saddle above. Paramount publicist Al Jeremy sits on the left. (Courtesy of the Oklahoma Historical Society.)

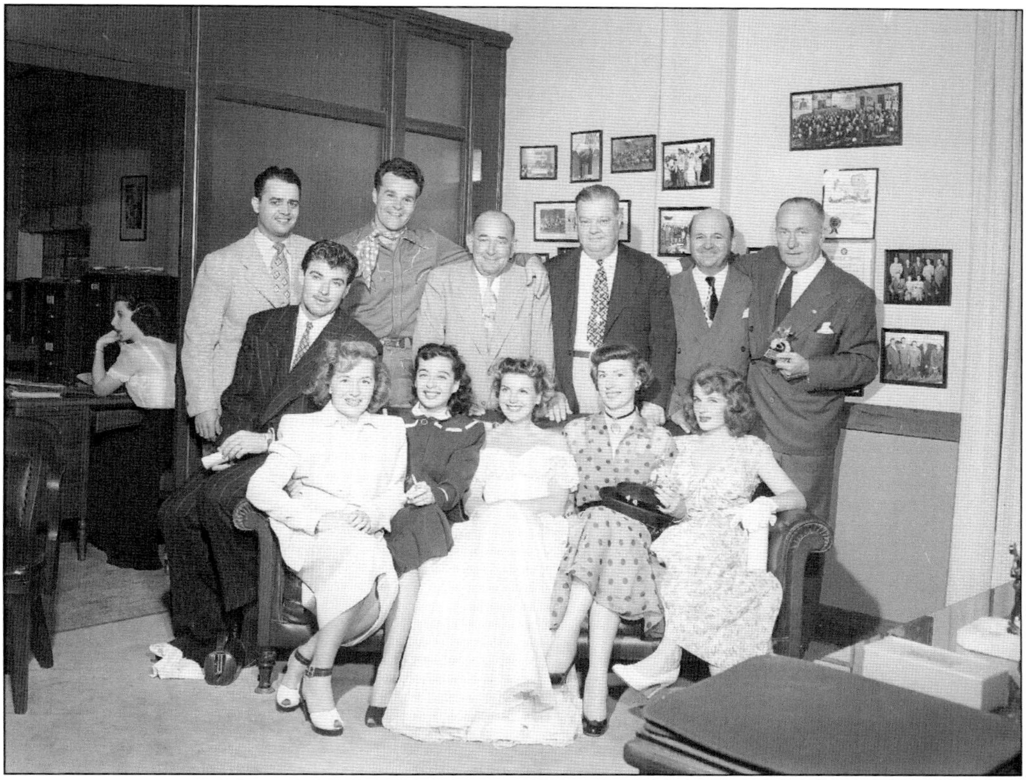

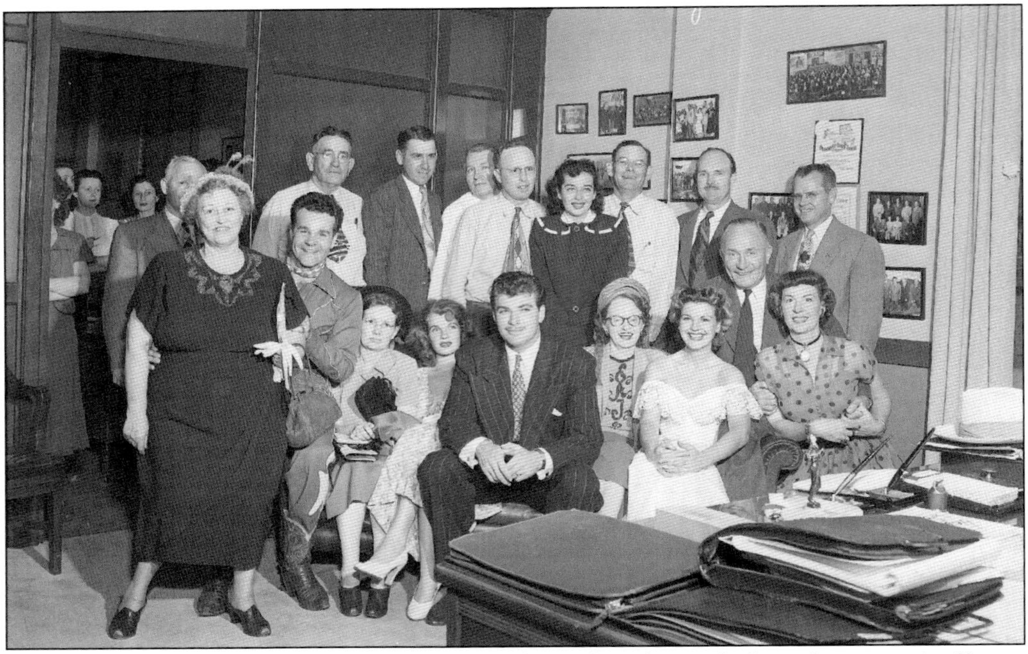

Paramount Pictures Film Exchange employees and friends gather in the branch manager's office to pose with the *Streets of Laredo* touring party on May 23, 1949. Pictured in these images are actors Dick Foote, William Demarest, Gail Russell, Man Leslie, and Corine Calves, along with their Paramount publicity agent, Al Jeremy. (Both, courtesy of the Oklahoma Historical Society.)

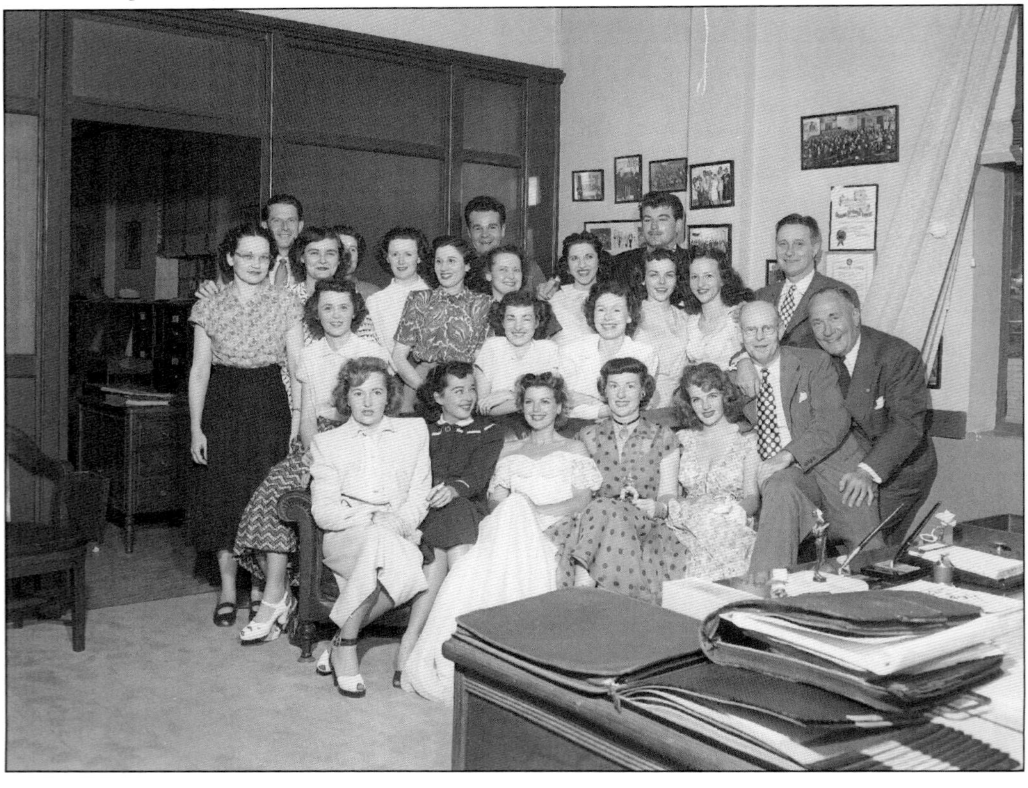

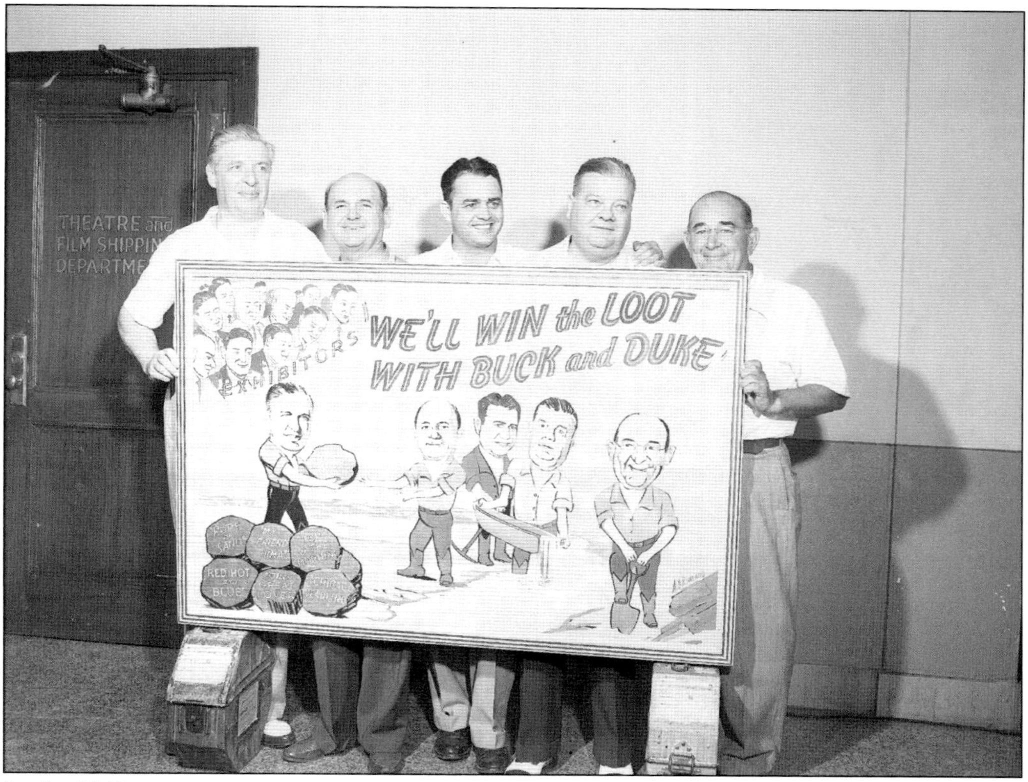

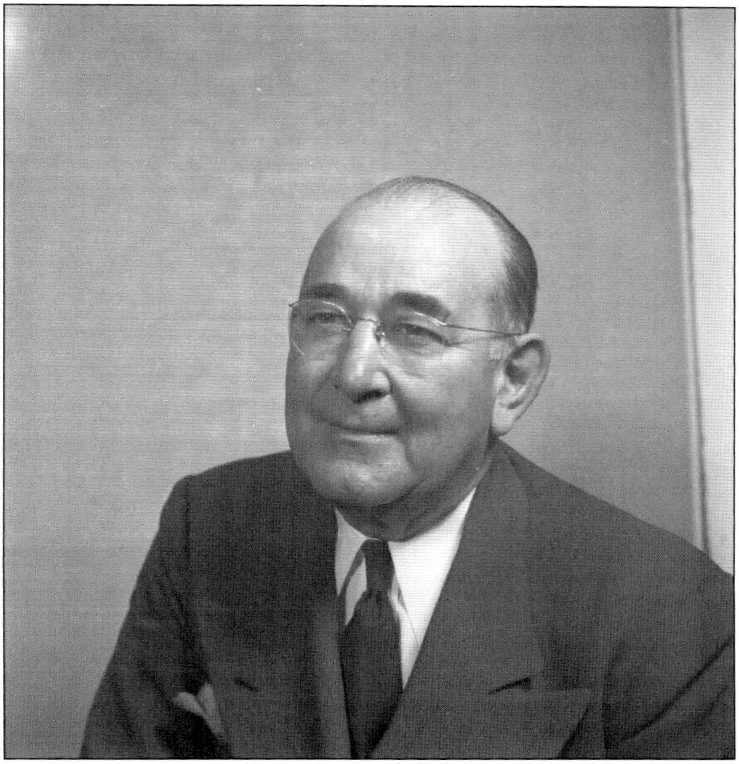

In the 1949 image above, Paramount Pictures Film Exchange management poses with a playful promotional sign depicting how, through their efforts, the exchange will bring in top film booking revenues. From left to right are Paramount Pictures distribution chief for the western United States Duke Clark, Paramount branch manager Carl H. "Buck" Weaver, and possible business partner Sam on the far right and in the portrait at right from November 21, 1949. (Both, courtesy of the Oklahoma Historical Society.)

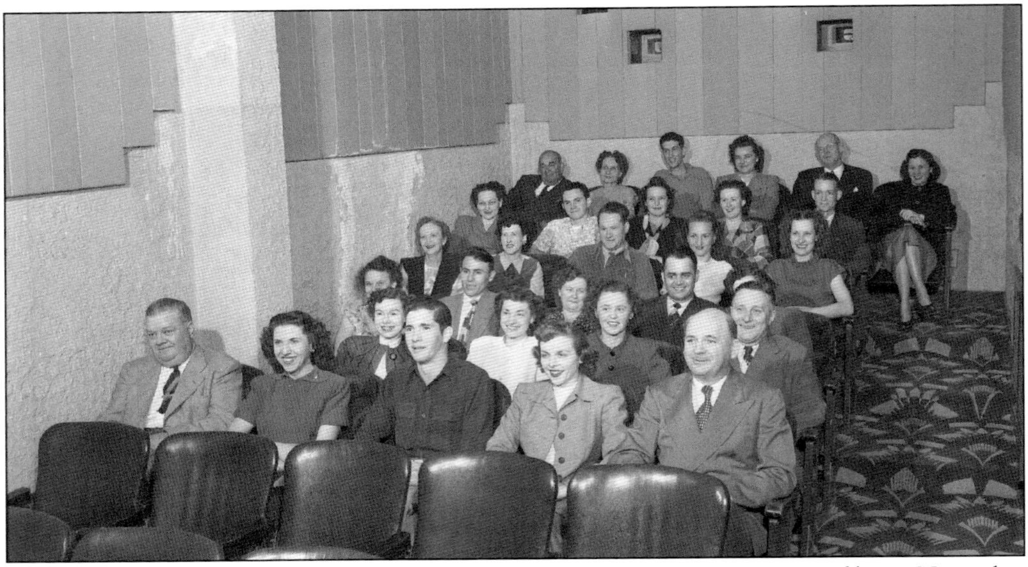

Paramount Picture Film Exchange employees and management prepare to screen a film on November 21, 1949. The screening room and equipment was owned by Paramount but operated by Russell Godwin. Godwin operated the screening room as a one-man show, maintaining equipment, films, screening logs, and janitorial needs. The room could seat up to 50 patrons consisting of theatre managers, theatre owners, film salesmen, exchange managers, film critics, management, and staff. Exhibited films were shown from numerous exchange studios present along Film Row. Paramount branch manager Carl H. Weaver sits in a front aisle seat on the right. Below, children prepare themselves for a screening treat. Carl Weaver sits in the back row. (Both, courtesy of the Oklahoma Historical Society.)

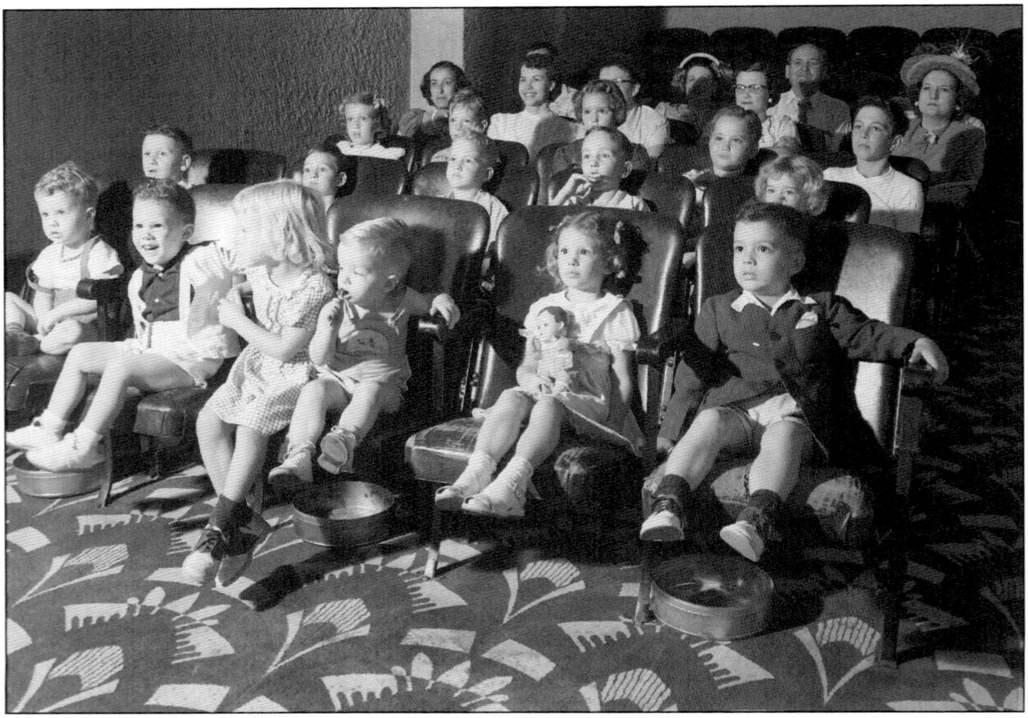

The November 21, 1949, image at right is of Carlton Howard "Buck" Weaver, Paramount Pictures Film Exchange branch manager. Weaver and his wife, Mignonet, were active members in Oklahoma City society. Weaver took charge of the Paramount branch in approximately 1938. Mignonet was an avid doll collector and travelled the world speaking about them. Their sons, Charles W. Weaver and Carlton H. Weaver Jr., served with distinction in the US armed forces during World War II, while their father served in World War I. According to Mrs. Carlton Weaver Jr., Carlton Senior was very kind and loved by all who knew him. Below are three fellow exchange managers. The man on the left may be Sam, while the other two are unidentified. (Both, courtesy of the Oklahoma Historical Society.)

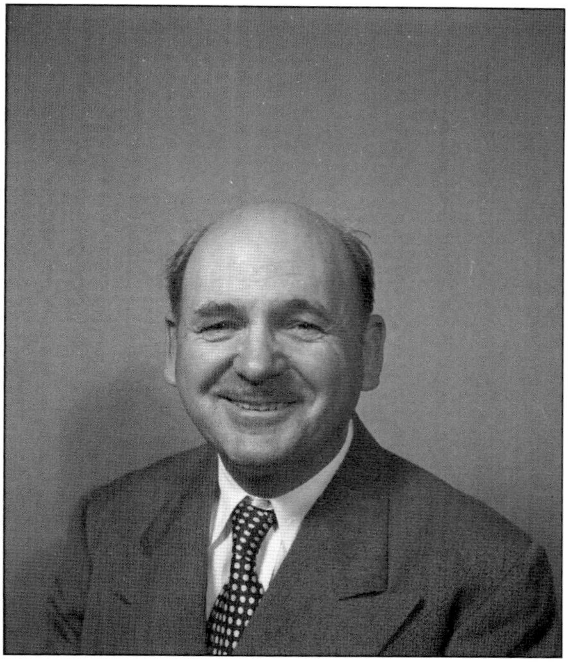

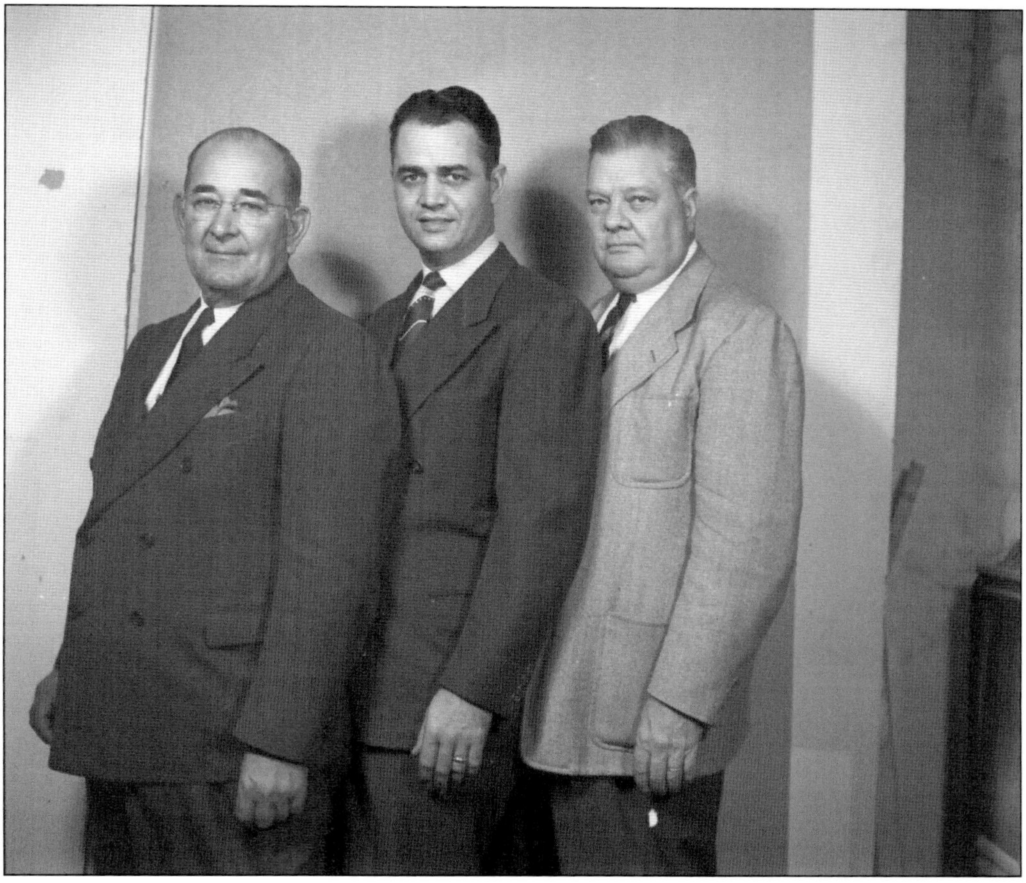

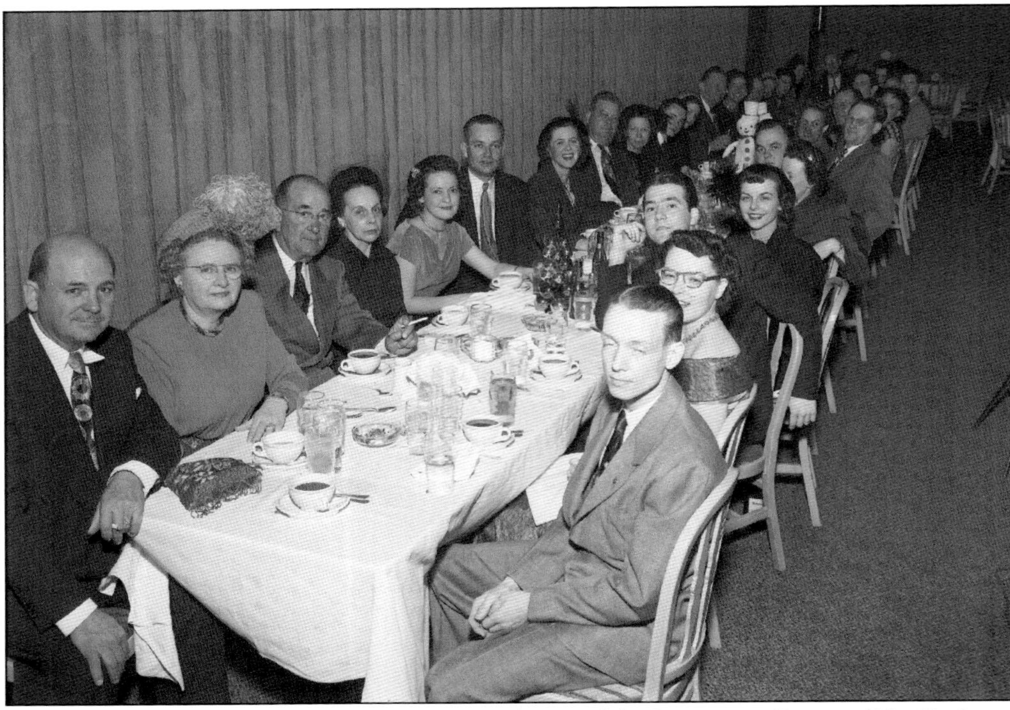

In this image, taken on December 10, 1949, employees of the Paramount Pictures Film Exchange celebrate Christmas in the Skirvin Tower's Persian Room at 101 Park Avenue. Above, branch manager Carl H. Weaver sits at the head of the table alongside his wife, Mignonet. Carlton H. Weaver Jr. sits across from them. (Both, courtesy of the Oklahoma Historical Society.)

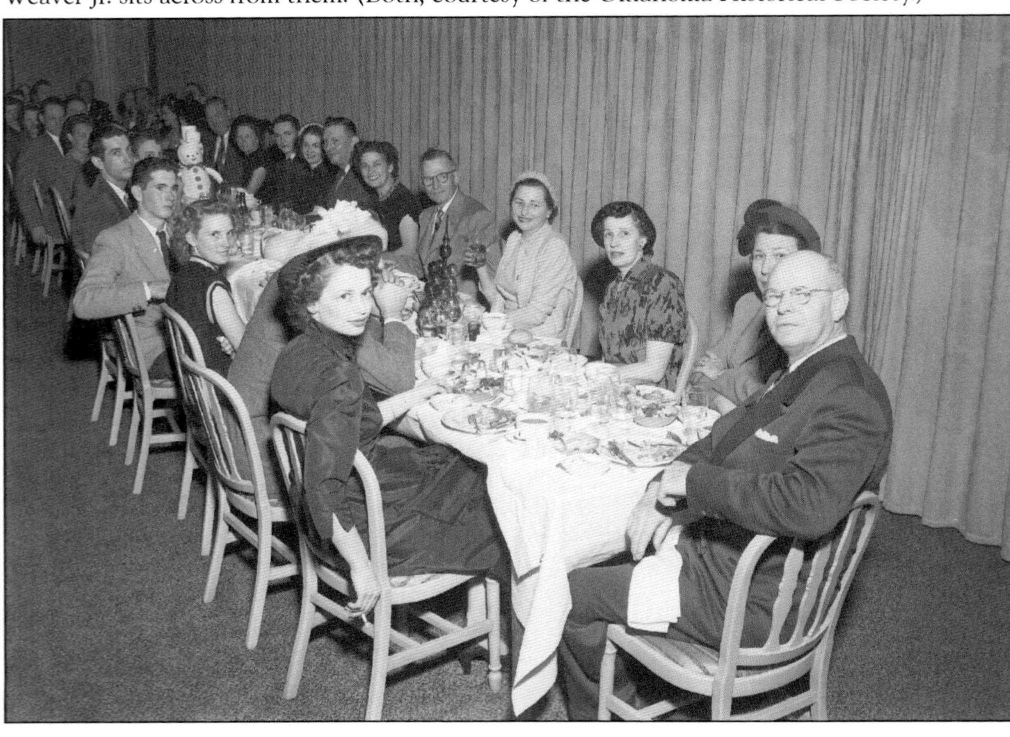

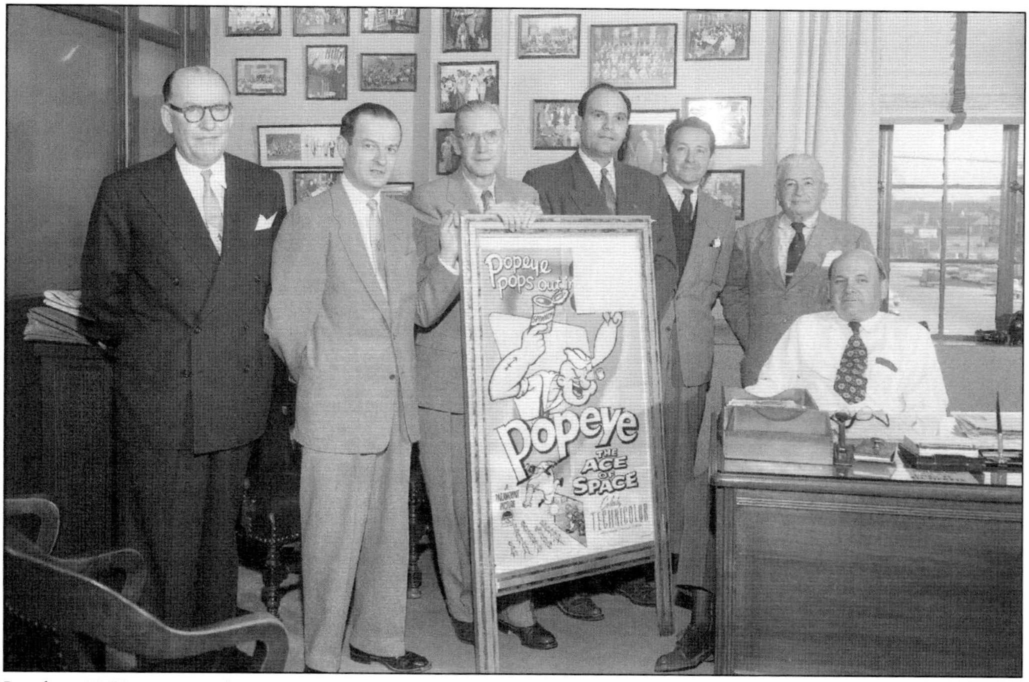

In this 1953 image, the Paramount marketing team poses with a framed *Popeye the Ace of Space* foldout promotional poster alongside them in branch manager Carl H. Weaver's office at 700 West Grand Avenue in Oklahoma City. (Courtesy of the Oklahoma Historical Society.)

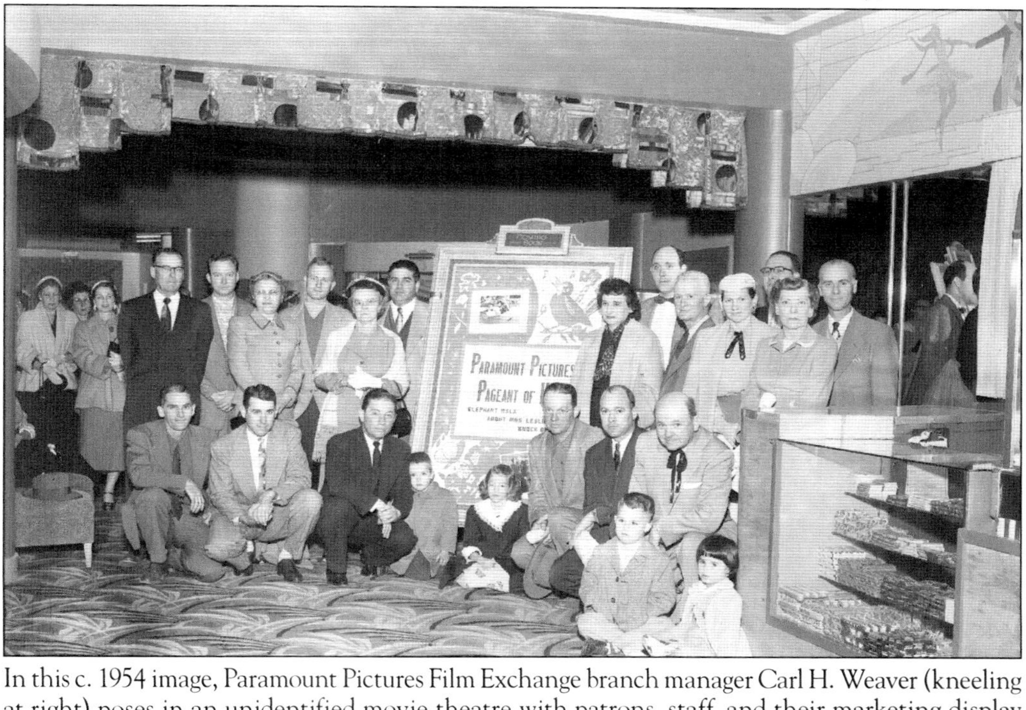

In this c. 1954 image, Paramount Pictures Film Exchange branch manager Carl H. Weaver (kneeling at right) poses in an unidentified movie theatre with patrons, staff, and their marketing display for Paramount's upcoming Pageant Week featuring *Elephant Walk*, *About Mrs. Leslie*, and *Knock on Wood*. (Courtesy of the Oklahoma Historical Society.)

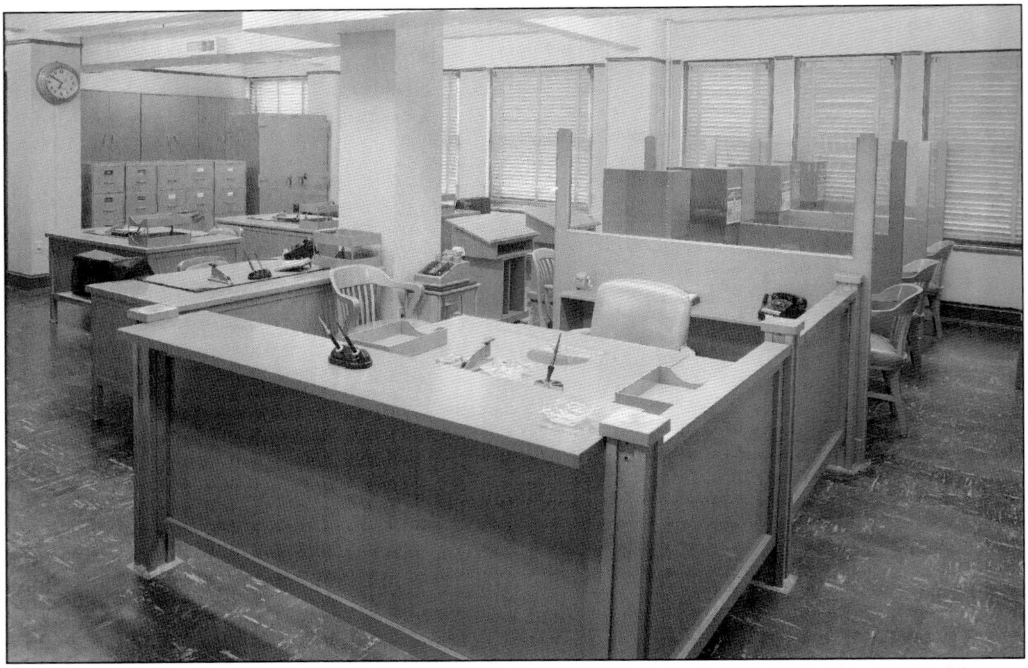

In 1956, the Paramount Pictures Film Exchange relocated to the Commerce Exchange Building at 130 West Grand Avenue in Oklahoma City while maintaining film storage and limited operations at 704 West Grand Avenue. The image above is of its new sixth-floor reception desk area, where the Paramount logo is emblazoned on the desk's blotter. The image below shows the main work space. Through the open door of the office in the background, film booking agents worked from two desks. (Both, courtesy of the Oklahoma Historical Society.)

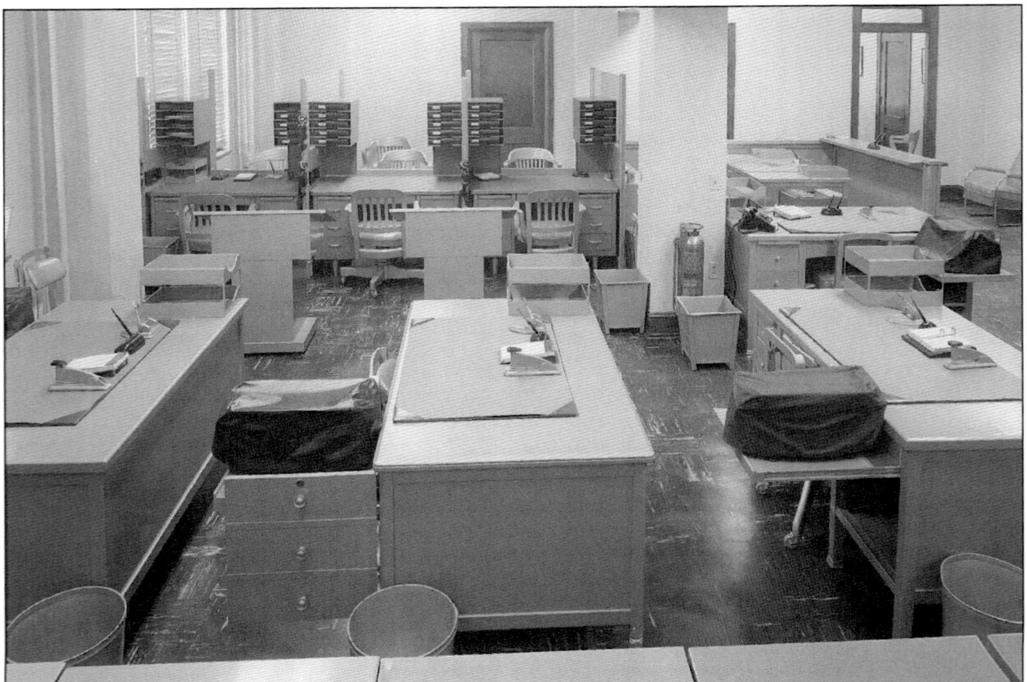

Four

That Movie on TV?

In 1919, a small amusement company owned by three brothers, Louis C. Griffith, Rupert E. Griffith, and Henry Griffith, launched the Oklahoma Specialty Film Company exchange. Over the next 20 years, Griffith Amusement Company, as the exchange would be known, amassed 156 theaters in 49 towns across Oklahoma, Texas, and New Mexico, becoming one of the largest independent theater circuits and distributors in the nation. Griffith based its operations at 621 West Grand Avenue in Oklahoma City until moving into its permanent home at nearby 11 North Lee Avenue.

Louis C. Griffith was an avid philanthropist and insisted that members of the company support their community and that his managers belong to the local chamber of commerce and civic organizations. In a Griffith brochure, he states, "We want you to be good citizens, trying at all times to make your community a better place in which to live, for what concerns your community also concerns you." Griffith backed his policy by paying for all membership dues. As a result, employees were both loyal and innovative.

The chain evolved into Video Independent Theatres after L.C. Griffith suffered a debilitating stroke in 1949. Henry Griffing, as Video's new chief operating officer, continued operations and encouraged change for the aging theater circuit. Through his leadership, Video changed theater operations, embraced television by investing in startup costs for Oklahoma's KWTV Channel 9, and created the first theater-supported television show and commercial, while conceiving and creating Telemovie, the precursor for today's cable television.

Over the course of 64 years, the Griffith Amusement Company and its legacies Video Independent Theatres, Video-Vumore TV, and Vumore TV would influence and shape the entire Midwest theater and television industry. Their personnel, offices, theaters, and fleet of service and delivery trucks dotted the southwest. Their philanthropic and innovative efforts continue touching Oklahoma, nearly 30 years after the curtain fell on the circuit's legacy.

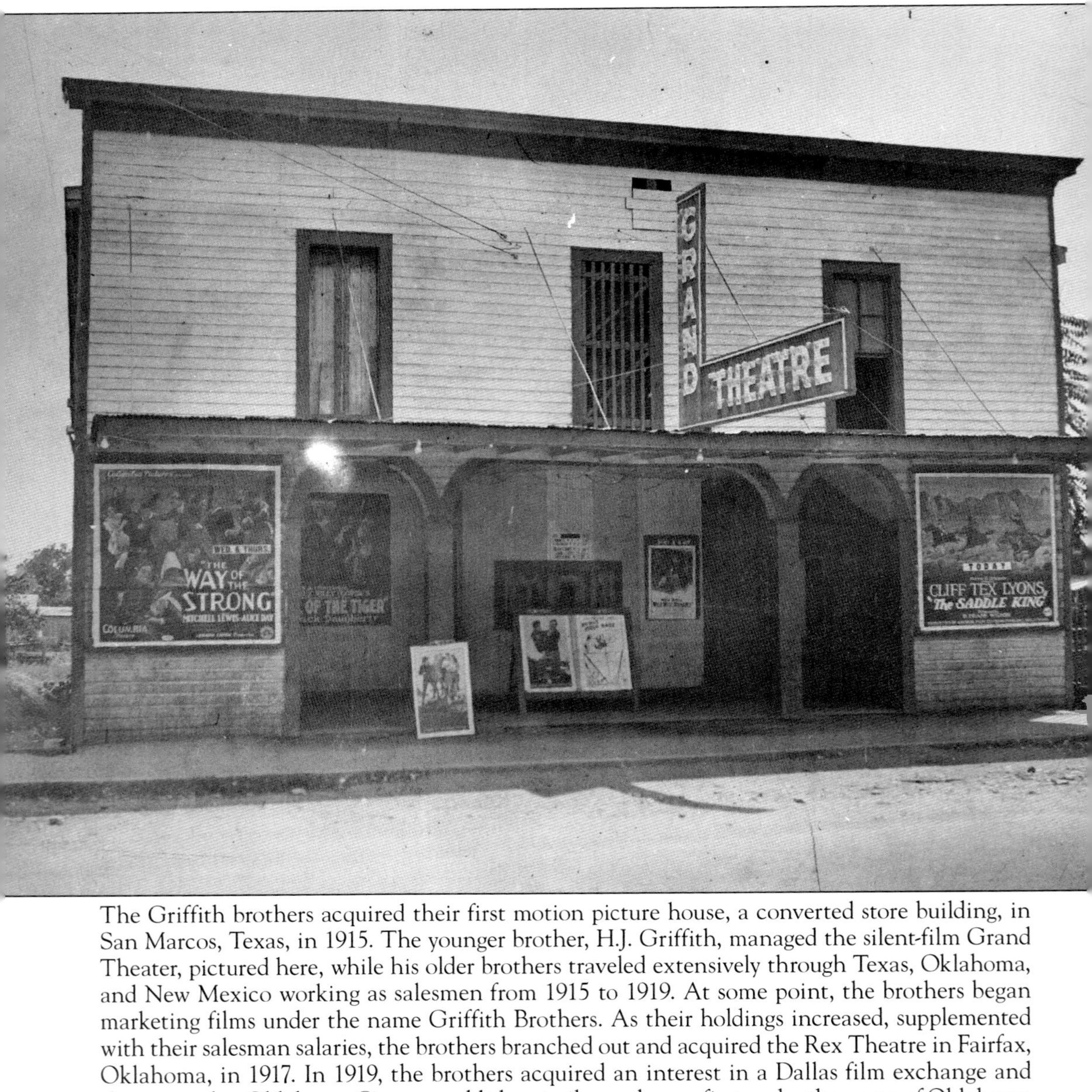

The Griffith brothers acquired their first motion picture house, a converted store building, in San Marcos, Texas, in 1915. The younger brother, H.J. Griffith, managed the silent-film Grand Theater, pictured here, while his older brothers traveled extensively through Texas, Oklahoma, and New Mexico working as salesmen from 1915 to 1919. At some point, the brothers began marketing films under the name Griffith Brothers. As their holdings increased, supplemented with their salesman salaries, the brothers branched out and acquired the Rex Theatre in Fairfax, Oklahoma, in 1917. In 1919, the brothers acquired an interest in a Dallas film exchange and then moved to Oklahoma City to establish a similar exchange first under the name of Oklahoma Specialty Film Company. (Courtesy of the Oklahoma Historical Society.)

Pictured at right is oldest brother Louis Clyde Griffith, and below is Rupert Earl Griffith. The two brothers, along with a third, Henry Jefferson Griffith, created the Griffith Amusement Company. Prior to motion picture sales, Louis served as either a salesman for a nonalcoholic extract or tobacco for the American Tobacco Company. The brothers started their own distribution company around 1919, after Louis served as a soldier in World War I. He then became a prominent philanthropist, founder of the Oklahoma City Variety Club, and a Shriner with India Temple. As an active member of the Oklahoma City Chamber of Commerce and vice president of the Young Men's Christian Association, he was a driving force behind construction of a new YMCA building at the corner of Northwest Fifth Street and Robinson Avenue. This building would later become one of 324 buildings destroyed or damaged from the bombing of the Alfred P. Murrah building in Oklahoma City on April 19, 1995. It was razed in 2001. (Both, courtesy of the Oklahoma Historical Society.)

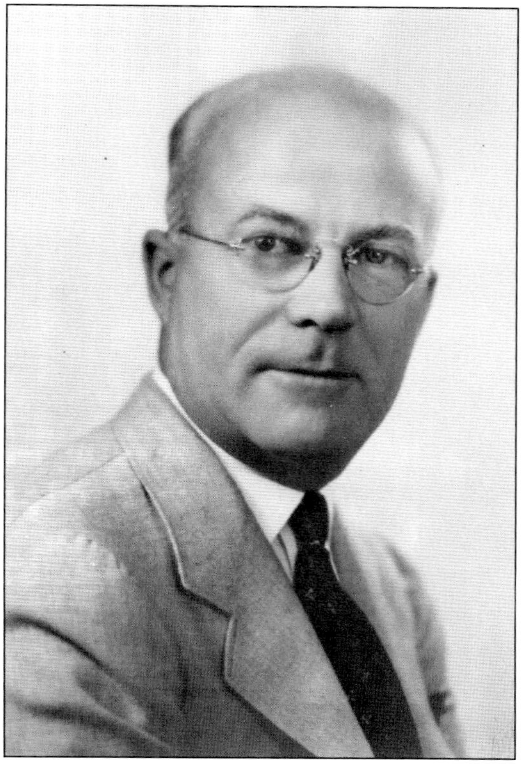

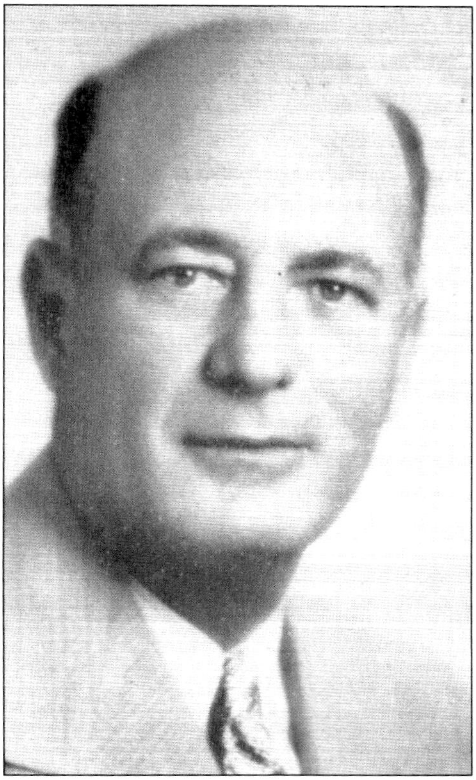

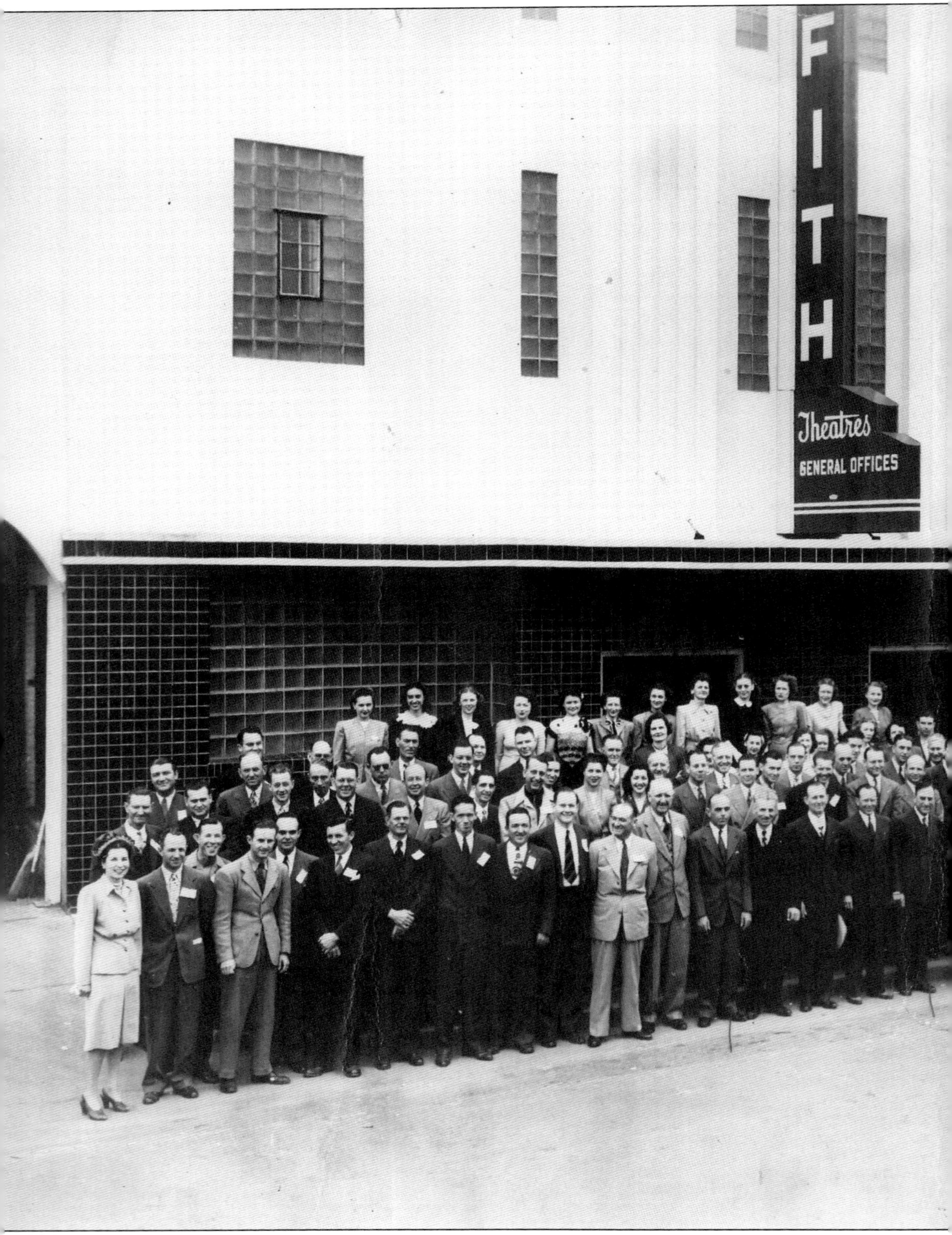
FITH
Theatres
GENERAL OFFICES

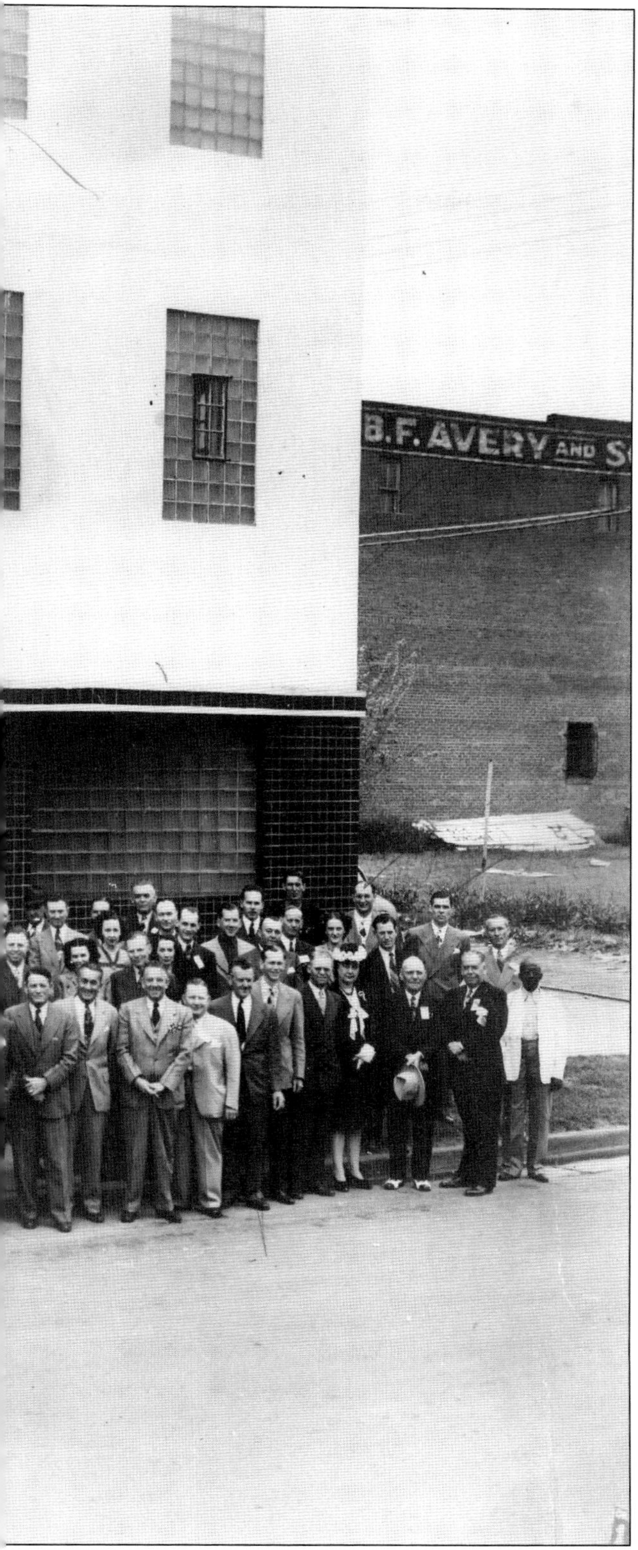

From April 10 to 11, 1946, Griffith Theatres hosted a state convention of theater managers and partners from its 54 theaters across the Southwest. Owner and brother Louis Clyde Griffith presided over the event. The convention celebrated the 31-year anniversary of Griffith Amusement. Here, attendees stand in front of the Griffith home offices at 11 North Lee Avenue. Louis Clyde Griffith stands in front, just right of center. The convention was hosted by the Skirvin Hotel and Beacon Club atop the First National Building. Approximately 175 attended the convention. (Courtesy of Steve Lackmeyer and RetroMetroOKC.org)

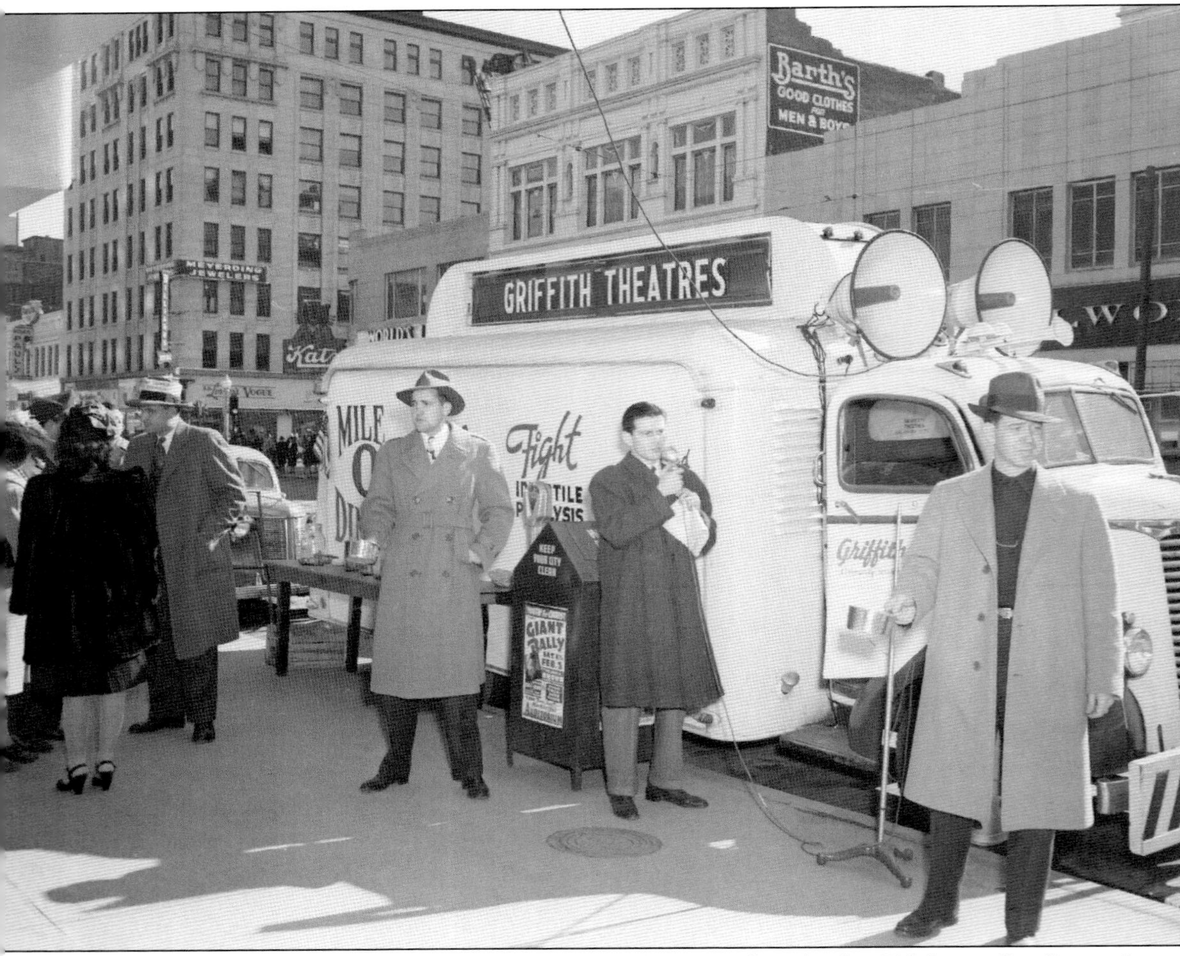

In 1946, this image was taken during sidewalk fundraising efforts by the Oklahoma City Jaycees' "Mile-O-Dimes" drive for the National Foundation of Infantile Paralysis. Griffith Theatres owner Louis C. Griffith initiated the drive in 1941 as its annual philanthropic company event. Griffith was president and campaign chairman of the Oklahoma division of the American Cancer Society. In 1946, he instituted a plan for public education about the disease through a state editorial writing contest. He personally contributed prizes for the four winning editors. The society adopted the idea nationwide the same year. Oklahoma's plan resulted in the formation of a mobile care unit that traveled the state and brought a free cancer detection clinic into its communities. (Courtesy of the Oklahoma Historical Society.)

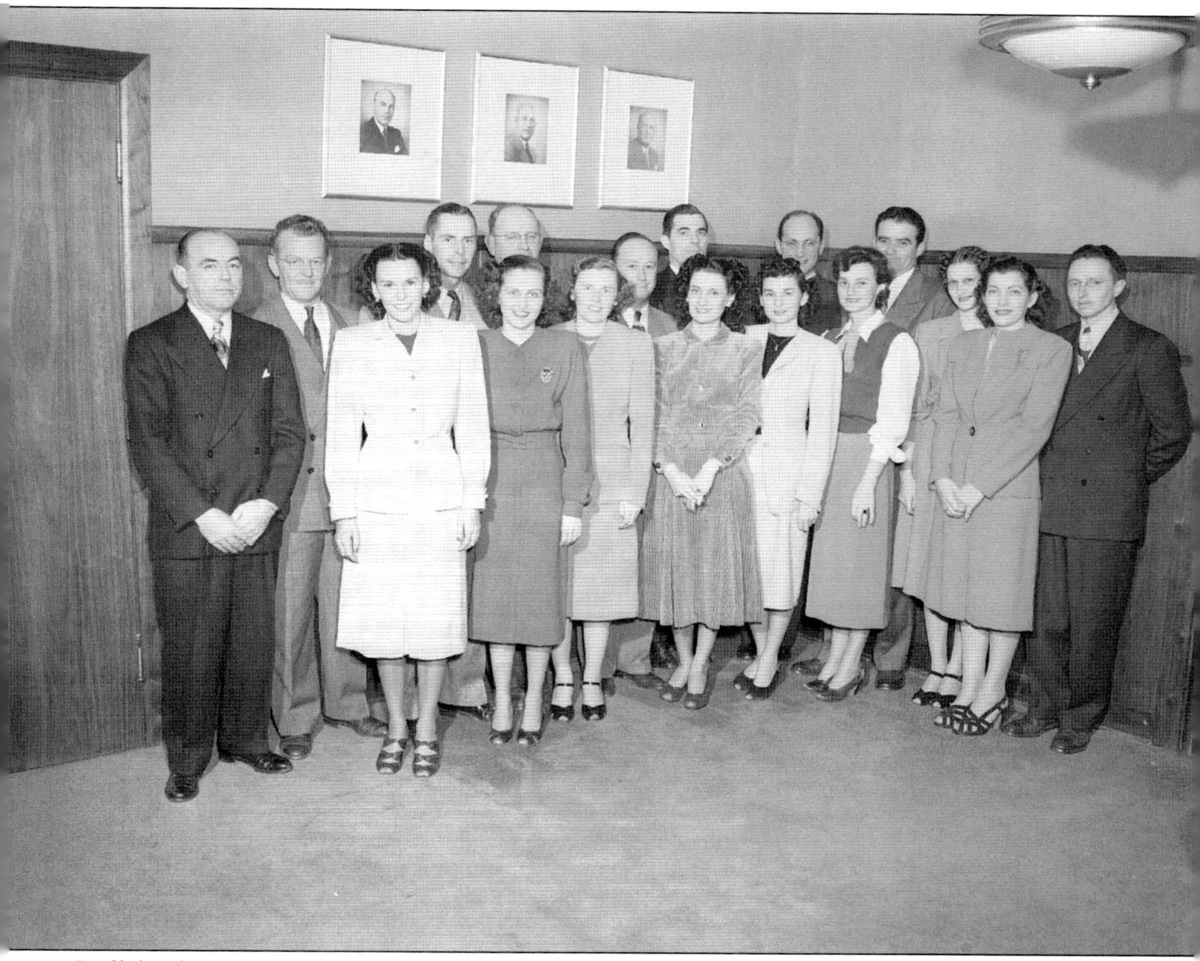

Griffith Theatres' home office administrative staff is pictured on December 5, 1947, in Charles Guthrie's office. From left to right are Claude Fulgham, director of theatre management and division manager; Amon Ince, director of construction and mechanical; Gertrude McGonigle, secretary to Claude Fulgham; Kenneth Blackledge, division manager; Fred Jackson, division manager; Allegra "Wee Gee" Thedford, receptionist and PBX operator; Fern Williams, secretary to Claude Motley; Claude Motley, theatre operations director; Henry Griffing, executive vice president and legal council; Betty Evans, secretary to Charles Guthrie; Nell O'Hara, concessions department clerk and screen advertising; Charles Guthrie, secretary-treasurer and personnel supervisor; Louise Wesson, concessions director and sub-rents; Robert Clark, assistant to Amon Ince; Mary Ragland, secretary to Amon Ince; Jane Harrison, concessions clerk and secretary to Louise Wesson; and Roger Rice, assistant to Claude Motley in film merchandising, exploitation, and publication of *Contact*. The wall photographs feature owners Henry Griffith, Louis Griffith, and Rupert Griffith. (Courtesy of the Oklahoma Historical Society.)

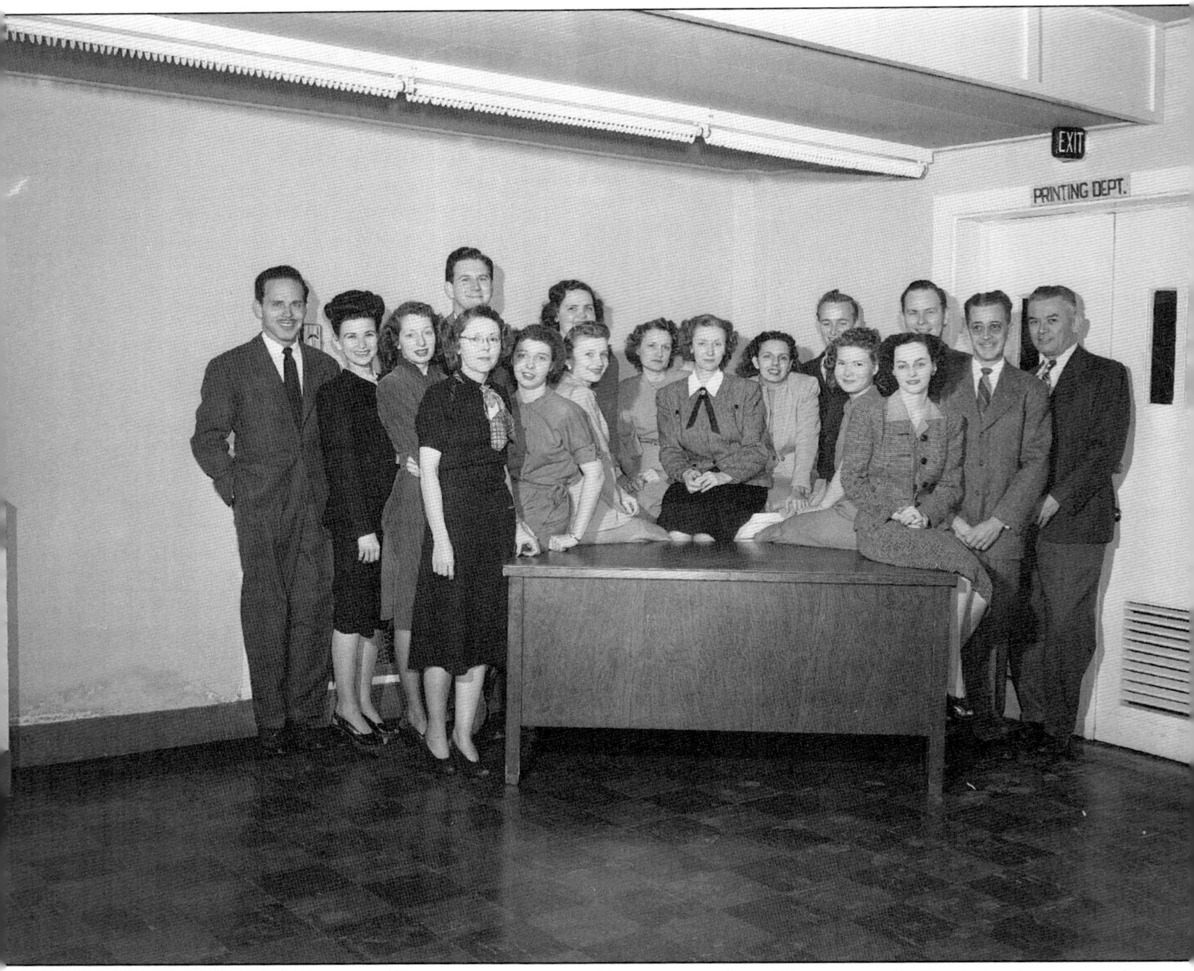

Griffith Theatres' home office accounting staff is pictured on December 5, 1947, in the general accounting offices. From left to right are Jack Brooks, office manager.; Juanita Henley, clerk; Mararet Moore, clerk; Evelyn Shaw, clerk; Samual Stone Jr., account assistant to Alva Horner; Jary Renshaw, secretary to Robert Bond; Imogene Moore, secretary to Jack Brooks; Jeannie Hollis, payroll; Evelyn Smith, insurance; Agnes Blackmon, payroll and personnel; Ruth Trosper, Comptometer operator; Don Wind, bookkeeper; Annebelle Thompson, Comptometer operator; Elma Best, Comptometer operator; Robert McGraw, auditor; Alva Horner, property accounts and construction records; and Green Bond, cashier, receipts, and disbursements. Not pictured is Evelyn Forgue, mail clerk and assistant to Evelyn Smith. (Courtesy of the Oklahoma Historical Society.)

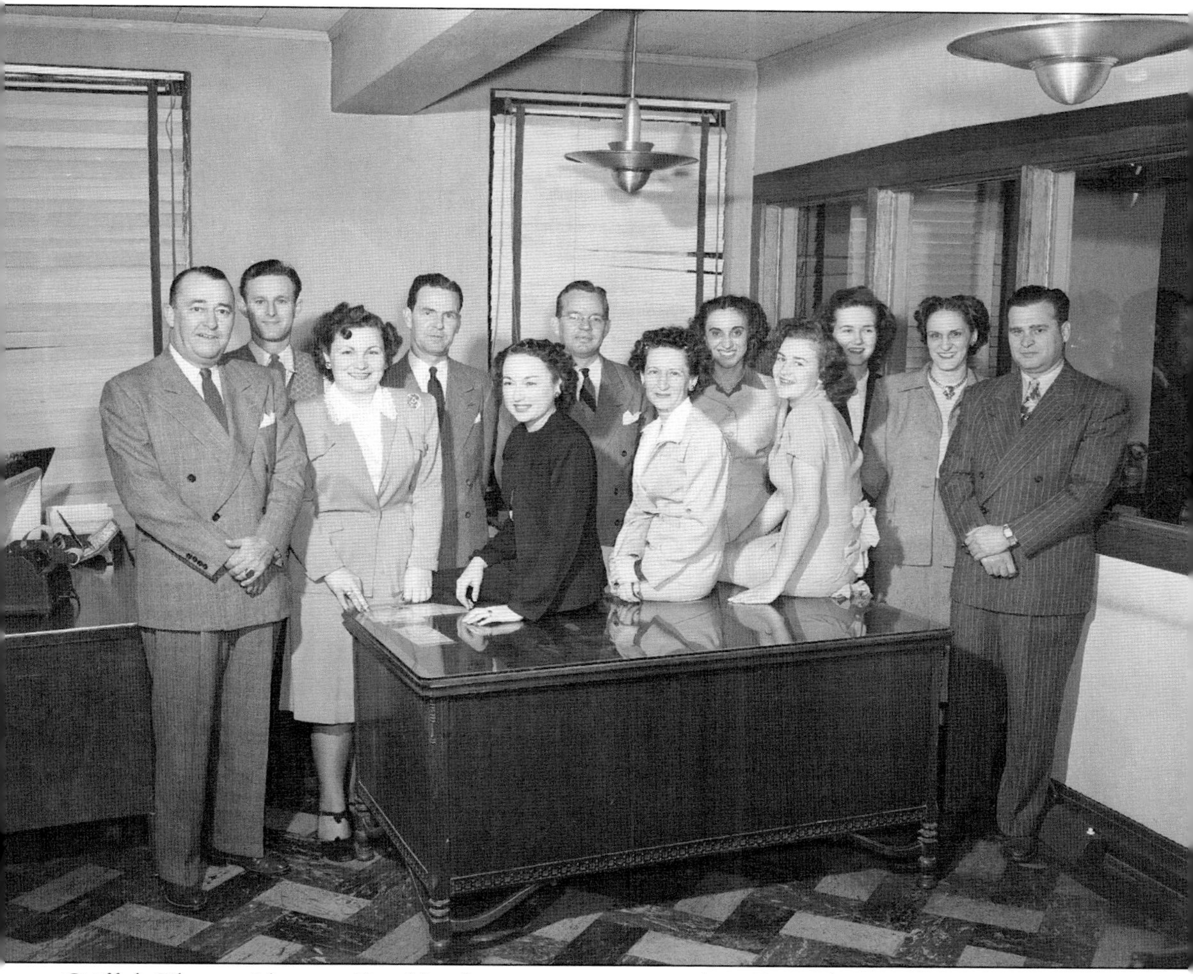

Griffith Theatres' home office film department is pictured on December 5, 1947, in the film department accounting room. From left to right are Lester Gibbs, feature booker; Bob Aldridge, film rental payment; Bernice Coley, secretary to John King; Frank McCabe, feature booker; Erlene Nahrgang, secretary to Frank McGabe and Roy Avey Jr.; John King, short subject booker; Evelyn Doty, film contracts and secretary to Cliff White Jr.; Mary O'Leary, secretary to Lester Gibbs; Helen Polly, assistant to Bob Aldridge; Betty Crawford, assistant to Marcella Proffit; Marcella "Ted" Proffit, analyst; and Roy Avey Jr., feature booker. Not pictured are Raymond Higdon, Dallas film buyer, and Cliff White Jr., assistant film buyer. (Courtesy of the Oklahoma Historical Society.)

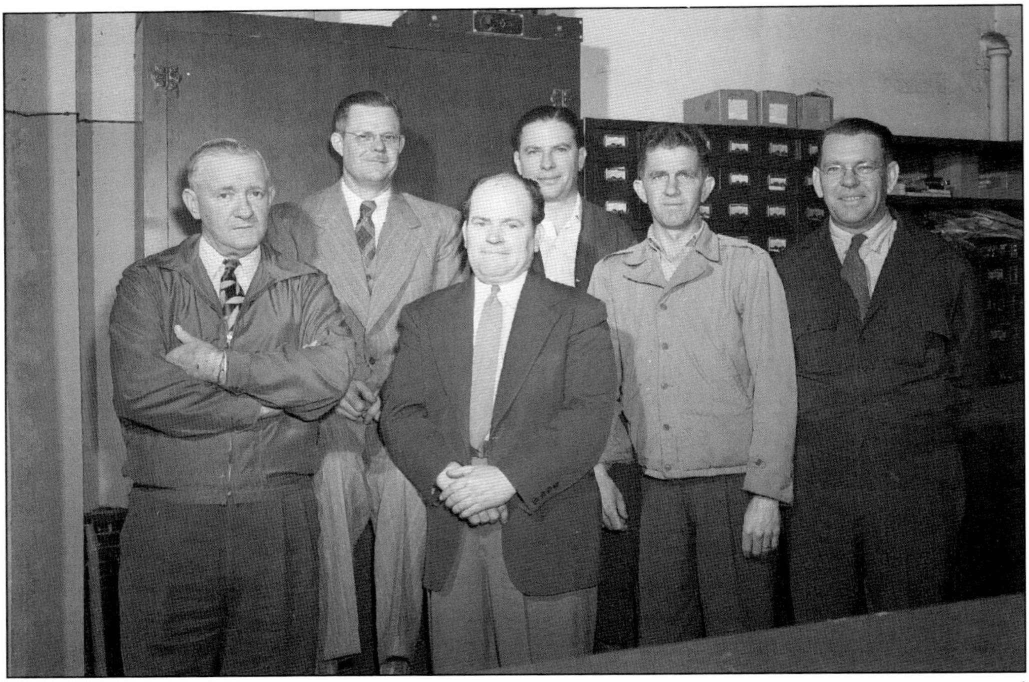

Griffith Theatres' home office mechanical, cabinet, drapery, and garage departments are pictured on December 5, 1947, in the mechanical department shop. From left to right are George Gaffaney, theatre operations mechanic; Doyle Stalcup, head of cabinet and drapery; Thomas Nelson, assistant to Doyle Stalcup; John Ormond, theatre operations mechanic; Earl Albright, building manager and home office maintenance; and Tom Kelley, head of auto maintenance, warehouse, and storage. (Courtesy of the Oklahoma Historical Society.)

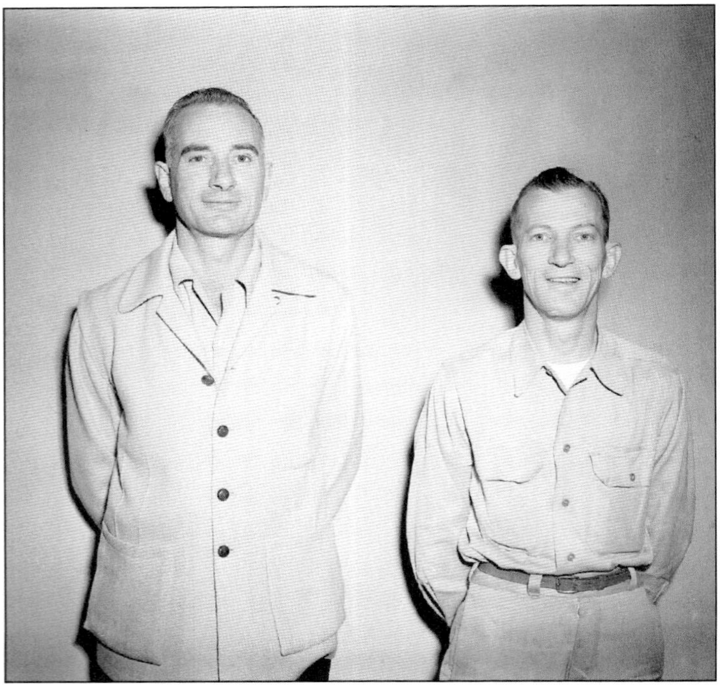

Robert Barthelemy Kiser (left) and Cecil Williams (right), theatre operations and tin shop mechanics, are shown on December 5, 1947, in the mechanical department shop. Williams also served as head of concession equipment repair after his return from 38 months as an Army signalman during World War II; he held the post at Griffith Theatres until his death. (Courtesy of the Oklahoma Historical Society.)

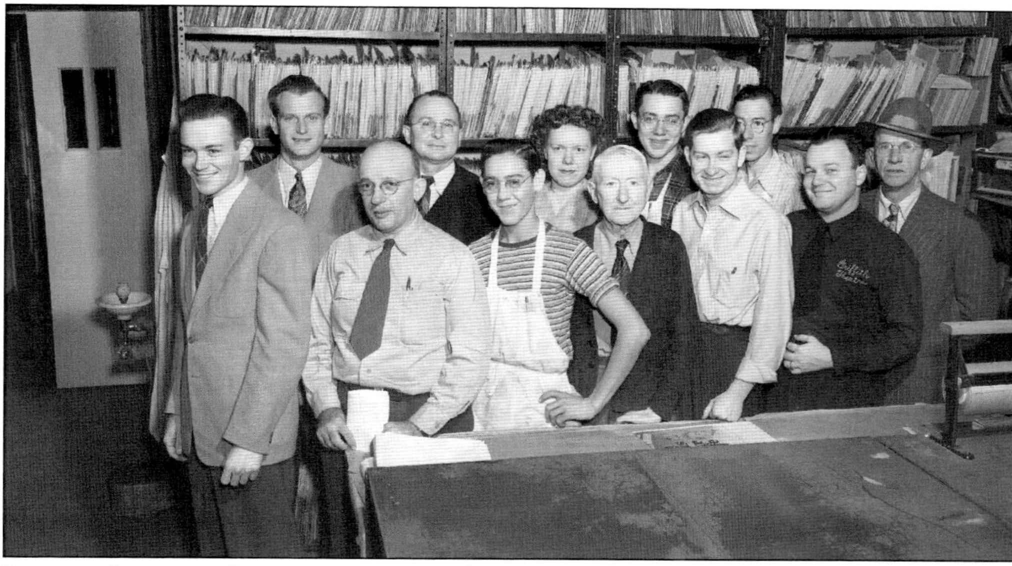

Poster and printing departments personnel are pictured at Griffith Theatres' home office on December 5, 1947, in the poster department's checking and wrapping room. From left to right are Elmer Pace Jr., printing and stationery department; Bernhart Jacobs, head of printing and stationery department; Hobart J. Rhoades, assistant to Leonard R. Bateman; Leonard R. Bateman, head of poster department; Harold Free, poster clerk; Aroma McNutt, secretary to Leonard R. Bateman; Frank Kelley, poster clerk; John Augustine, poster clerk; Bobby Head, poster clerk; Winifred White, poster clerk; Charles Tharp Jr., poster clerk; and Sam Lupo, poster clerk. (Courtesy of the Oklahoma Historical Society.)

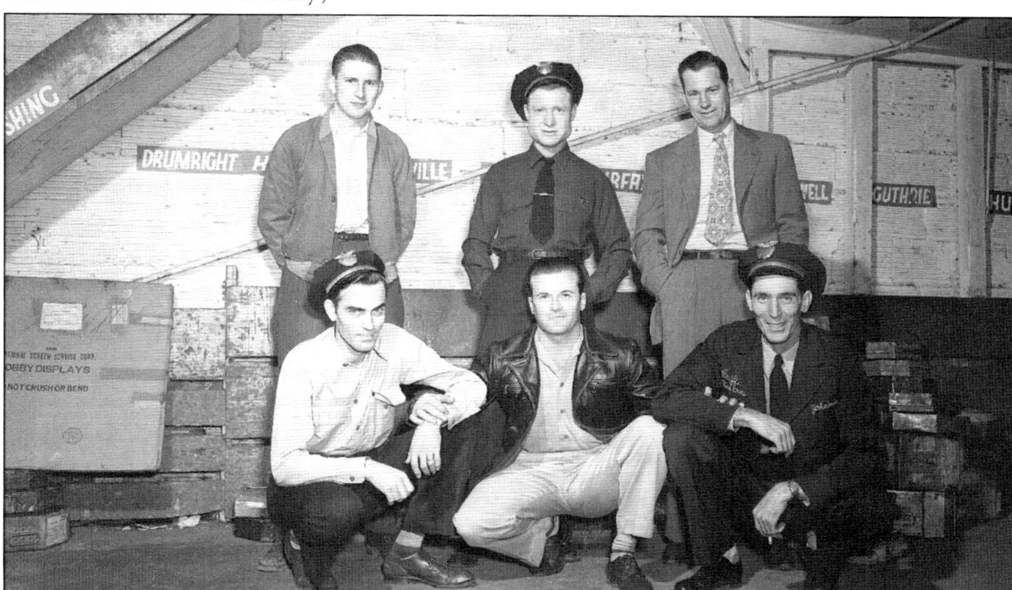

The shipping department of Griffith Theatres' home office is shown on December 5, 1947, in the shipping room. From left to right are (first row) Charles Stipe, driver, west run; Guy Porter, head concession, equipment, and warehouse shipments; and Claude W. Johnson, driver, south run; (second row) William Raymond, first shipper; J.D. McNutt, driver, north run; and Alfred Baird, head of shipping department. (Courtesy of the Oklahoma Historical Society.)

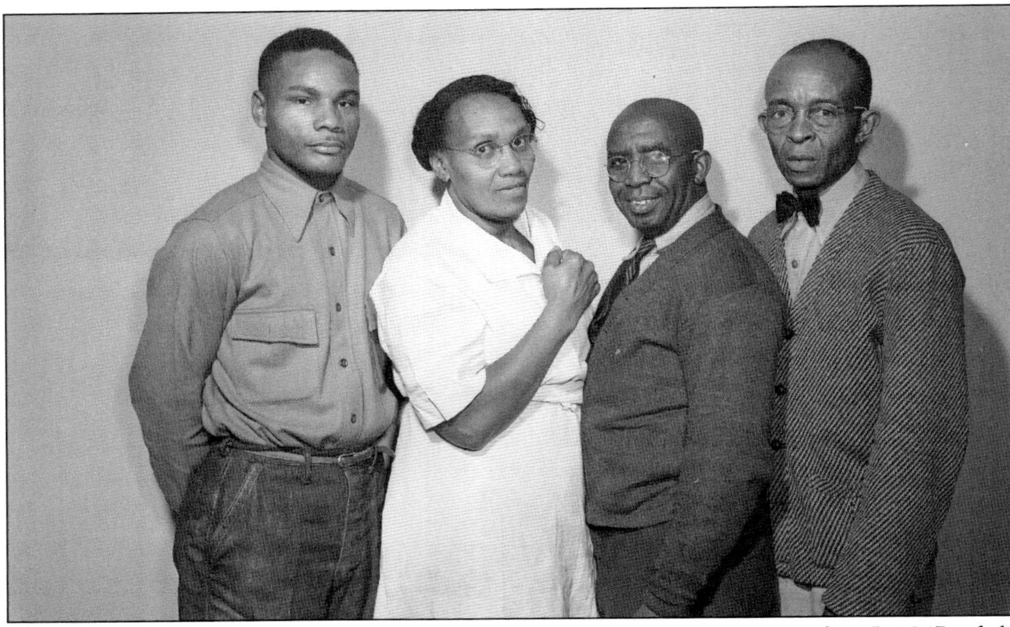

This picture was taken in Griffith Theatres' accounting room on December 5, 1947, of the maintenance and porter section of 11 North Lee Avenue. Pictured from left to right are Wilbert Parker, Carrie Kimbrough, Willie Johnson, and Thaddeus Nolan. The home office consisted of three stories and would later add Paramount Pictures' two-story building and numerous west side additions—a large responsibility for a team of four.

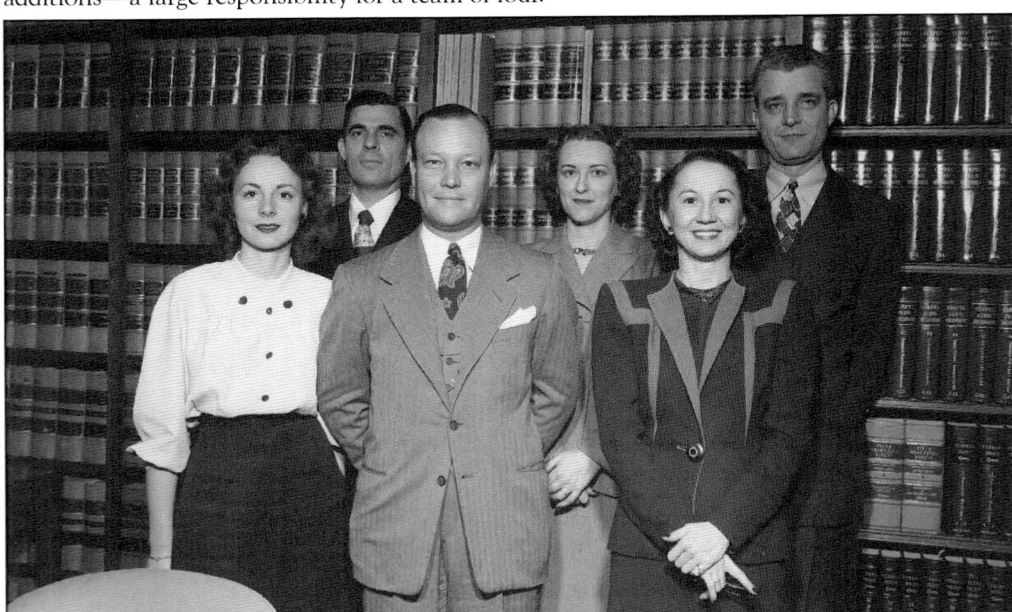

The Video Independent Theatres legal team poses in its First National Building offices. Along the back row at far left stands Henry Griffing, who took the helm of Video in the 1950s. During his term, he helped Video heal from its extensive legal troubles and introduced the drive-in theatre to the Midwest region. Griffing moved his team to 11 North Lee Avenue after extensive remodeling in 1953. (Courtesy of the Oklahoma Historical Society.)

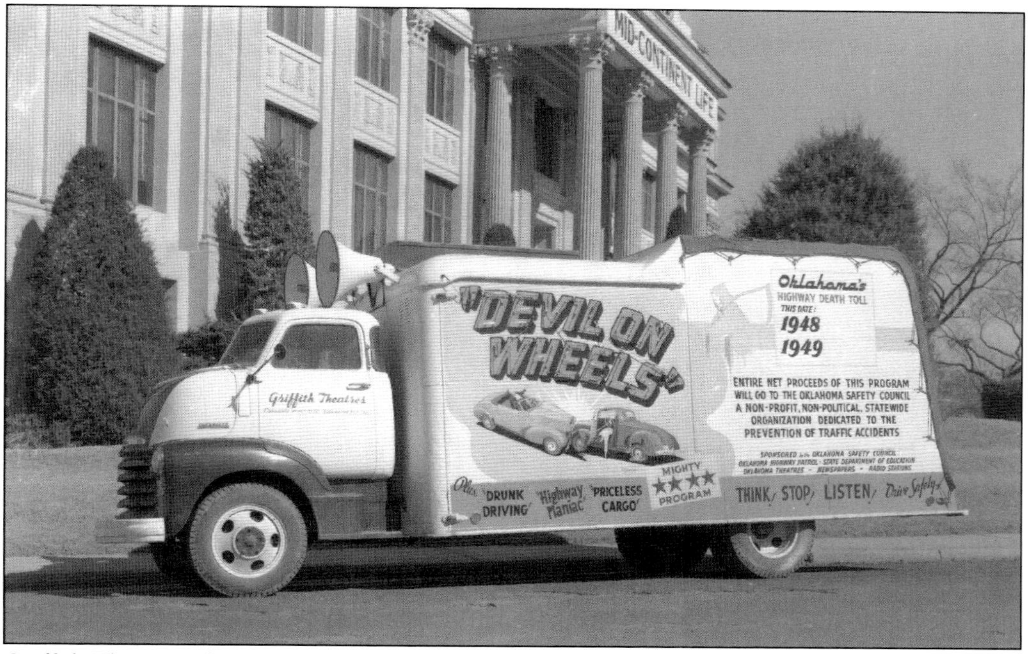

Griffith Theatres often promoted upcoming films or events with trucks hosting a variety of special features, including a generator to power sound, neon lights, signs, banners, and custom-installed searchlights. Outside the Mid-Continent Life building at 1400 North Classen Boulevard in the February 9, 1949, image above, special screenings of *Devil on Wheels* raised awareness to the dangers of reckless driving, with proceeds going to the Oklahoma Safety Council. Below, Video Independent Theatres, a subsidiary of Griffith, offered a road show truck for the jubilee movie week of June 10, 1950. This truck shows a platform stage where speakers and promoters talked up the films and presented prizes from the truck's rear. Such trucks often drew large crowds. This image is in front of the Griffith fleet shop at 701 West Grand Avenue in Oklahoma City. (Both, courtesy of the Oklahoma Historical Society.)

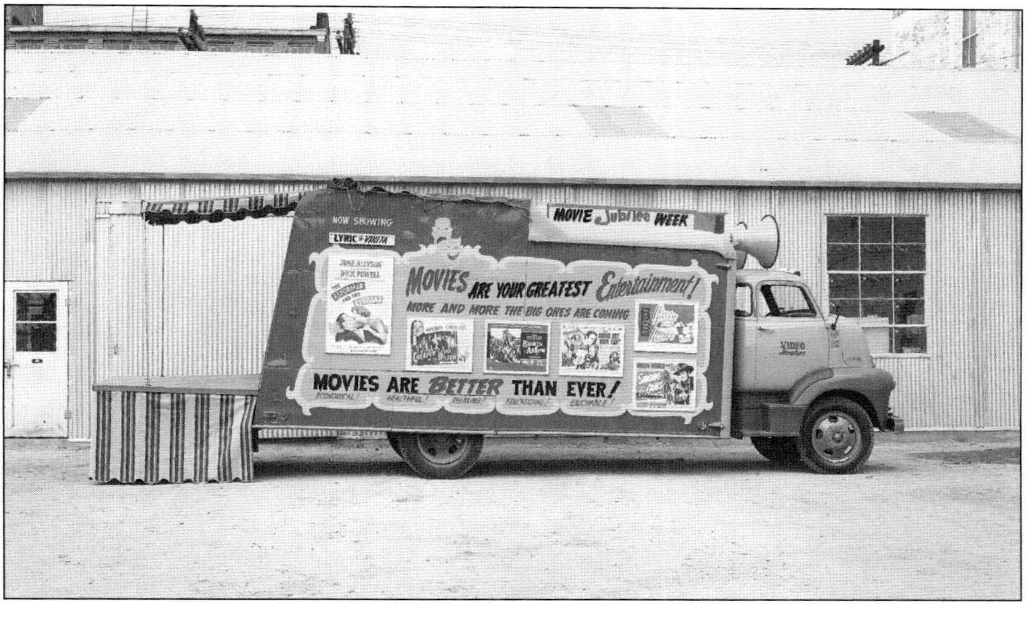

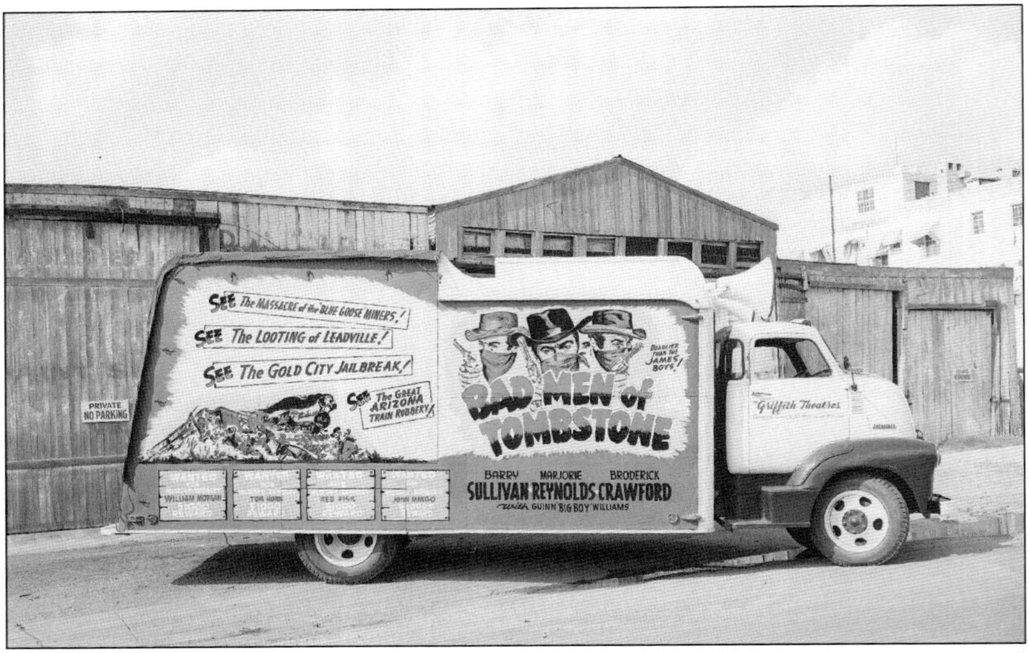

Griffith and, later, Video Independent Theatres dominated the Oklahoma theatre circuit, and although there was little competition, the chain would take measures to keep them in the lead. The most common campaign involved Griffith or Video road show trucks. These trucks festooned with promotional posters and lights were common among rural towns. The theatre chain would go as far as keeping closed houses in operating condition in rural towns, and if a competitor opened a theater, Griffith or Video would reopen the formerly closed house. In one extreme case, Griffith purchased the Paramount-owned Inca Theater in Okmulgee during the 1930s just to remove the competition. Shown here are two road show trucks. Above, this June 19, 1949, image markets *Bad Men of Tombstone*. The truck below promotes *Savage Splendor*. (Both, courtesy of the Oklahoma Historical Society.)

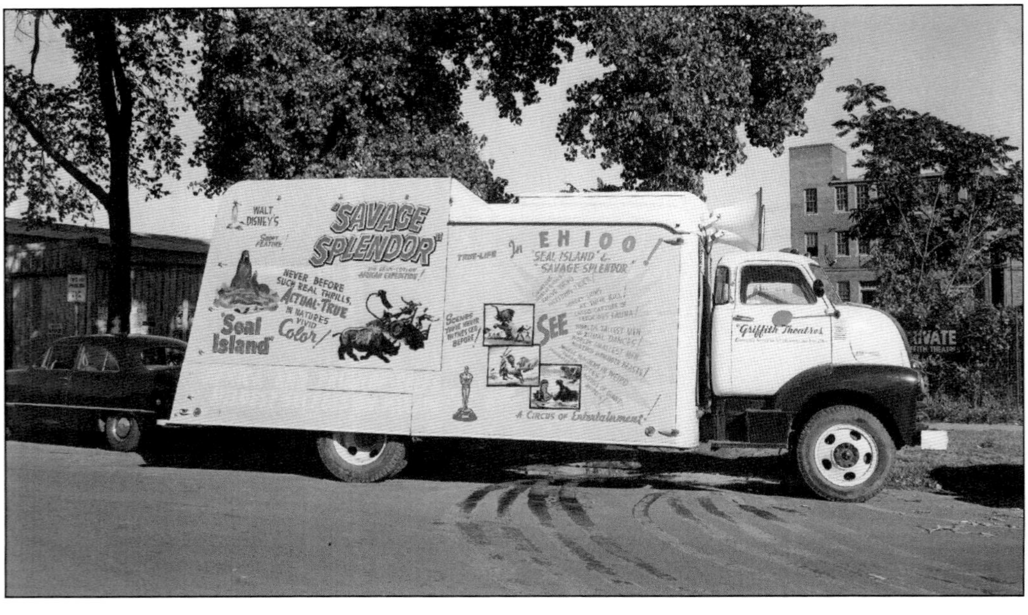

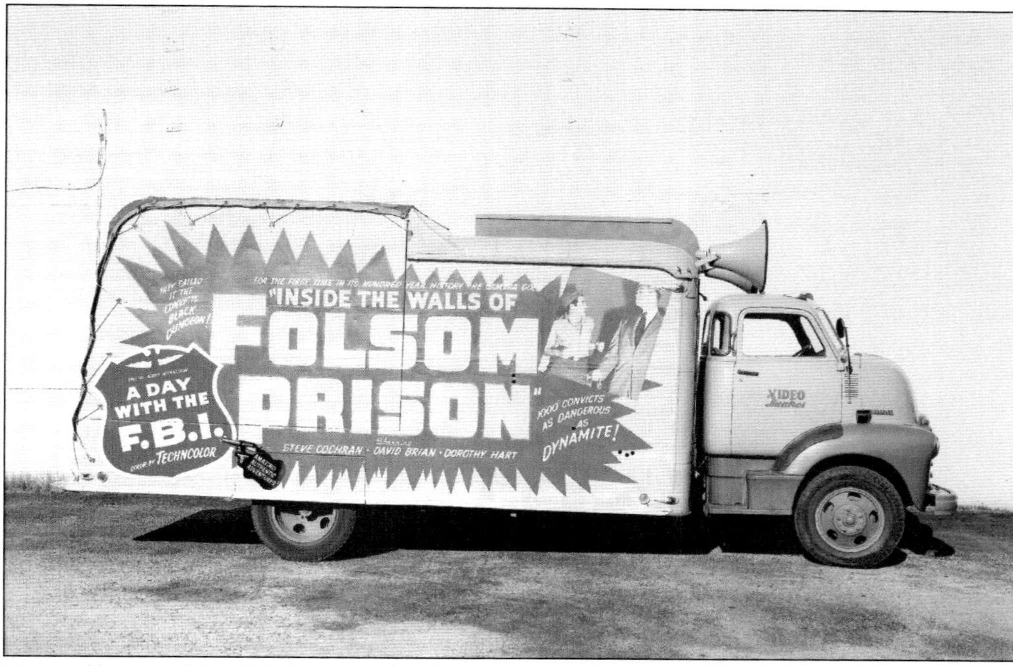

Pictured here on July 15, 1951, is another Video Independent Theatres road show truck promoting *Inside the Walls of Folsom Prison*. This particular rig carried a search light with a weather-protected back and a special set of front promotion boards and roll-out banner. The photograph was taken along the west side of the Paramount Pictures building. Following World War II, Griffith Theatres purchased a large number of surplus searchlights for use in its many drive-in theaters, road show trucks, special events, and outside conventional movie houses. During summer operating times, aircraft flying over Oklahoma would see numerous strobes sweeping the night skies. (Both, courtesy of the Oklahoma Historical Society and Roger E. Rice.)

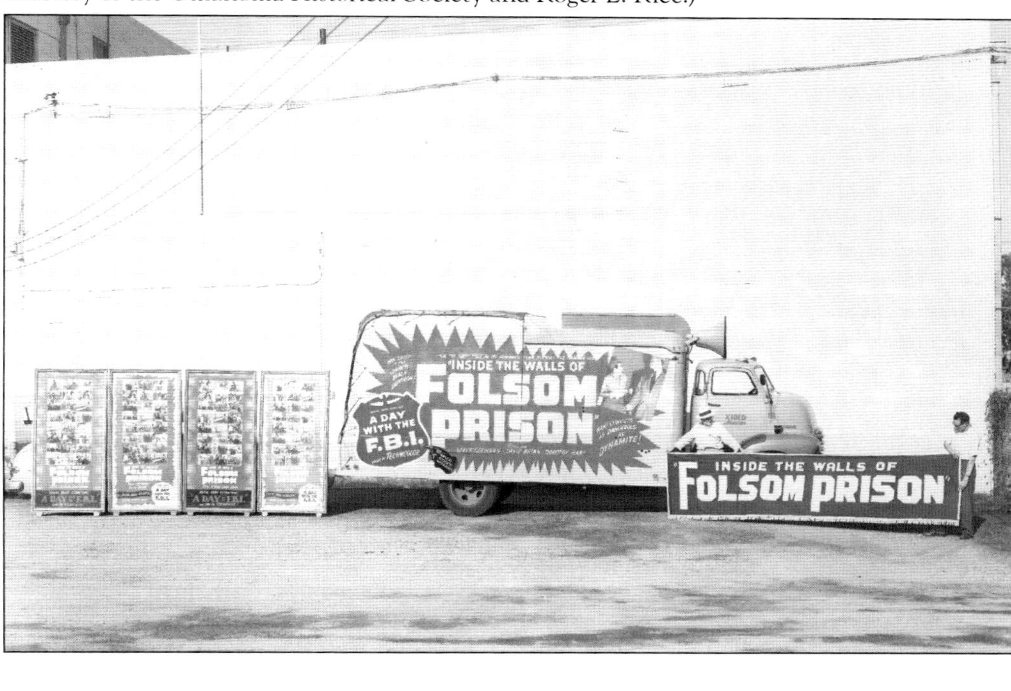

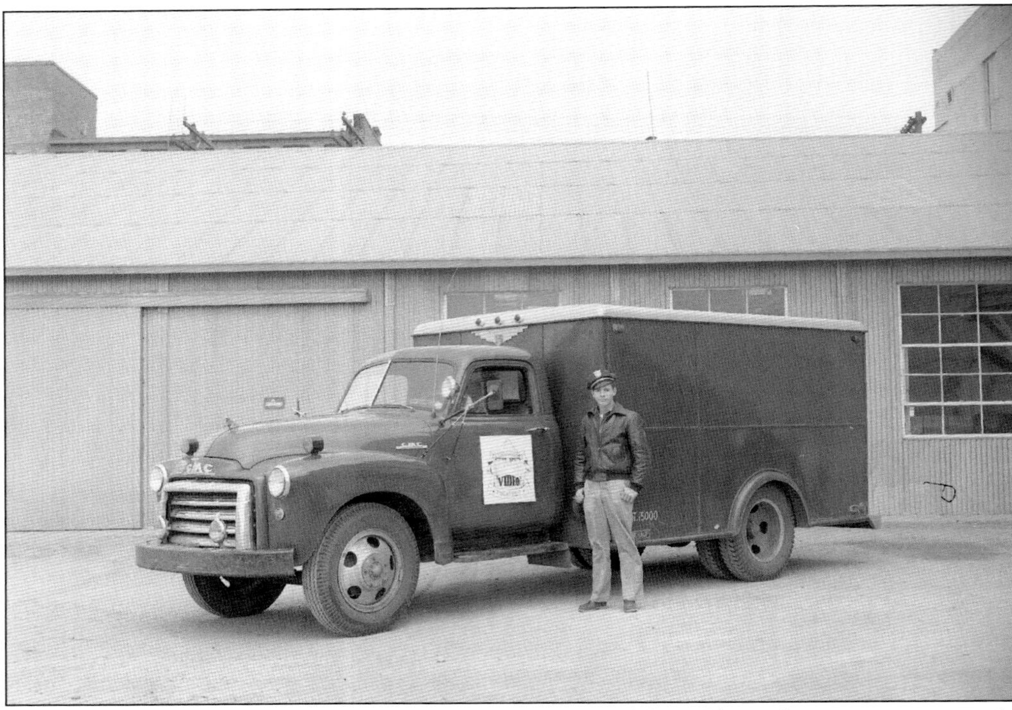

Video Independent Theatres employed a fleet of trucks to deliver film reels or services across the Video circuit daily, as seen in these two images with unknown drivers. Sometimes, an ambitious driver striving to get a set of reels to a theater in time for its 1:00 p.m. Sunday matinee would be stopped by Oklahoma's Highway Patrol for excessive speeding. A quick call to the shipping manager, Earl Albright, would often get the driver back on the road with little more than a warning and a promise to drive at least 70 miles per hour. (Both, courtesy of the Oklahoma Historical Society.)

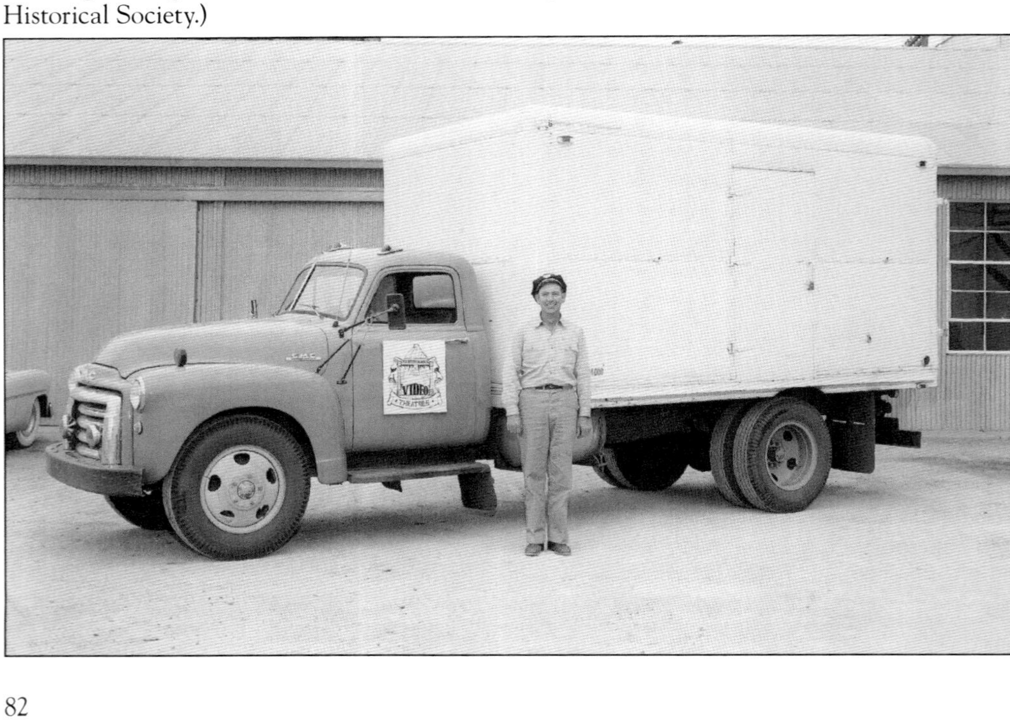

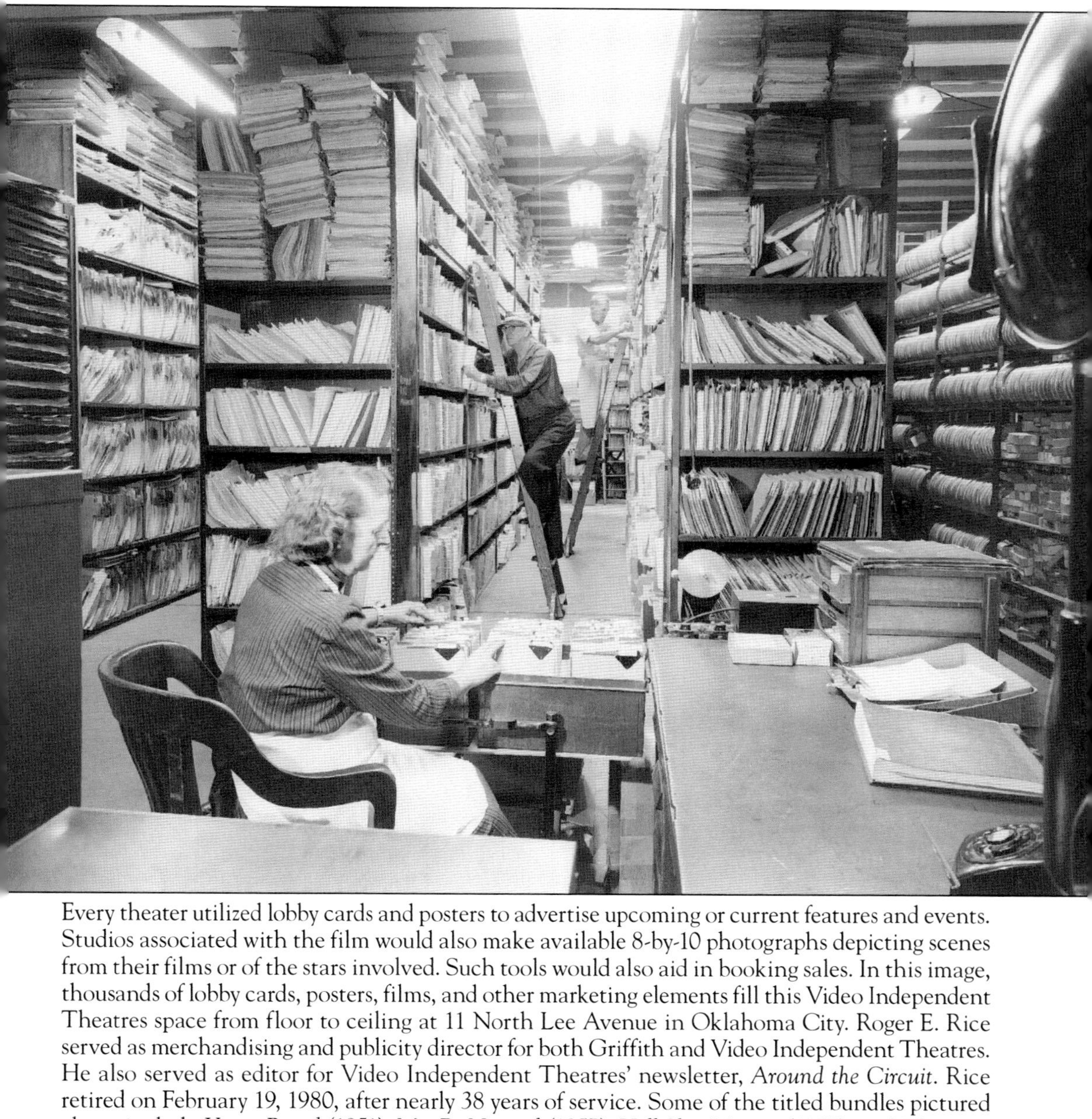

Every theater utilized lobby cards and posters to advertise upcoming or current features and events. Studios associated with the film would also make available 8-by-10 photographs depicting scenes from their films or of the stars involved. Such tools would also aid in booking sales. In this image, thousands of lobby cards, posters, films, and other marketing elements fill this Video Independent Theatres space from floor to ceiling at 11 North Lee Avenue in Oklahoma City. Roger E. Rice served as merchandising and publicity director for both Griffith and Video Independent Theatres. He also served as editor for Video Independent Theatres' newsletter, *Around the Circuit*. Rice retired on February 19, 1980, after nearly 38 years of service. Some of the titled bundles pictured above include *Korea Patrol* (1951), *Mr. B. Natural* (1957), *Hell Ship Mutiny* (1957), and *The Man with My Face* (1951). (Courtesy of the Oklahoma Historical Society.)

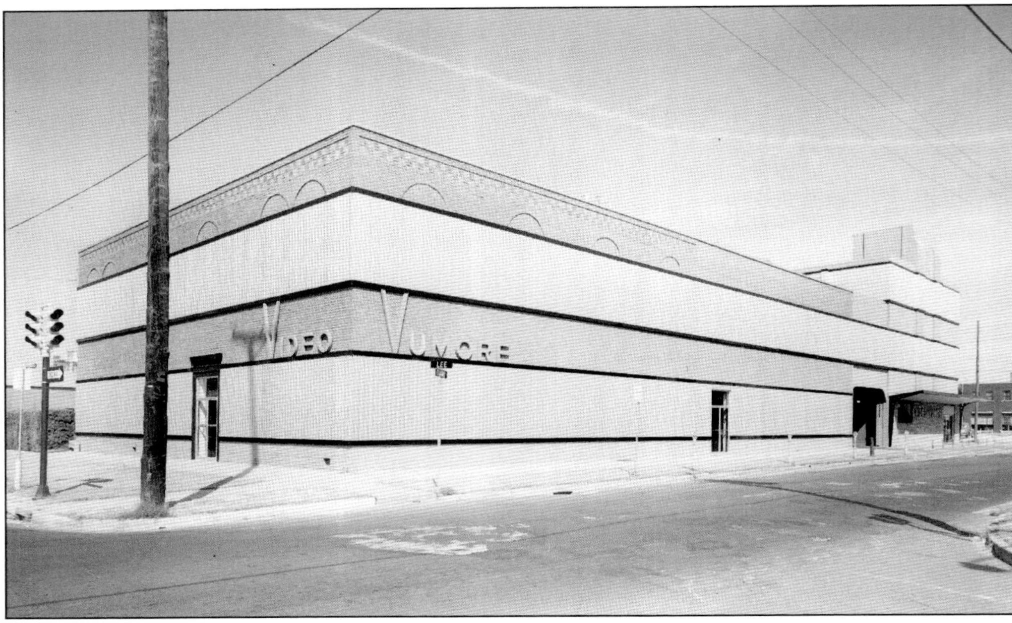

In 1953, Video Independent Theatres acquired the former Paramount Pictures building facing Grand Avenue and incorporated it into its existing 11 North Lee space, creating an all-encompassing general office for Video and Vumore subsidiary operations. Support structures and more parking were added to the west, and extensive remodeling expanded facilities for the administrative, accounting, shipping, printing, concession warehousing, posters, accessories, construction, and mechanical repair departments. A remodel of Paramount's former screening room removed its Grand Avenue entrance and upgraded its projection room. For years, George "Snowman" Snow, a former Russian soldier and survivor of a Nazi POW camp, worked as a Video projectionist and concession equipment repairman. He became a huge fan of Sophia Loren and posted photographs of her throughout his west-side workspace. In this 1954 image, the former red brick of Paramount's first and second floors are wrapped in stainless steel. This steel would remain until property owners initiated restoration efforts in 2007 and uncovered the original Paramount facade. (Both, courtesy of the Oklahoma Historical Society.)

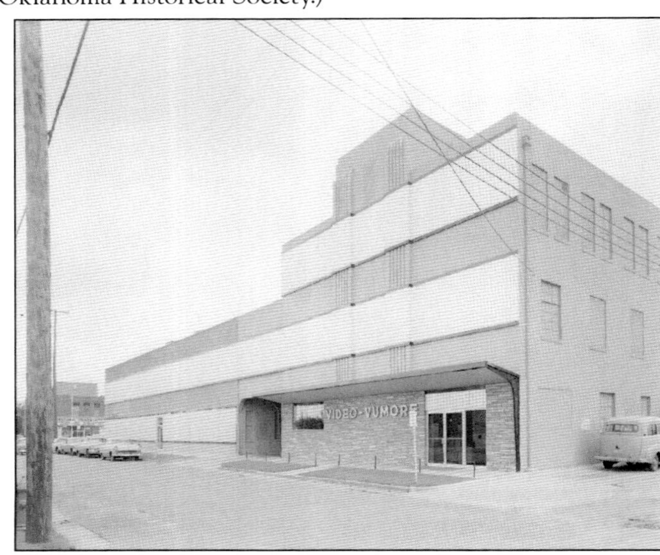

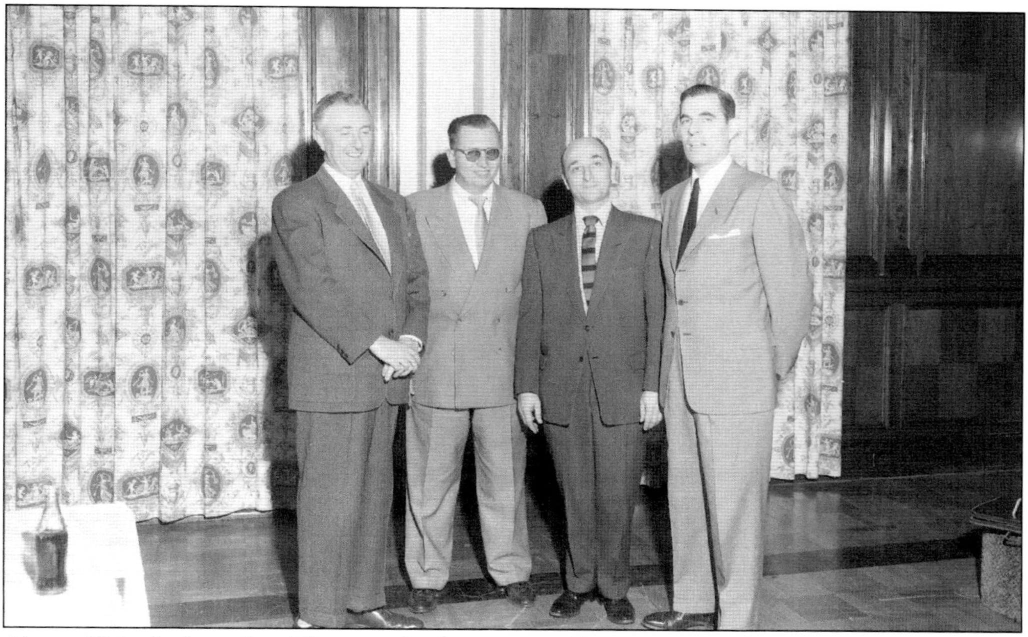

Above, Video Independent Theatres chief operating officer Henry Griffing (far right) stands with speakers from Metro-Goldwyn-Mayer's 1955 convention at the Skirvin Hotel. Griffing, unlike his predecessor, Louis Griffith, shunned publicity but worked quietly behind the scenes. Through his guidance, Video became involved with the construction of Oklahoma City's KWTV Channel 9 studios while securing over 12-percent interest in the studio for Video. Channel 9 was the CBS affiliate in Oklahoma City, and Griffing served as a director. In 1954, Video sponsored a 13-week Thursday night program called *All American Football* on the station. It was the first theater-sponsored show on television, and during the winter of 1954–1955, Video put its name and circuit advertising on an exclusive half-hour Sunday show with Hollywood news and celebrity interviews, where it would also produce the first 2 1/2–minute commercial about the emerging Cinemascope process. (Both, courtesy of the Oklahoma Historical Society.)

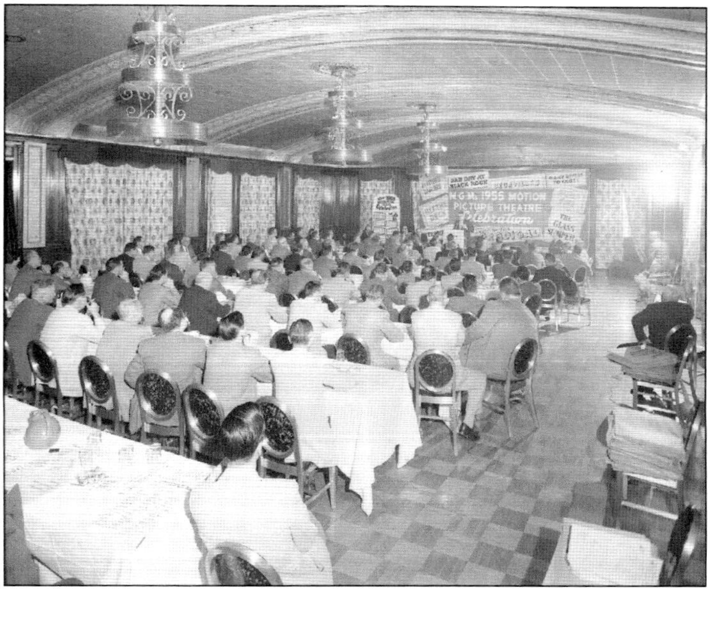

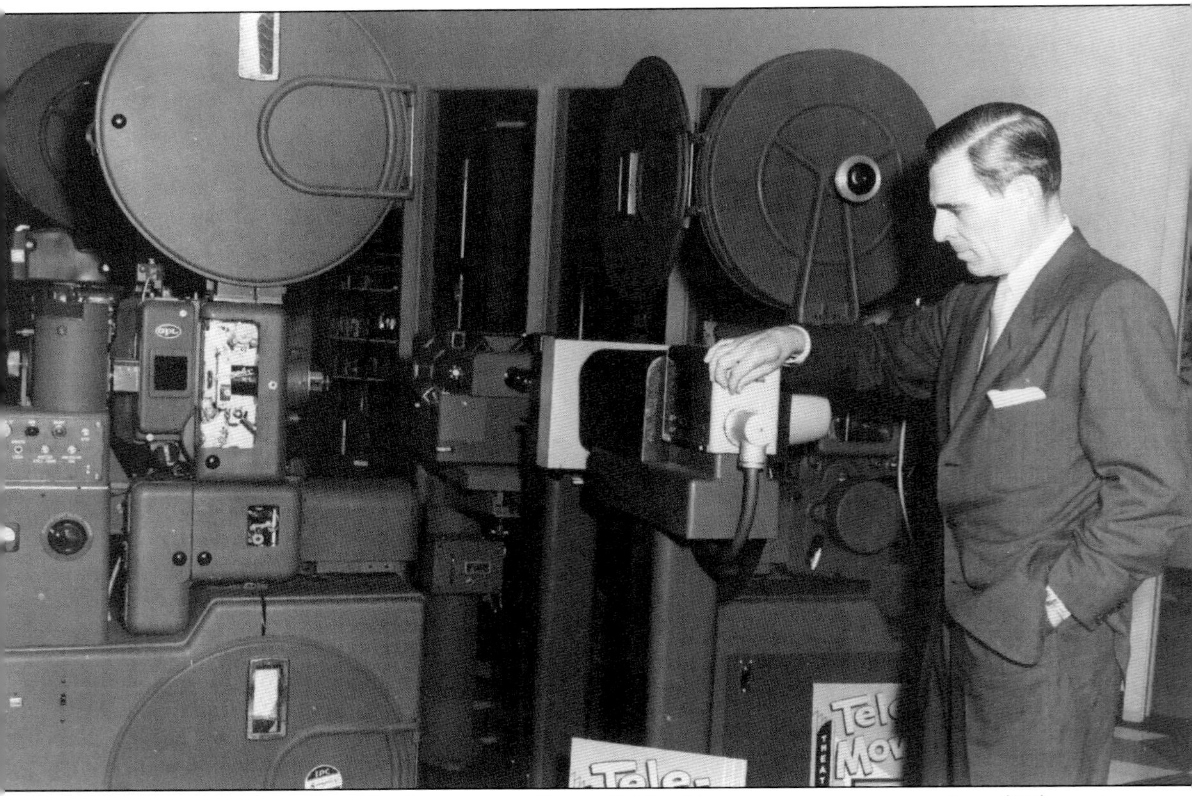

Here, Henry S. Griffing, chief executive officer of Video-Vumore, is starting operation of Telemovies on September 3, 1957, in Bartlesville, Oklahoma. The first broadcast film was Doris Day's *Pajama Game*. The new technology and concept was ahead of its time but were ignored when Griffing approached major studios seeking films for viewing. The potential of the system may have been vastly different decades before cable television became standard in most households if not for the tragic and untimely loss of Griffing, his wife, and two children after their small plane crashed into the side of a mountain during a return flight to Oklahoma from Pennsylvania in 1958. Henry Griffing was a benefactor to Oklahoma City as a silent backer of aspiring politicians, cofounder and officer of the Beacon Club atop the First National Building, and cofounder and builder of Casady School, where he chose its first headmaster. He was also cofounder of All Souls Episcopal Church, where he was first warden and served on the vestry numerous times. (Courtesy of the Cablecenter; Barco Library.)

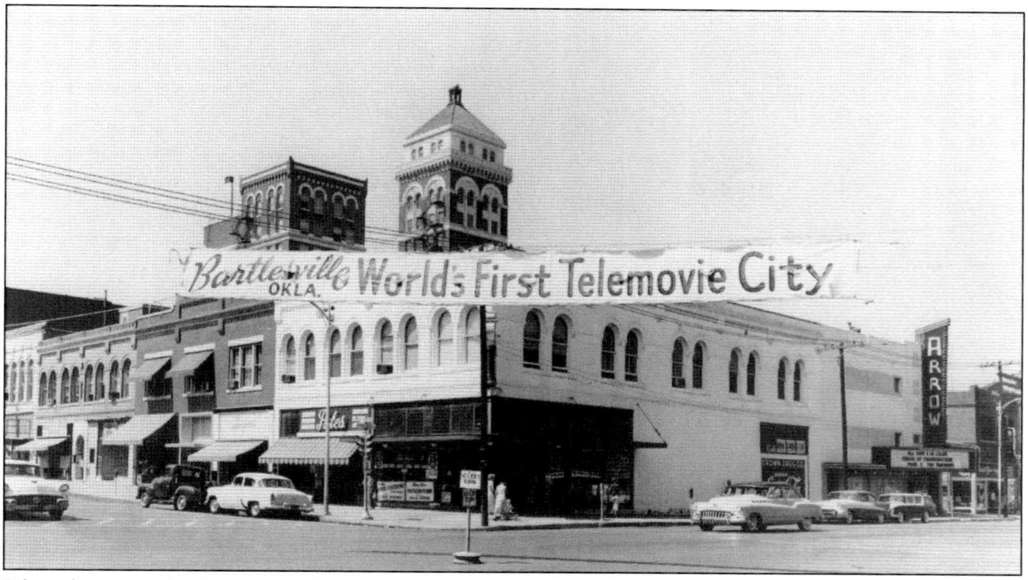

The photograph above is of Bartlesville's main business intersection and its 800-seat Arrow Theatre. The street banner was maintained for 30 days. Below is the bannered truck carrying the studio equipment for the Telemovie experiment, which arrived with a police escort. Several providers, particularly in the lower Midwest and Southwest, put up a microwave receiver or mini point-to-point network and cabled content to their subscribers, thereby giving them access to the existing three network broadcasts without the use of kinescopes as an intermediate transfer step. The Bartlesville experiment started this way, but added something new—content. Video Independent Theatres negotiated deals with movie distributors to provide first-run films that Video would project on to their coax system for distribution. Video charged a pay-per-view rate, giving a legitimate claim that Bartlesville had the first cable television system in the nation. The experiment received worldwide media attention. (Both, courtesy of the Cablecenter; Barco Library.)

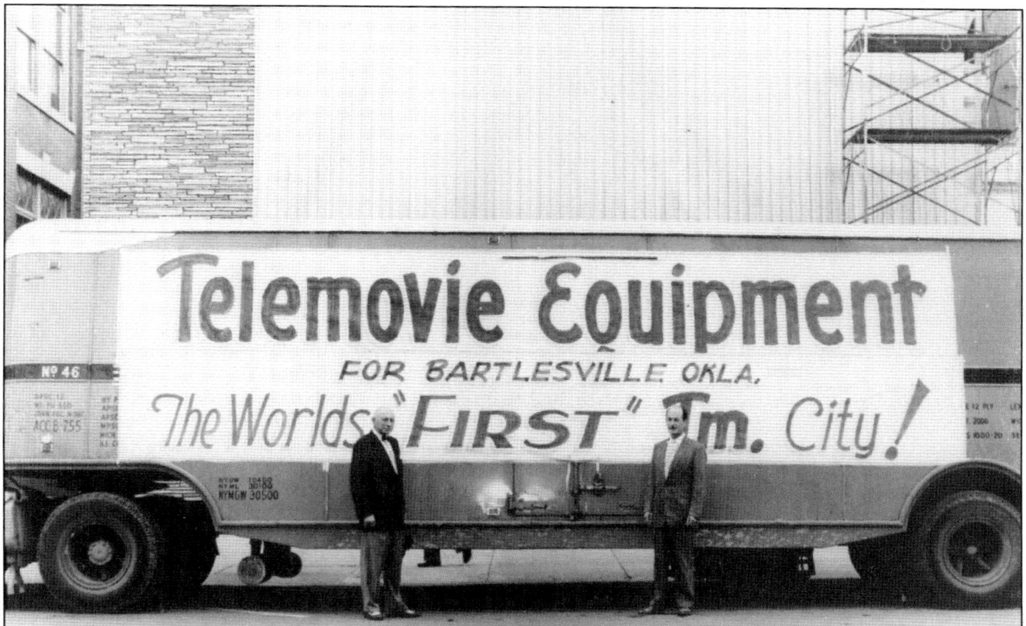

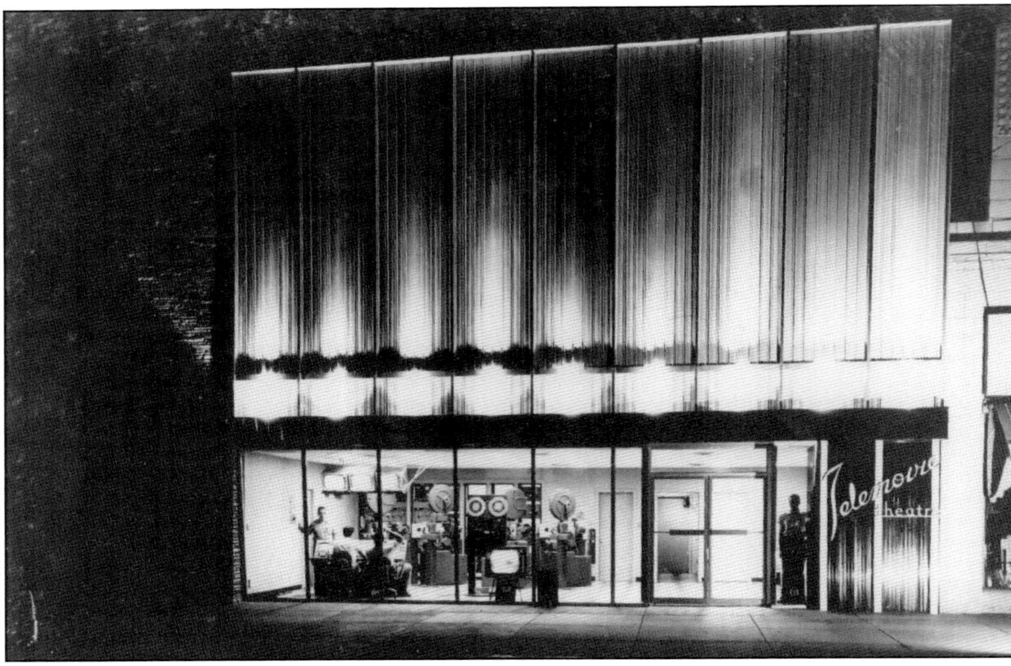

The Telemovie equipment was installed in the converted former Lyric Theatre at 325 Dewey Avenue, above, which also served as a studio and central office. Special development and manufacture of transmission and set conversion adapters were necessary as well as building the actual cable delivery system. The complete system entailed a gathering mast or tower mounted at a high spot between broadcasting stations and the towns and cities to be served, a studio with refining and amplifying capabilities, and a delivery network of coaxial cables and drop lines into the homes and receiving sets, all for a flat monthly fee. Below is an interior view of the studio in full operation. (Both, courtesy of the Cablecenter; Barco Library.)

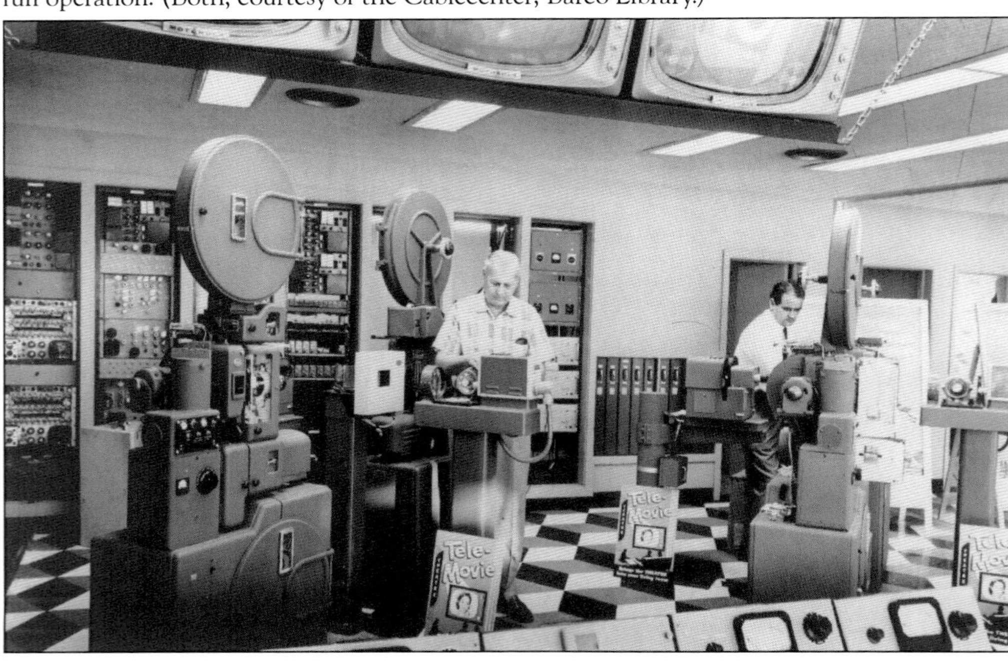

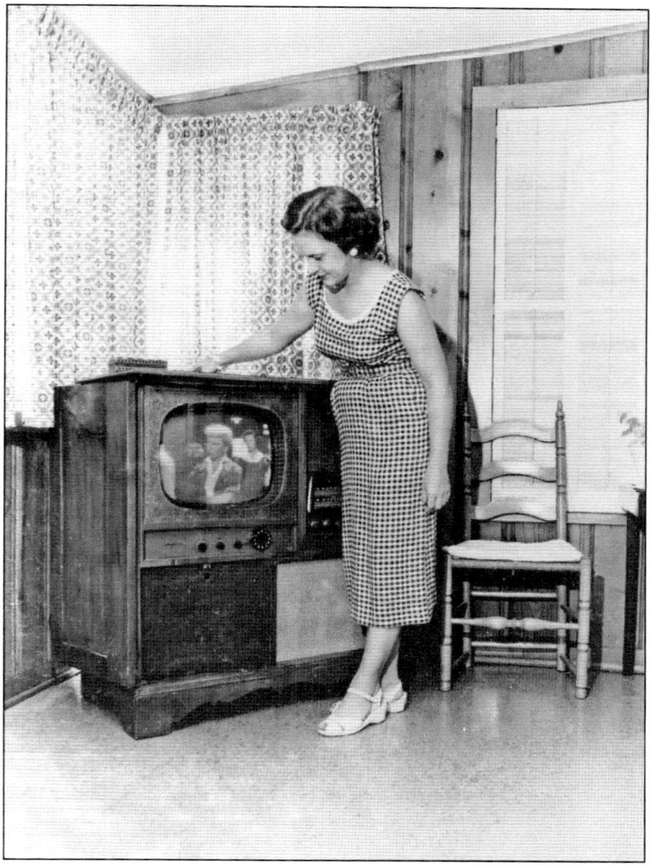

Telemovie broadcasts were delivered over a coaxial system that was contract-built at the insistence of utility pole owners. The entire network then had to be sold to Southwestern Bell and leased back for $10,000 per mile, per year. The service sold for a flat rate fee of $9.50 per month and was reduced to $4.95 and enhanced with the addition of an antenna service carrying continuous news, weather, and time with audio background and mood music as operations waned. The television set in the above photograph shows Doris Day from the first-run film *Pajama Game*. The photograph below shows a television console awarded as a prize to first subscribers. (Both, courtesy of the Cablecenter; Barco Library.)

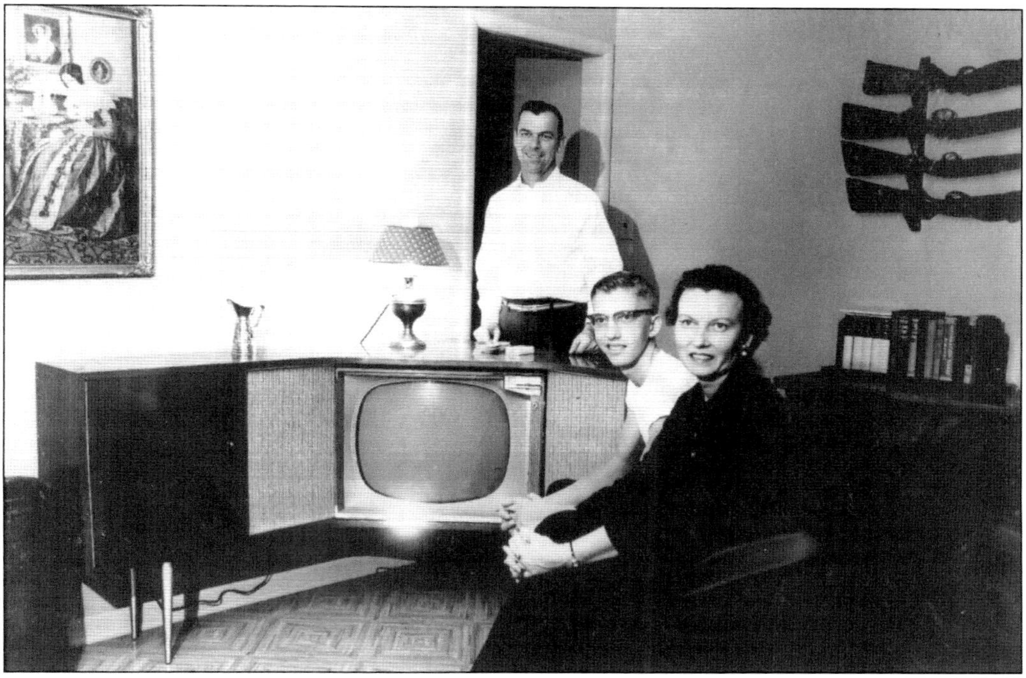

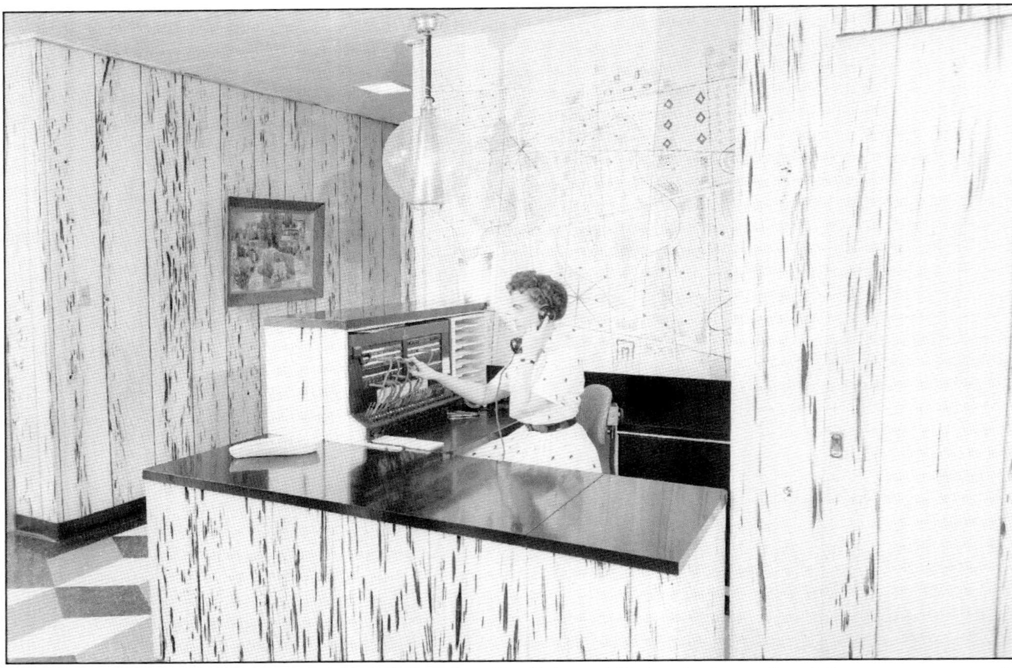

Here sits Allegra "Wee Gee" Thedford-McCabe, Griffith and Video Independent Theatres receptionist and PBX operator. Wee Gee was married to Frank William McCabe, feature booker and film buyer for Griffith Theatres. This photograph was taken on August 17, 1958. (Courtesy of the Oklahoma Historical Society.)

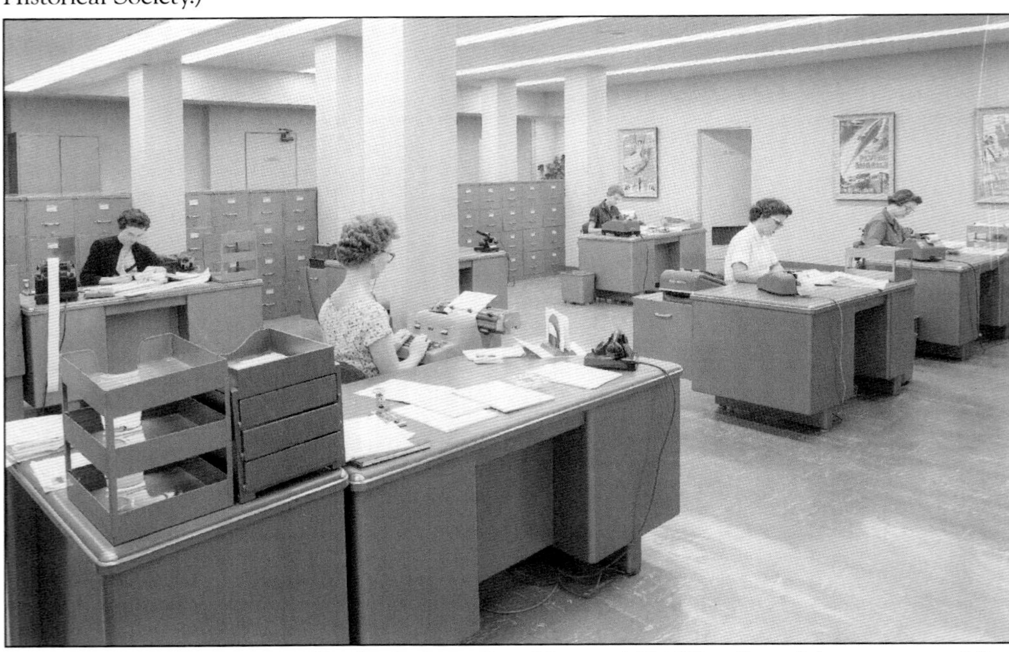

This is an August 1958 view of Video Independent Theatres' 701 West Grand Avenue second-floor workstations. The employees are, from left to right, Alma Best, Auvella Maxey, unidentified, Dottie Lilly, and Betty Hugo. The posters along the far wall depict *Slightly French* (1949), *The Flying Missile* (1950), and *Hans Christen Anderson* (1952). (Courtesy of the Oklahoma Historical Society.)

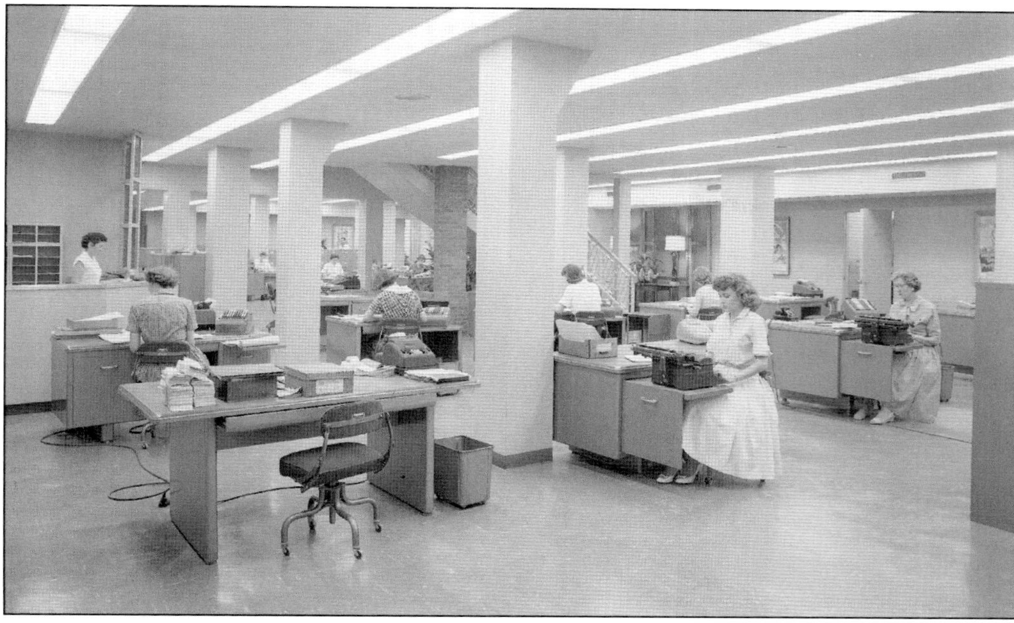

These images were taken on August 17, 1958. The above view is of the Video Independent Theatres 701 West Grand Avenue second-floor workstations and employees. From left to right are Jane Harrison; Anna "Ann" B. Cooper, property accountant; unidentified; Effie Ritter, purchasing agent; Dottie Lilly; Paul Edward Cornwell, vice president theatre operations; unidentified; Betty Hugo; two unidentified; Beverly Moon; and Agnes Blackmon, insurance department head and clerk. Below is an unidentified secretary. (Both, courtesy of the Oklahoma Historical Society.)

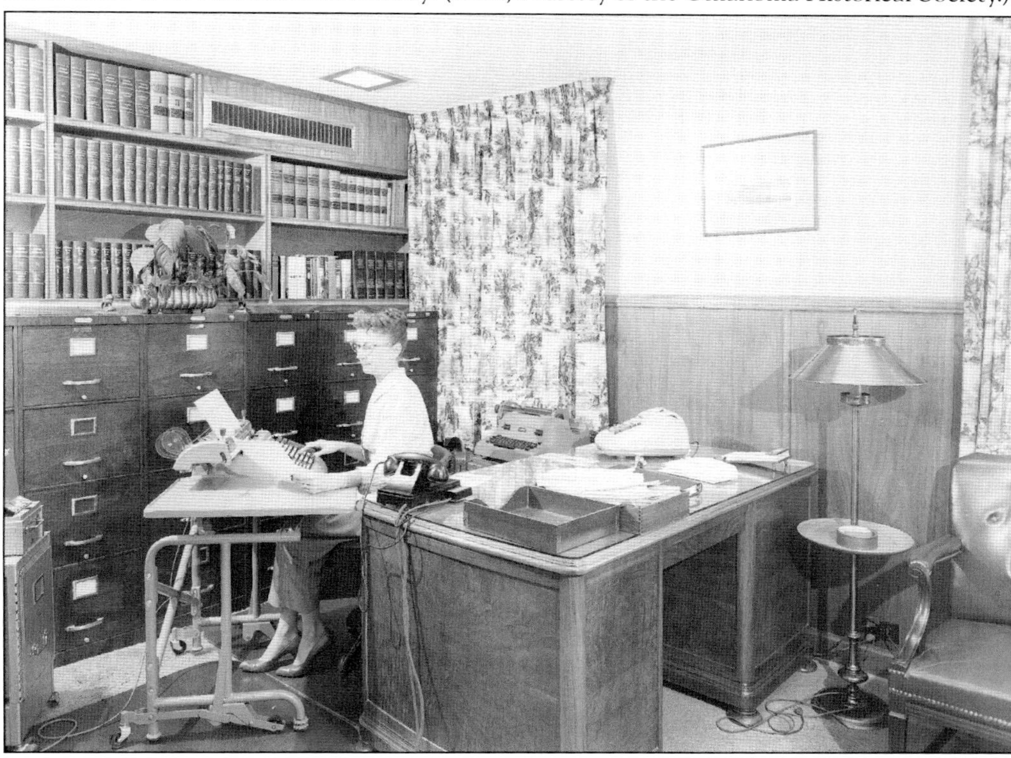

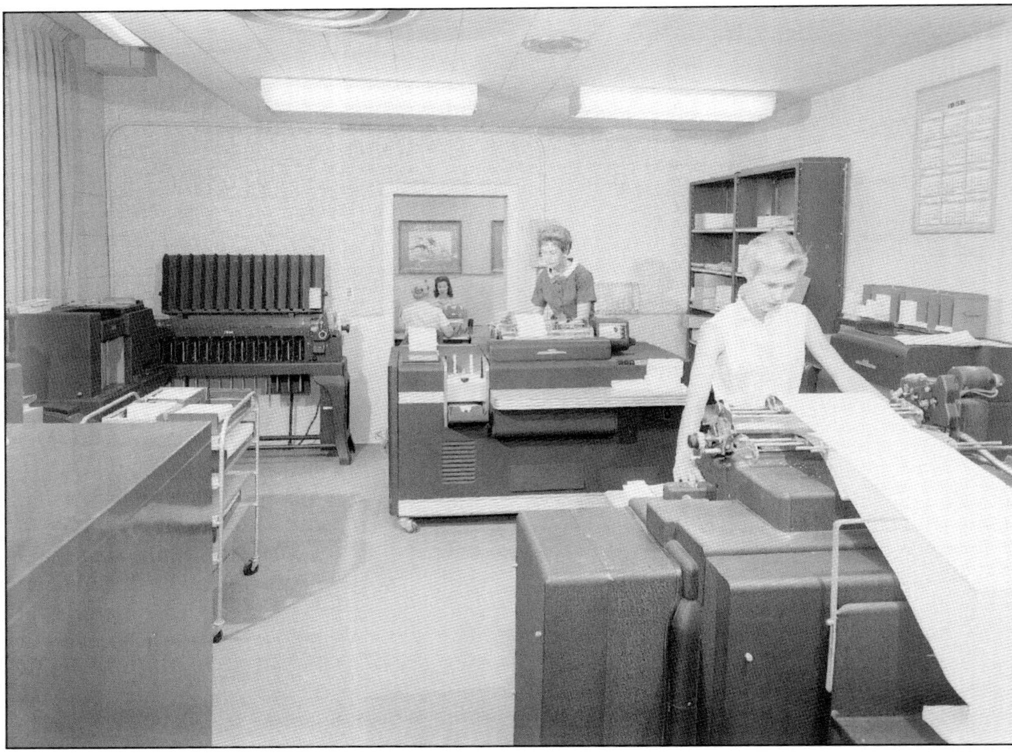

Above is an August 1958 view of the Video Independent Theatres 701 West Grand IBM accounting computer print room with Dorothy Ellen Pfeiffer (left) and Shirley Henson (right). Through the rear door is the IBM 026 key punch room and its operators, also seen below. Such devices were used to manually enter the theatre chain's accounting data on punch cards. There was a great demand for full-time keypunch operators, who were usually women. (Both, courtesy of the Oklahoma Historical Society.)

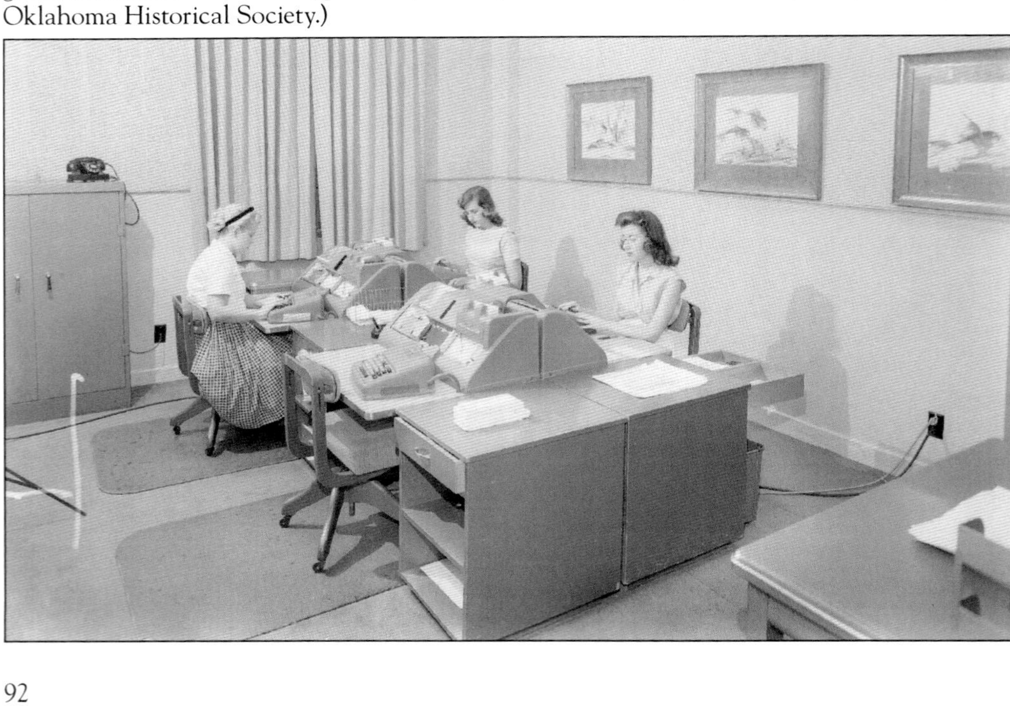

At right sits William Bondies Turk Jr., Griffith and Video Independent Theatres divisions manager, in his second-floor Video Independent Theatres office at 11 North Lee Avenue on August 17, 1958. Turk served as a regional manager until World War II, when he served in the infantry. He returned in 1943 and cofounded Video Independent Theatres. He retired from Video on May 3, 1983, after 47 years of service. Paul Edward Cornwell, Griffith and Video Independent Theatres division manager and cofounder, is in the photograph below from August 17, 1958. He retired after 49 years. (Both, courtesy of the Oklahoma Historical Society.)

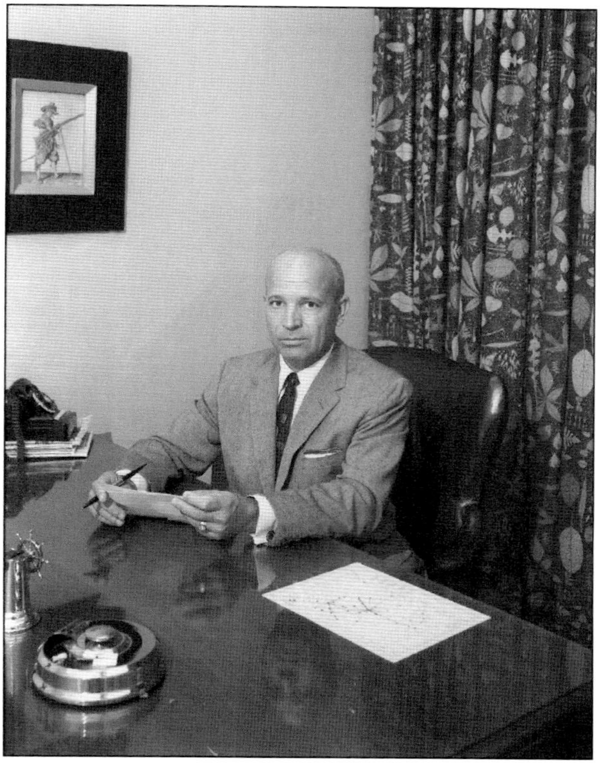

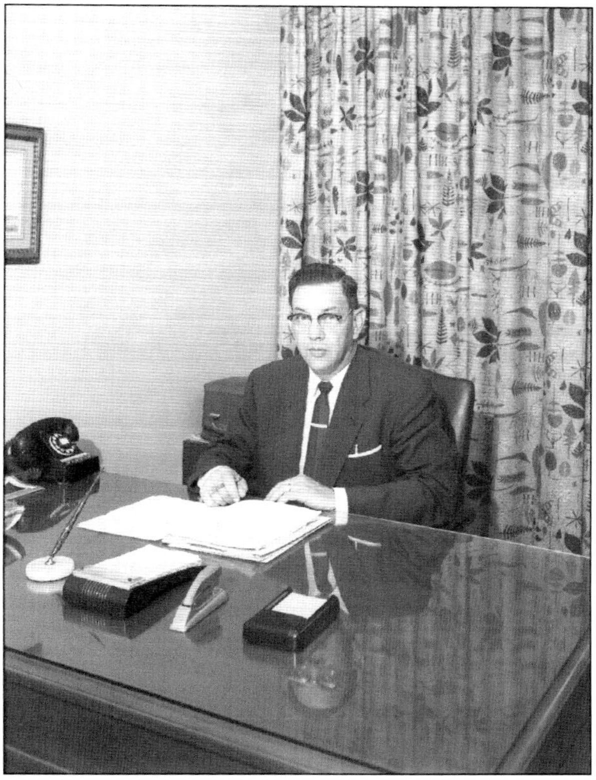

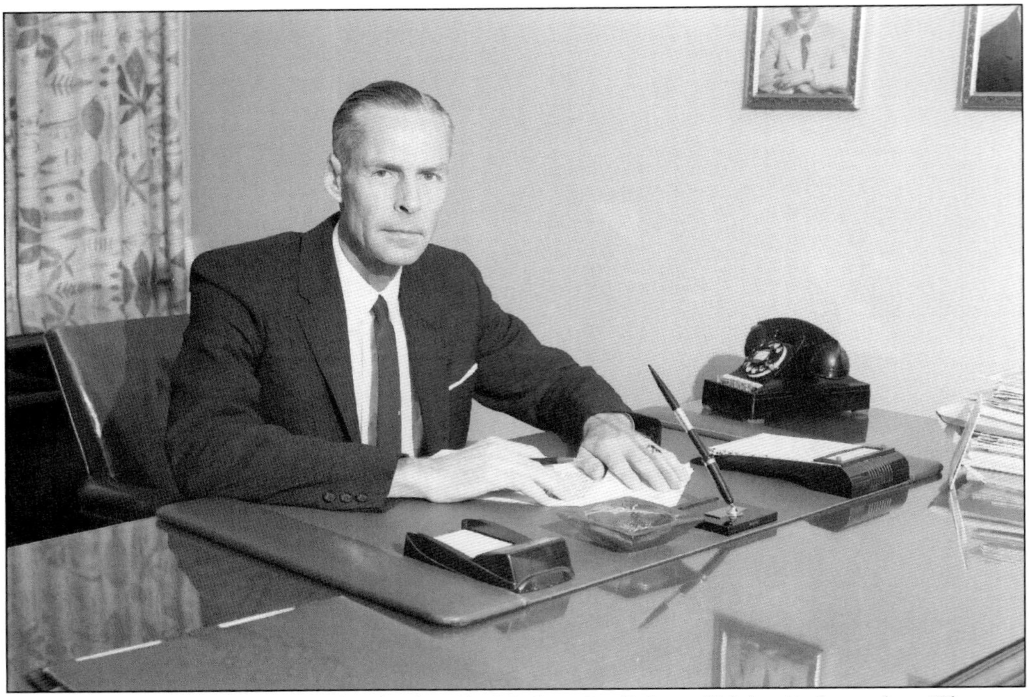

Photographed above is Kenneth Charles Blackledge, Griffith and Video Independent Theatres division manager and Video cofounder. He became president of Video on April 1, 1963. His son Larry Blackledge was an architect who designed numerous Video theatres, among them the Esquire in Enid, Oklahoma. Kenneth retired from Video on January 31, 1976, after 47 years. Below is Comella "Louise" Wesson, head of concessions for Video, who rose through the ranks from Griffith Theatres' film pay department and is remembered to have always driven Cadillac automobiles. Wesson retired on November 30, 1975, after 33 years of service. These photographs were taken on August 17, 1958. (Both, courtesy of the Oklahoma Historical Society.)

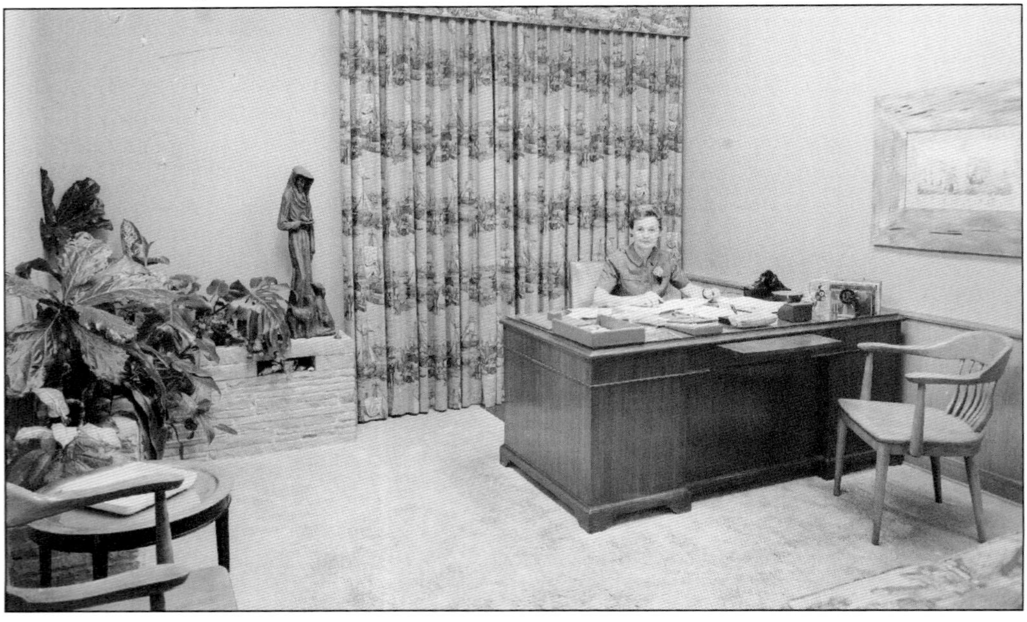

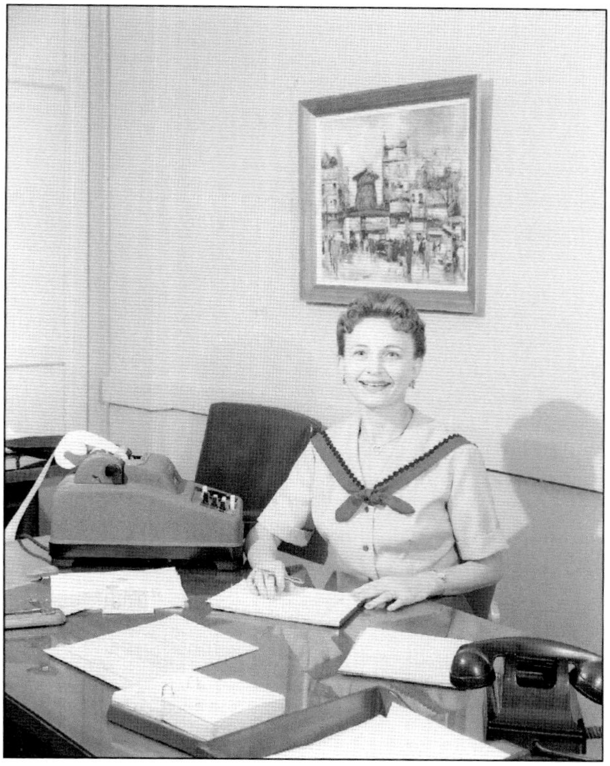

In the photograph at right is Video Independent Theatres insurance manager Evelyn Smith. Below is William "Earl" Albright, head of Video's shipping department, surrounded by photographs of his fleet of trucks and the many national and state awards won by the company and drivers for safe and accident-free operation. Albright served Video in numerous roles, including the poster, mechanical, record, concession, and shipping departments. He was a veteran of the US Navy in World War II. Both photographs were taken on August 13, 1958. (Both, courtesy of the Oklahoma Historical Society.)

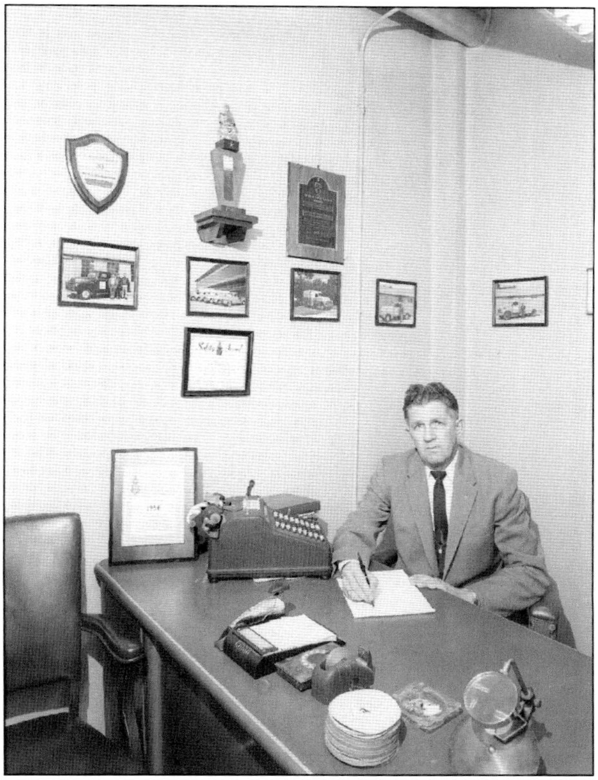

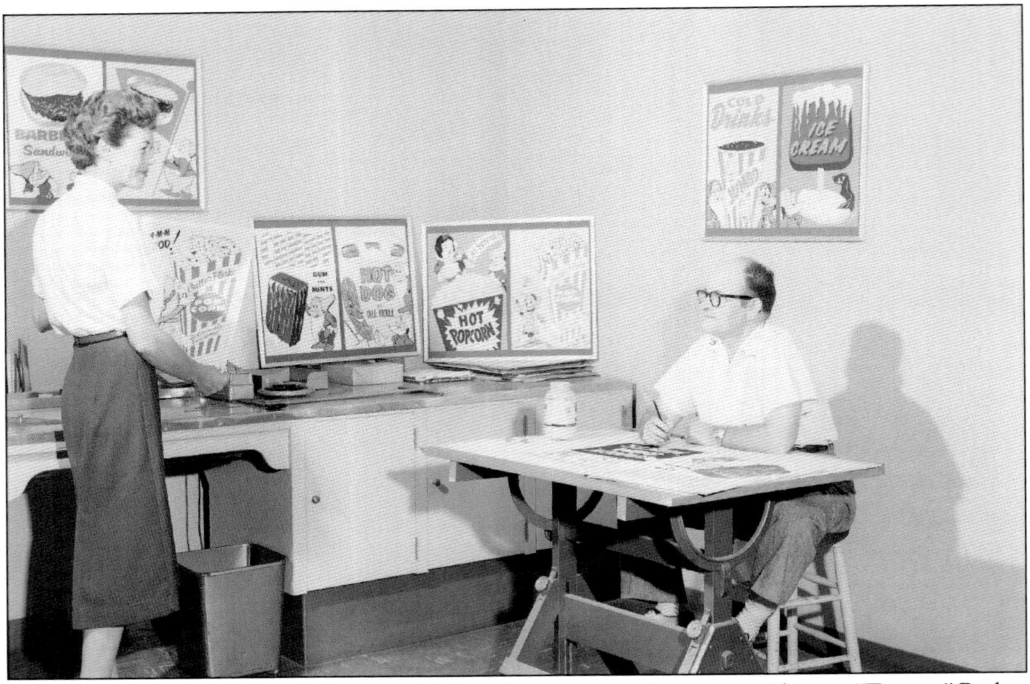

Here, Dorothy Ellen Pfeiffer, Vumore Company IBM operator, looks on as Thomas "Tommy" Berlyn Nelson, head of Video Independent Theatres' art and printing department, is seen designing concession posters for display in theaters in Video-Vumore's home offices at 701 West Grand Avenue on August 13, 1958. The exchange was responsible for the marketing and promotional lobby cards, posters, and signage needed by its theaters. The company also printed its own stationery. The department used the three printing presses seen below. The press on the left has just completed the stack of ice cream display posters on the adjacent table, while the press to the right is printing lobby posters promoting a film. There were approximately 12 employees for this single department. It was phased out on August 15, 1965. (Both, courtesy of the Oklahoma Historical Society.)

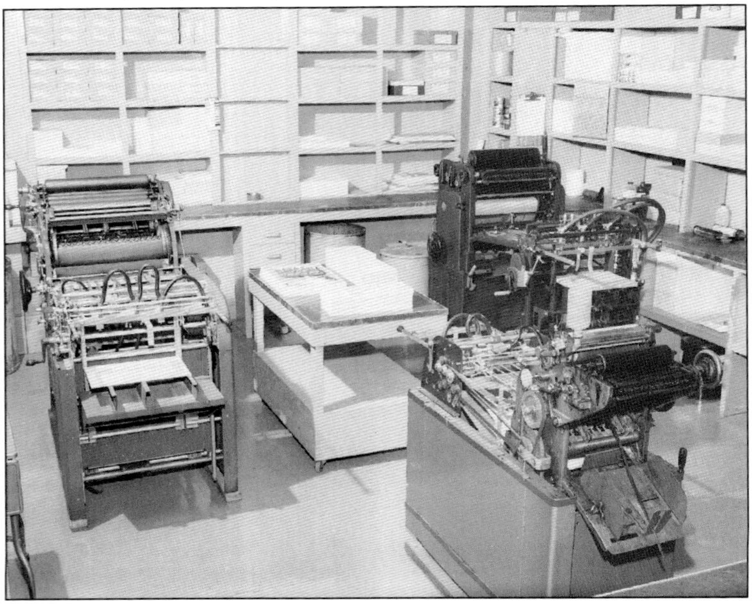

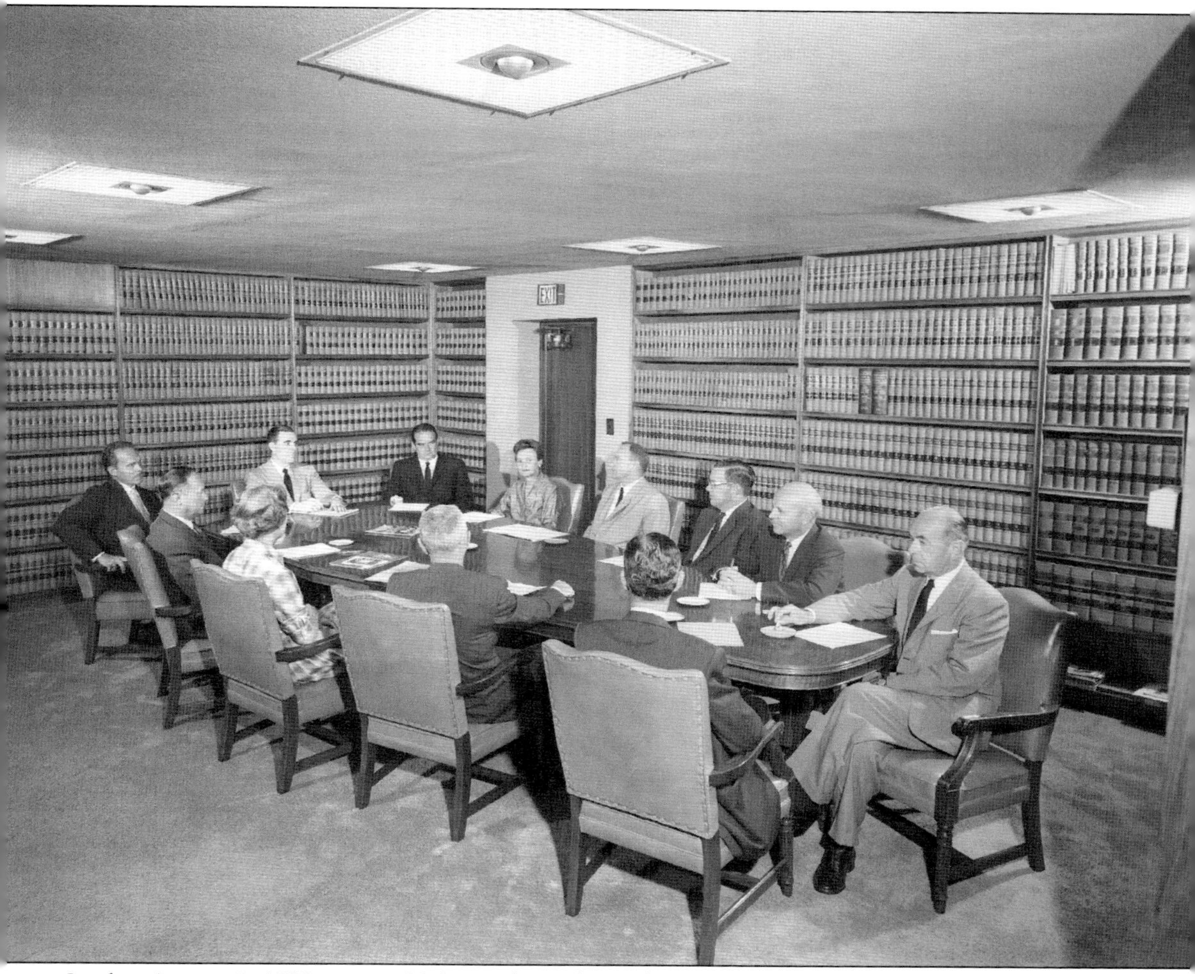

In this August 9, 1958, image, Video Independent Theatres management holds an executive session in their third-floor conference room. Clockwise from head of the table at left are chief executive officer Henry S. Griffing; Robert M. Clark; concessions director Comella "Louise" Wesson; Vumore president Larry B. Boggs; division manager Paul E. Cornwell; division manager William B. Turk; theatre operations director Claude O. Fulgham; assistant film buyer Frank McCabe; head film booker Cliff White Jr.; Griffing's executive secretary, Lois McColgin; Claude F. Motley; and company treasurer Jack E. Brooks. Less than two weeks later, Henry Griffing and his family were killed in a small plane crash. For two weeks afterward, search and rescue efforts looked for Griffing's plane while Video's management and employees worried about the future of the company. RKO General, a subsidiary of General Tire, purchased the company in 1961 to add to its own cable television business. (Courtesy of the Oklahoma Historical Society.)

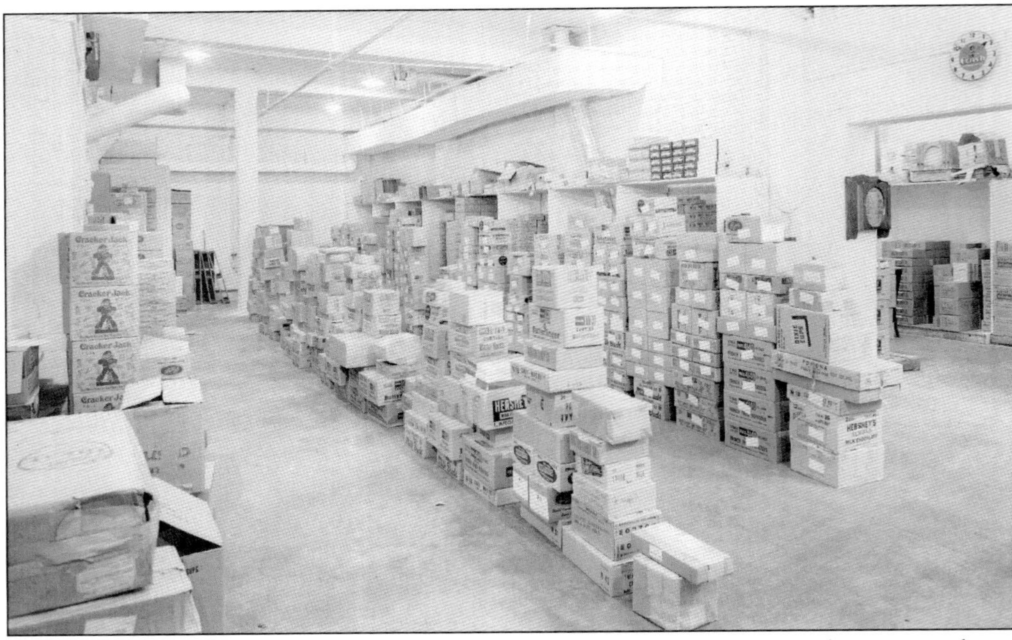

Concession sales revenue far exceeded that of ticket sales. Video Independent Theatres' warehouse, as seen in these two images, carried numerous selections for shipping across the circuit. Clerks would pull and sort orders for loading in shipping and receiving. The most popular concession items were popcorn and soft drinks. Louise Wesson, head of concessions, directed theaters to use cheaper paper sacks for popcorn during matinees and reserve the more expensive popcorn boxes for evening shows. Video Independent Theatres' concession prices ranged on average from 1¢ to $1, as it was hoped that even children would not leave the theater with money still in their pocket. (Both, courtesy of the Oklahoma Historical Society.)

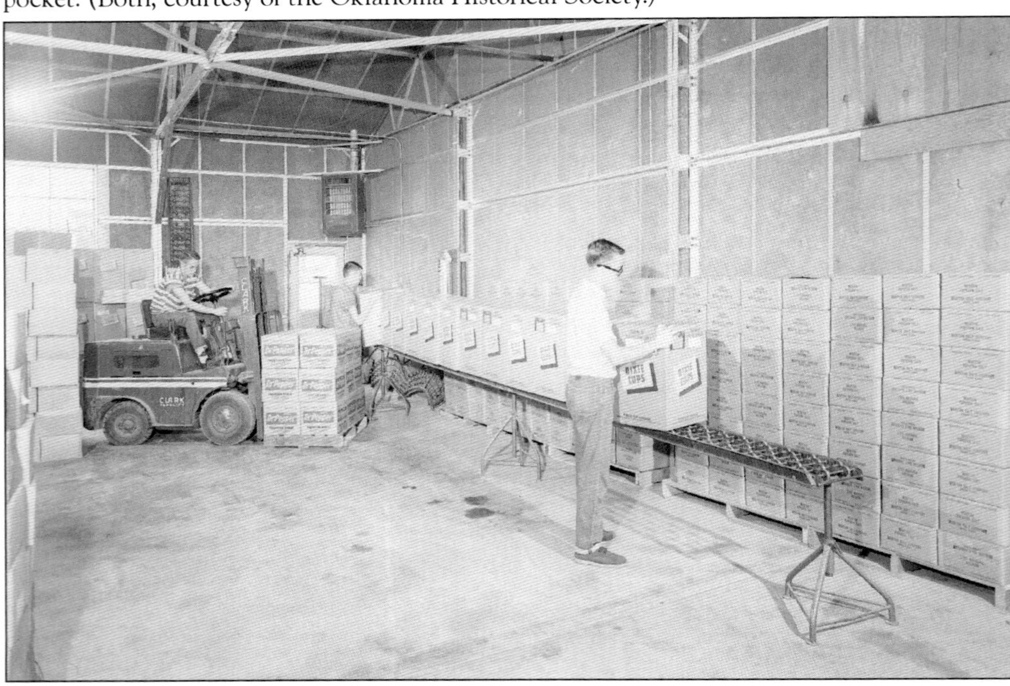

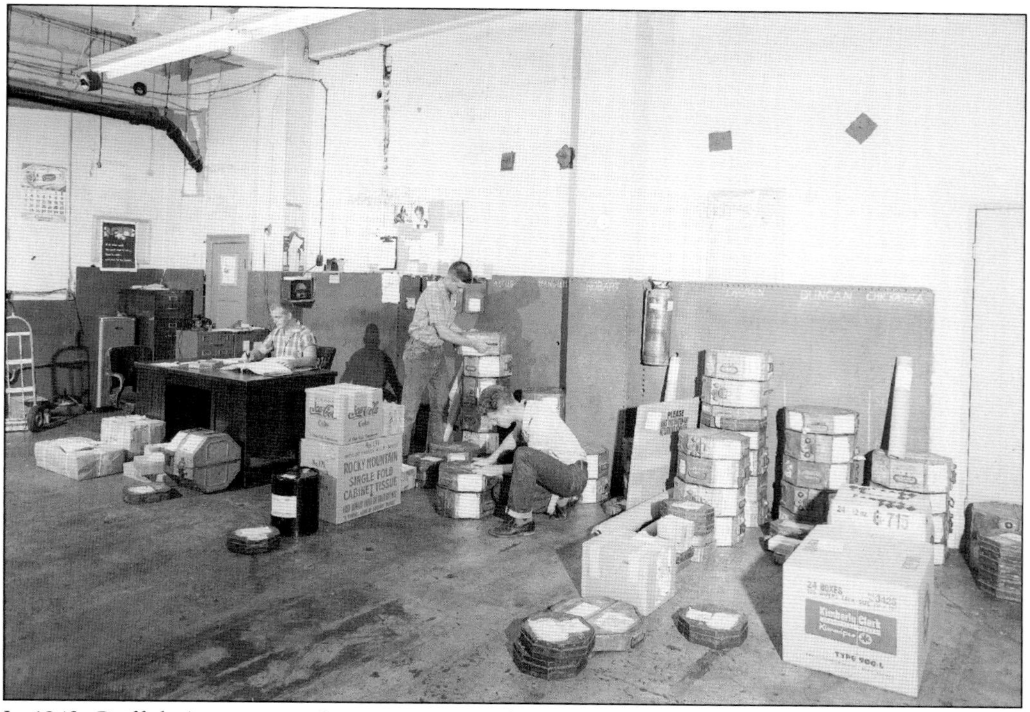

In 1943, Griffith Amusement Company operated 156 theaters in 49 towns. After Louis C. Griffith suffered a debilitating stroke at a downtown Oklahoma City barbershop in 1946, he could no longer manage day-to-day operations of the company. On December 1, 1949, Video Independent Theatres formed out of Griffith Theatres and took charge of 143 screens, including the growing number of drive-in theaters. The clerks above sort and place film cans, theater supplies, and concessions under the destination's name along the walls. Below, numerous film cans sit ready for distribution among Video's circuit of theaters. (Both, courtesy of the Oklahoma Historical Society.)

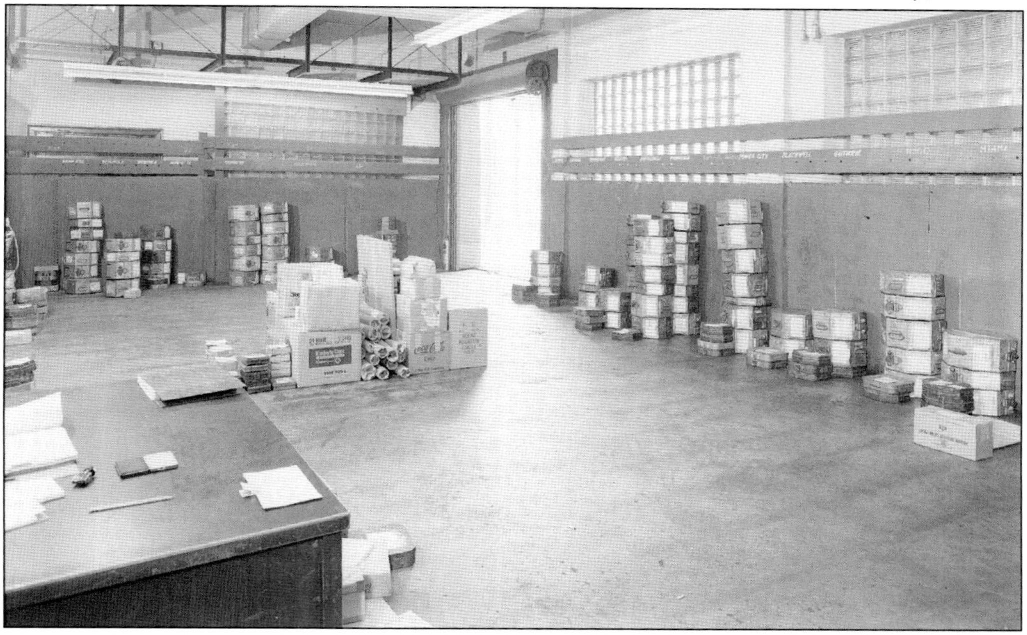

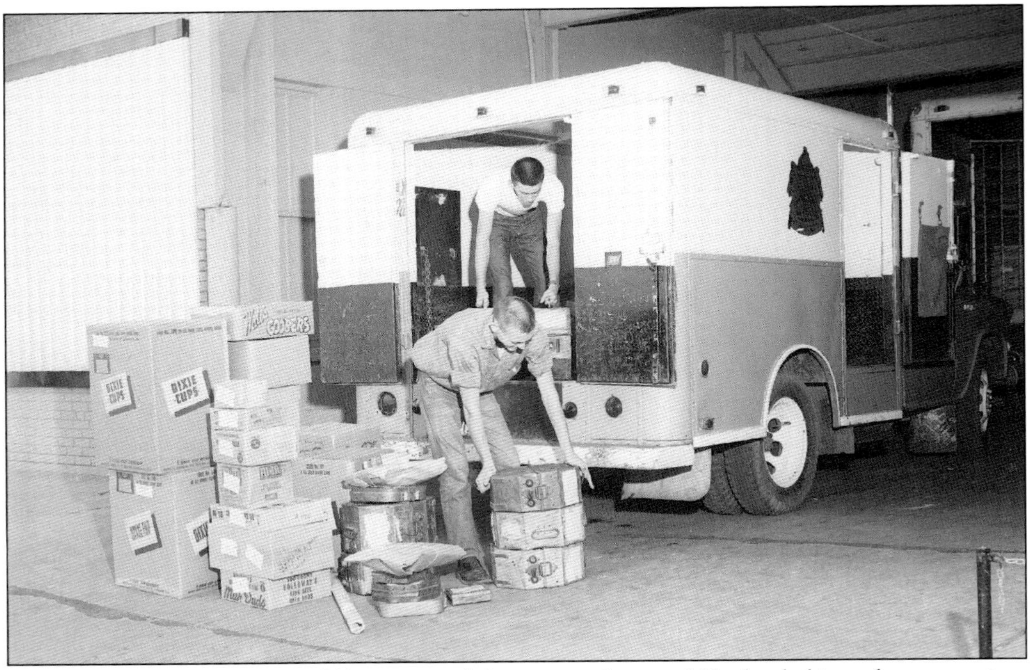

After sorting, the collection of film cans and theater supplies would be loaded into the appropriate destination truck. Above, employees of Video Independent Theatres load their trucks outside of the 11 North Lee Avenue loading docks. The trucks ventured all across the region and to more than one theater per trip. The film cans seen here protected the reels of stock from scratches and were still required to be in metal cans at all times, although cellulose triacetate safety film was now in use by most studios. (Both, courtesy of the Oklahoma Historical Society.)

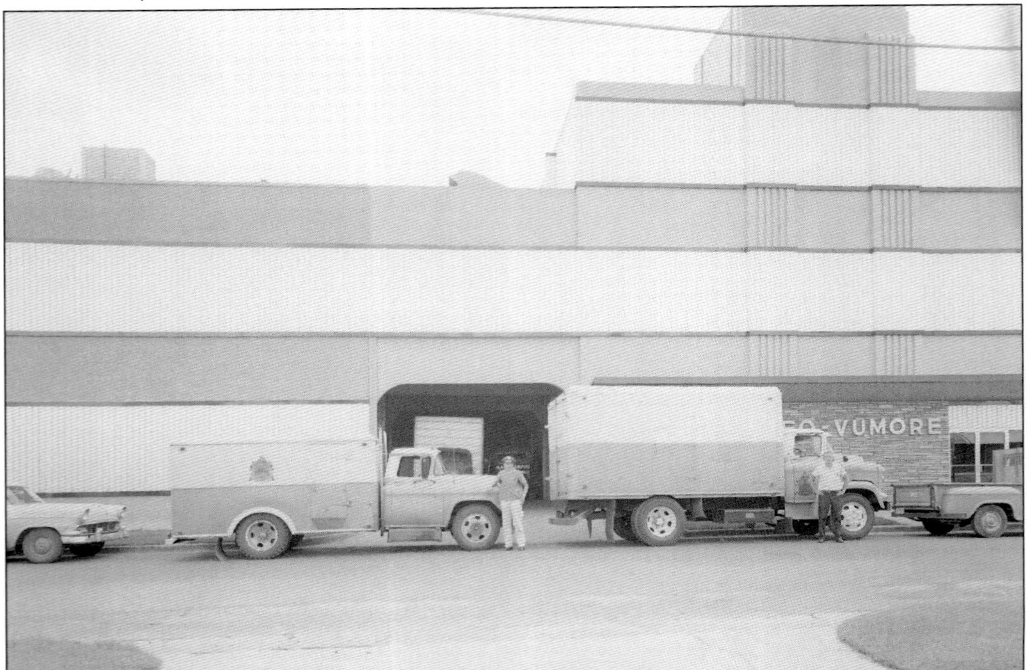

Five

Reel to Real

In 2003, efforts inspired by rediscovery of Film Row's unique history enabled a small group to approach the Oklahoma City Planning Department with a bold new plan for the area. The plan originally focused on the former Film Exchange building at 700 West Sheridan Avenue and its unique history. The concept was to build a synergy around the building as private investment transformed it into loft apartments and ground-floor retail space. This synergy would help develop the rest of the street and surrounding area into a new downtown business district.

City planners were excited about the idea. Shortly afterwards, the Oklahoma City Film District Task Force formed to look into and discuss the possibilities with the assistance of numerous professionals and volunteers. Over the next few years, a plan began to materialize.

Ironically, as new planning initiatives began, the Oklahoma Theatre Supply Company, the last business from the bygone era of Film Row, closed its doors after 74 years of single-owner operation. The last surviving owner, Maxine Peek, passed away by spring 2005. If not for the Oklahoma Theatre Supply Company, McKenzie Tees, and the International Crystal Manufacturing Company occupying former film exchange spaces, Film Row would have been lost completely.

By 2006, many of the derelict properties started their revitalized transformations by new and established owners, and Oklahoma City declared the 600–700 blocks of Sheridan Avenue "Historic Film Row" and its surrounding blocks the "Film Exchange District." Planning and development opened to public input that same year in a series of design charrettes, outlined in the first issues of the district's newsletter, the *Row*. Efforts by volunteer professionals in 2007 allowed Oklahoma to list the Film Exchange District on the National Register of Historic Places in 2008.

In 2009, ongoing development by property owners, move-ins by new businesses, and city streetscaping efforts were well underway. In the spring of 2011, streetscaping and private development completed the transformation of Historic Film Row, and today, its unique history is preserved while the synergy and support from its flourishing businesses serves to keep its story alive for future generations.

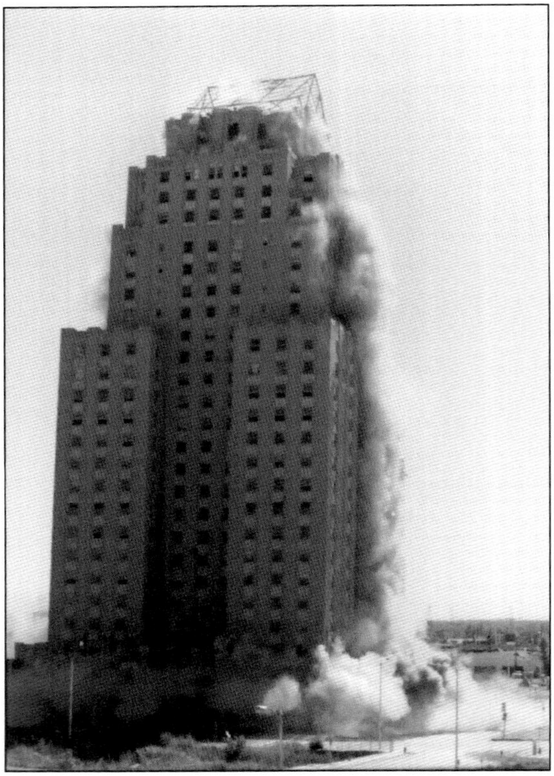

On October 17, 1977, Oklahoma City's Biltmore Hotel came crashing down after a series of timed explosions were detonated along its lower floors. The demolition was scheduled after the hotel's purchase by the Urban Renewal Authority of Oklahoma City for the sum of $1 million. Thirty thousand citizens gathered to watch the 26-story structure built in 1932 collapse in no more than seven seconds. It was the tallest steel-reinforced structure in the world at that time to be brought down with explosives. The cleanup would take nearly four months. The Biltmore was brought down after years of vacancy and neglect to make room for the Oklahoma City Myriad Gardens, a botanical wonder encased in a cavernous capsule and surrounded by a landscaped park. (Both, courtesy of the Oklahoma Historical Society.)

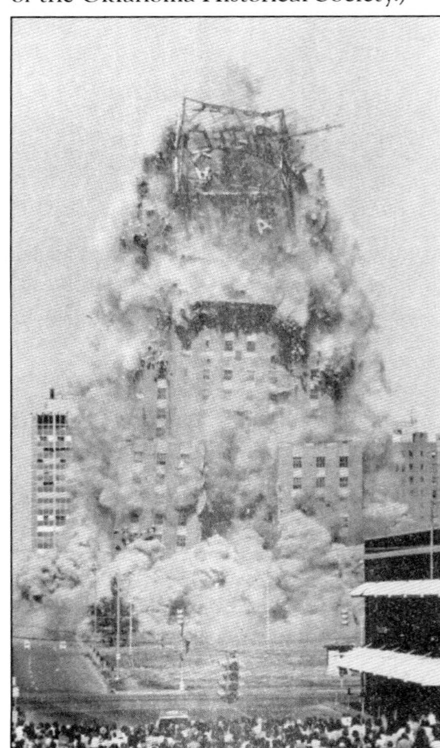

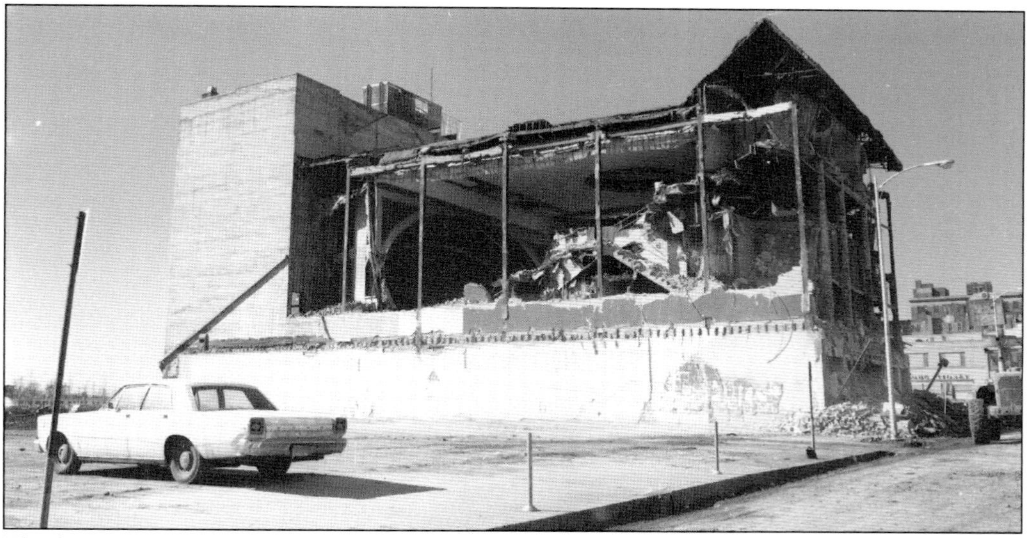

The former Criterion, "a symphony in brick and stone," stands partially demolished. The stripped exterior walls allow a glimpse of its once-elaborate interior, including its stage. The Criterion was among the last victims of the disastrous downtown program of urban renewal, which resulted in destruction of the aging Sheridan Avenue theater district and numerous other structures. A massive shopping mall called the Galleria was intended for the area until renewal money could no longer afford more than its parking garage. This left downtown Oklahoma City with vacant lots where Victorian brownstones once stood, as seen below. (Both, courtesy of the Oklahoma Historical Society.)

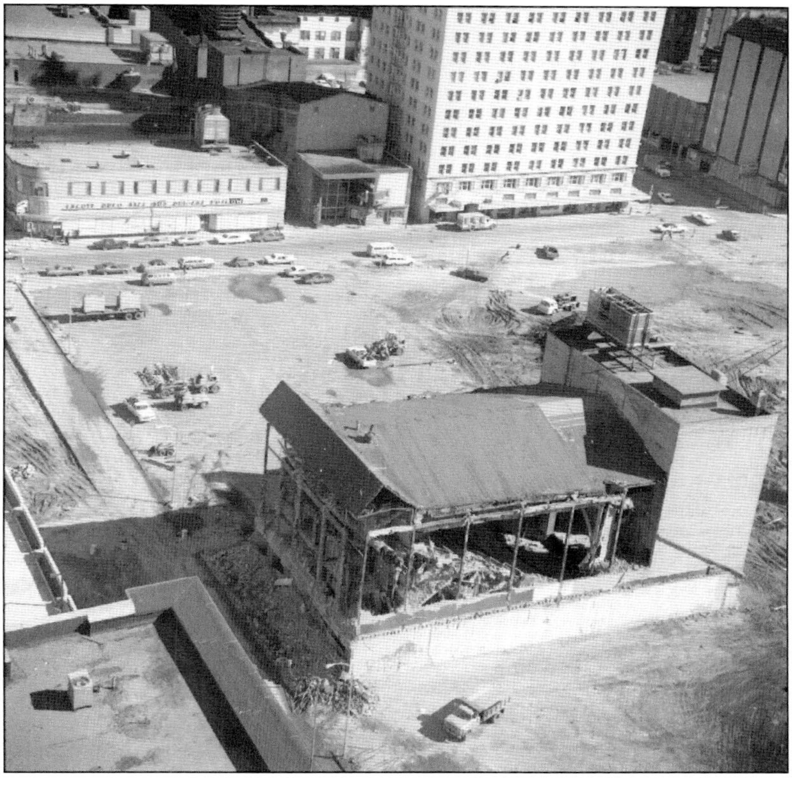

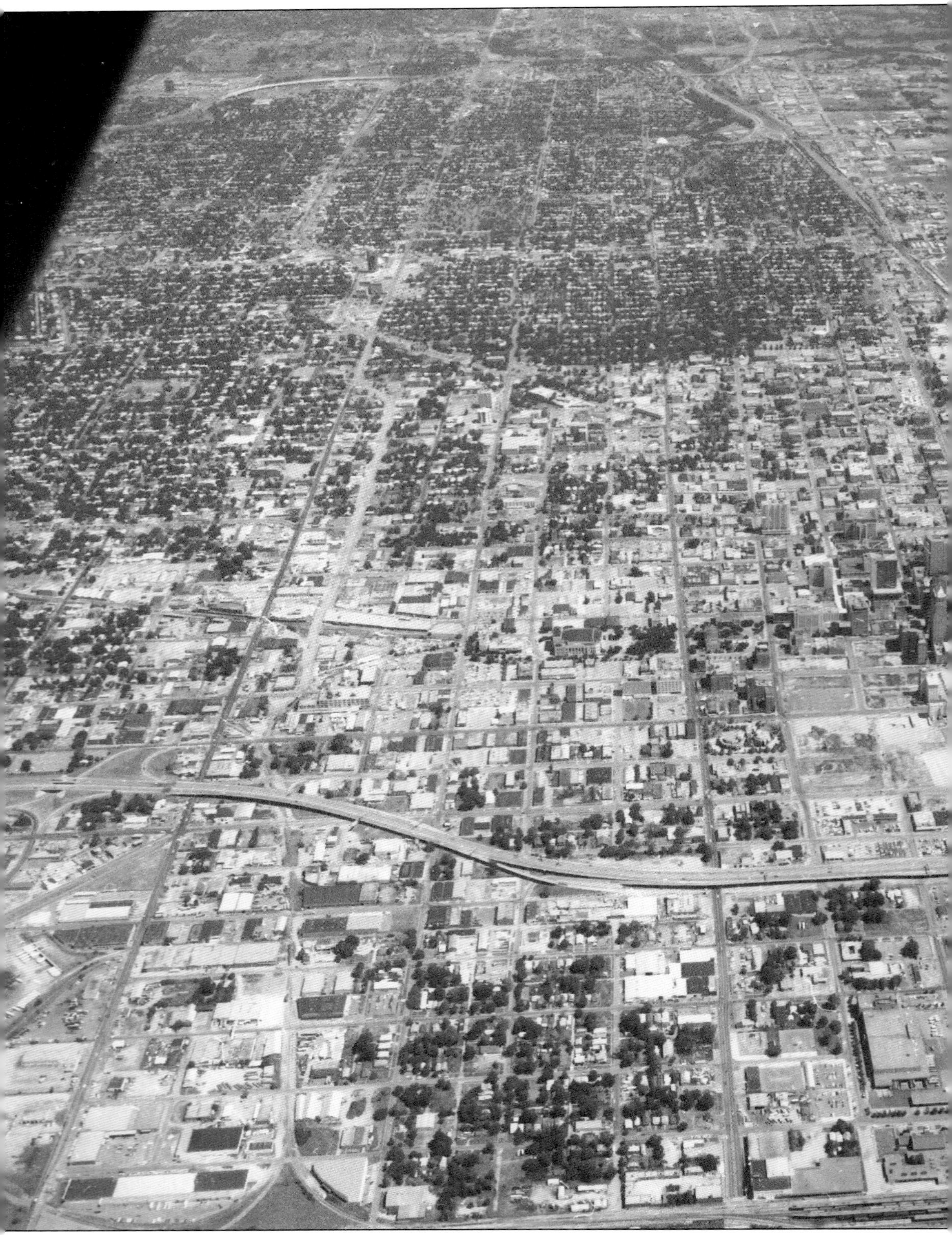

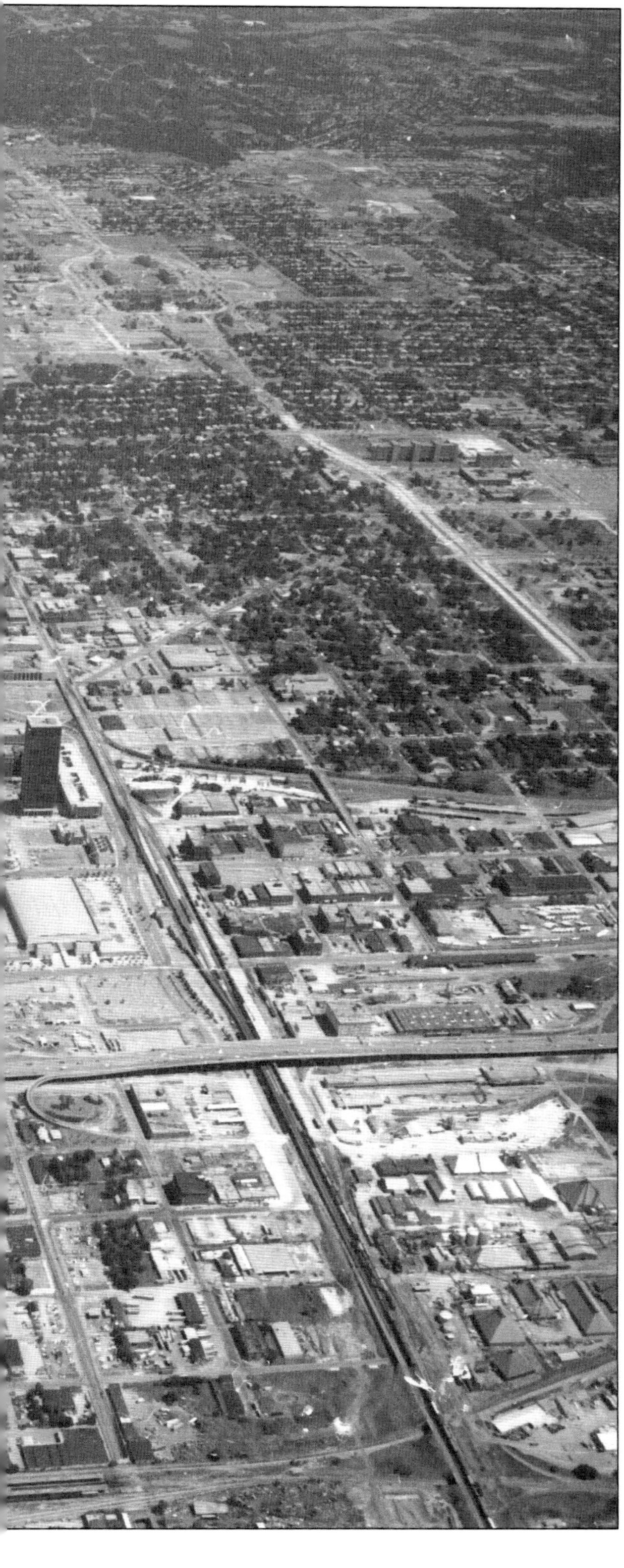

This rare aerial image of downtown Oklahoma City shows the swath of destruction left behind after urban renewal failed. The 1970s and 1980s were periods of stagnation for downtown and periods of affluence and explosive development for the suburbs. With the exception of the Myriad Gardens, little was done to improve the inner city or the central business district during this time, even as the oil boom of the late 1970s brought a flood of money into the area. At the far right rests Film Row, which had been slated for destruction in the aggressive renewal plans. Ironically, over the next 30 years, downtown slowly recovered and saw a surge of growth near the end of the 20th century while Film Row remained vacant and nearly destroyed by blight. (Courtesy of the Oklahoma Historical Society.)

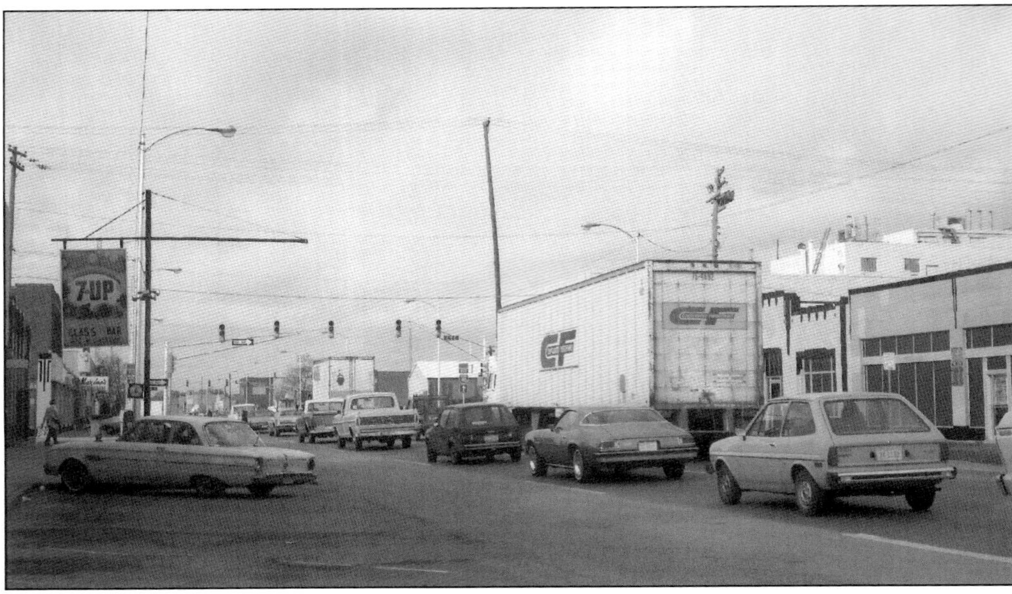

The images above and below were taken by Oklahoma Theatre Supply owner J. Eldon Peek about 1978. They show Sheridan Avenue and the former Film Row, obscured by rush hour traffic. The image above faces west. On the left is Maxine's Film Coffee Shop, former Film Exchange, and Warner Brothers buildings. Along the right is the Video-Vumore and the former MGM building. Just right of MGM starts Poverty Row. Below, facing east along the left is the former MGM and Poverty Row exchange offices, now occupied by the International Crystal Manufacturing Company. Poverty Row consisted of addresses 619–629 West Grand Avenue and included the Tower Pictures, Monogram Pictures, Republic Pictures, Southwestern Theatres, Syndicate Pictures, United Artists, Universal, and Loew's film exchanges. The Oklahoma City Shipping and Inspection Bureau occupied 623 West Grand Avenue in 1956. The city skyline in this photograph is devoid of many structures due to the onslaught of urban renewal. (Both, courtesy of the author's private collection.)

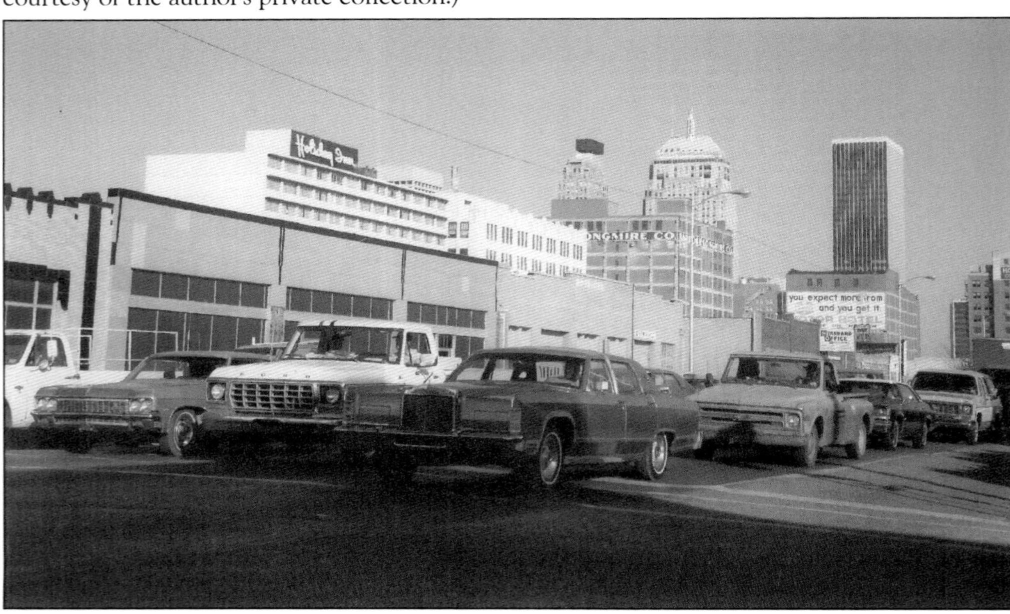

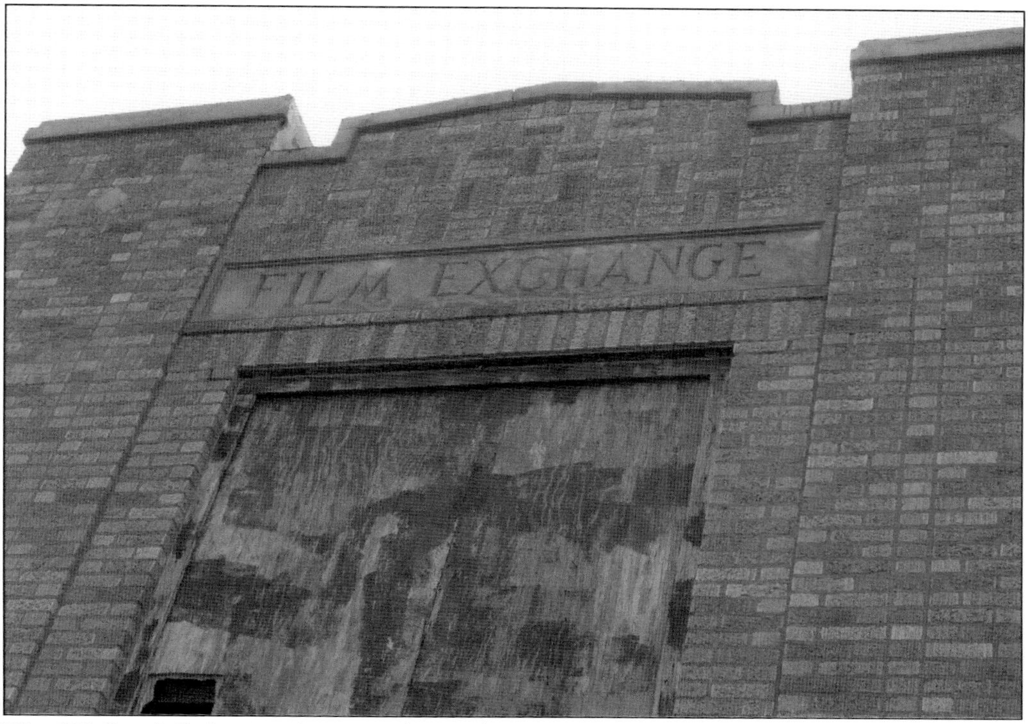

The 523 South Robinson Avenue Film Exchange sat vacant for approximately 25 years. The City Rescue Mission relocated many years ago to facilities along West Reno Avenue. The image above shows the Art Deco–styled film exchange lentil. The interior film vaults and nearly all its interior walls are gone, but the structure and floors were well constructed and composed of nearly 12-inch-thick brick and mortar. This exchange once hosted nearly 20 film exchanges. A citywide revitalization of downtown called Project 180 and Maps 3, at the time of this writing, threatens to demolish the building. (Both, courtesy of the author's private collection.)

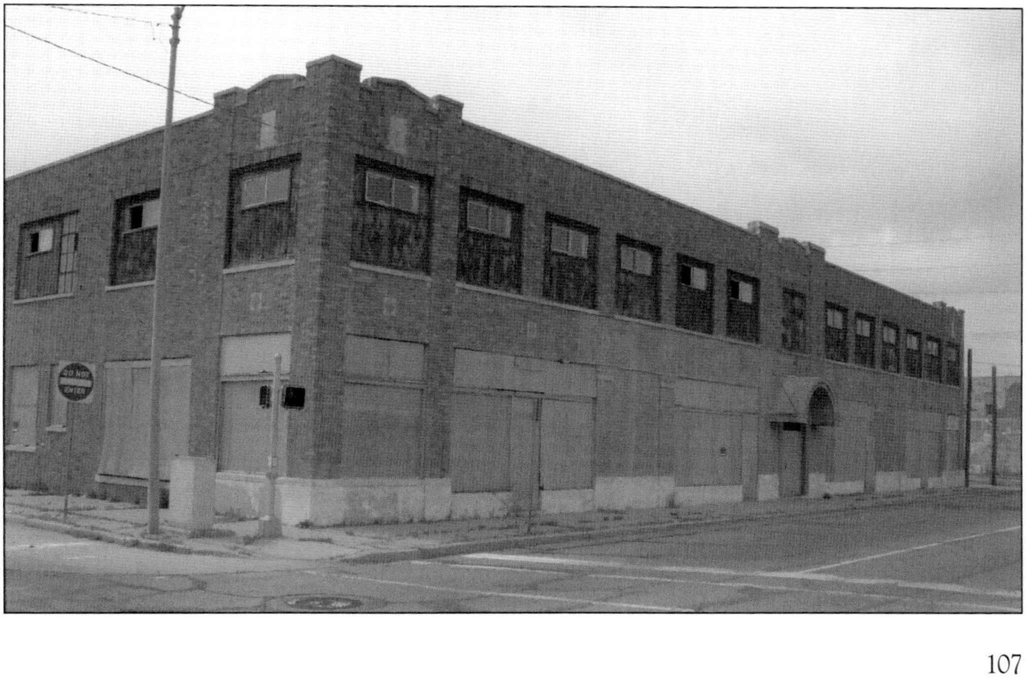

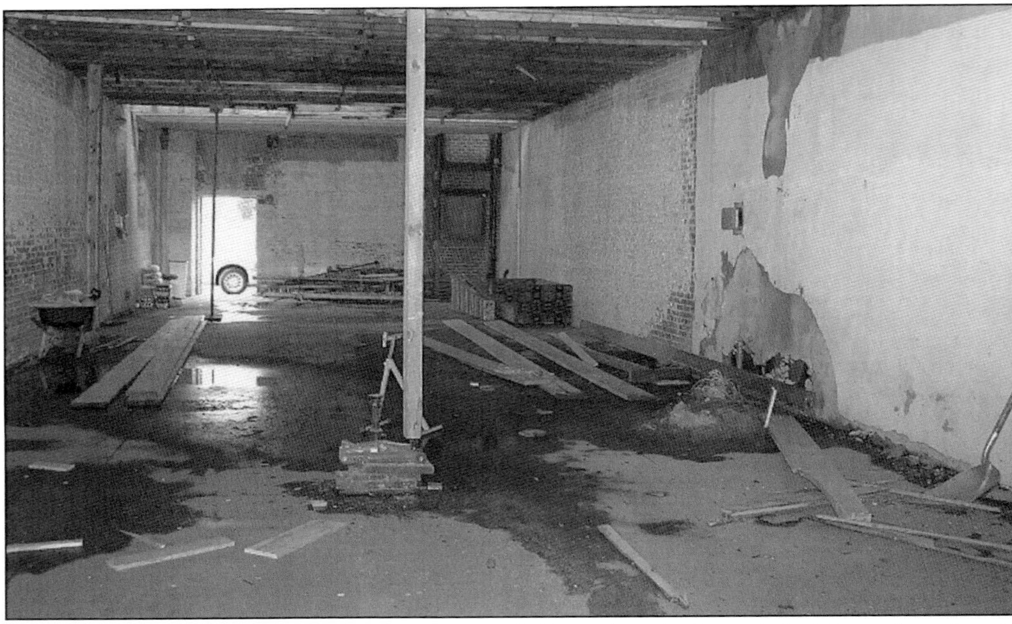

The history of Film Row began to reemerge in 2003, and as the historic buildings that played a role in its past were located, the amount of blight and neglect over the course of 30 years or more was painfully obvious. In this series of photographs, the former Film Exchange building's interior is seen in disrepair. The spaces have been used for squatting and are heavily vandalized and covered in detritus. These images are of 700 West Sheridan Avenue, the former home of National Theater Supply, Simplex Bludworth, Vitagraph, Warner Brothers, First National Features, and Anderson Theatre Supply. The view from this space would have looked upon every film exchange surrounding the building in one glance. The upper floors may have been used for wartime cotton grading. Note the cotton bale elevator in the distant right corner in the above photograph. (Both, courtesy of the author's private collection.)

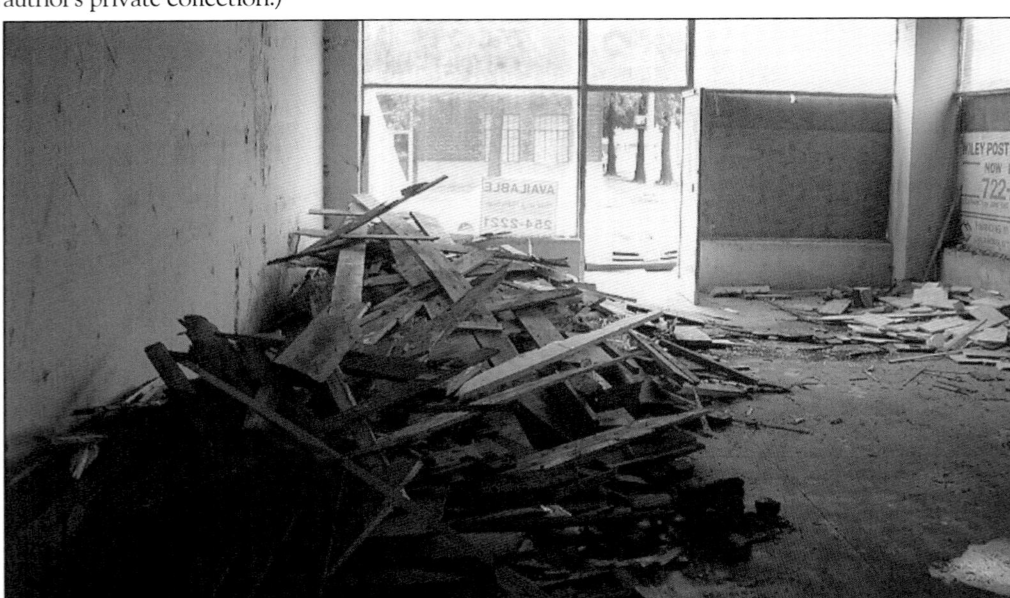

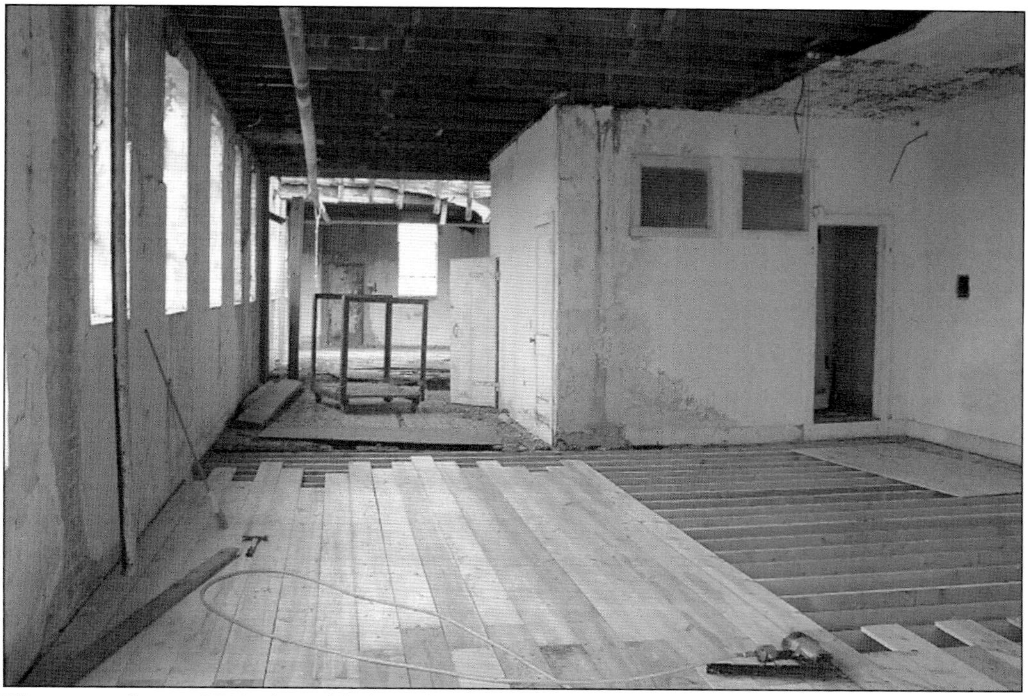

The views above of 702 1/2 and below of 702 West Sheridan Avenue show the ruin of the former Allied, Liberty Special, and Columbia Pictures film exchanges and the former upstairs Simplex Screening Room. The roof and skylights pictured above were practically nonexistent due to rot and neglect. Prior to revitalization and restoration efforts underway in these 2005 images, the upper floor was covered in large amounts of bird droppings and was unsafe to walk upon. The door at the far right in the image below lead to five film vaults and an inspection room. (Both, courtesy of the author's private collection.)

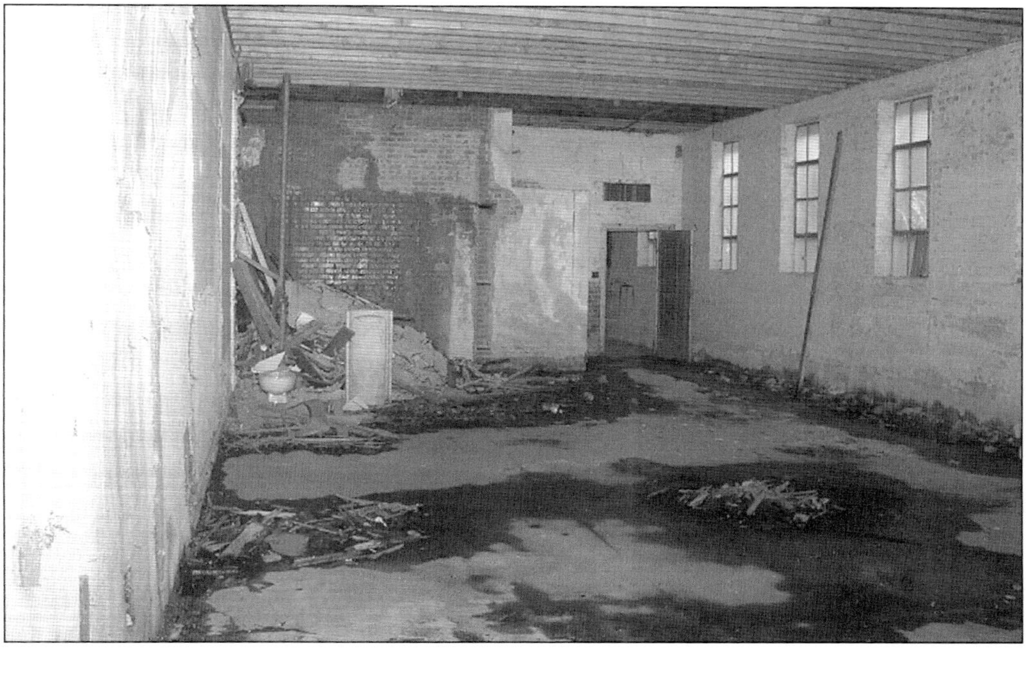

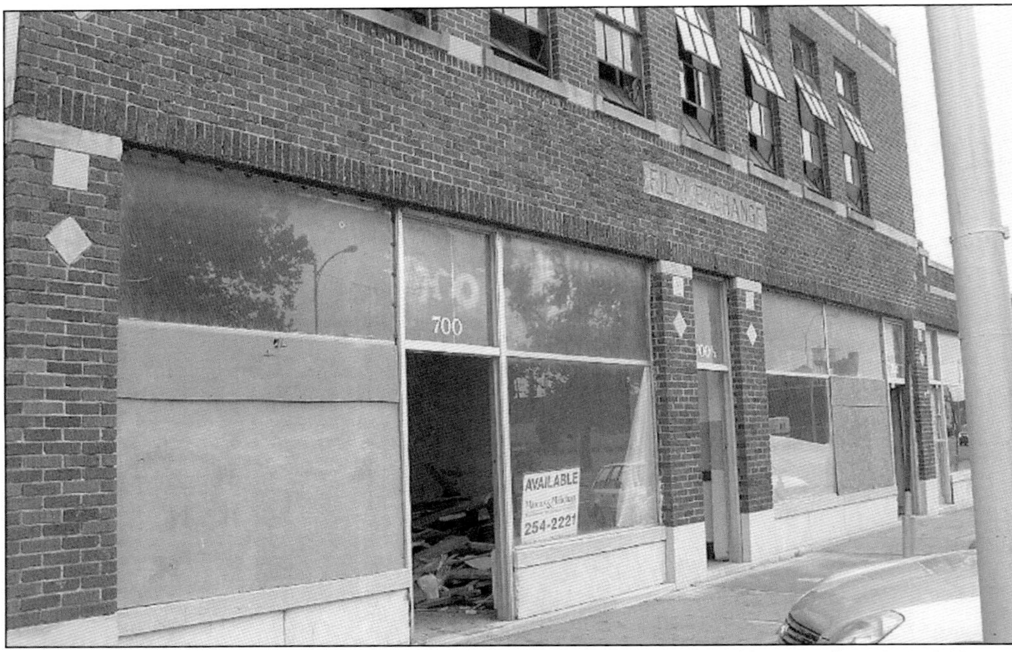

These two 2005 images show the exterior of the Film Exchange building and its 700, 702, and 702 1/2 West Sheridan Avenue spaces. The lentil reads "Film Exchange," but is difficult to read due to decades of grime. The space was often used for nefarious purposes by area transients, and windows were constantly being broken. Columbia Pictures moved into the 702 West Sheridan Avenue space and remained for more than 40 years. It was the last studio film exchange and departed from the cityscape in 1971. (Both, courtesy of the author's private collection.)

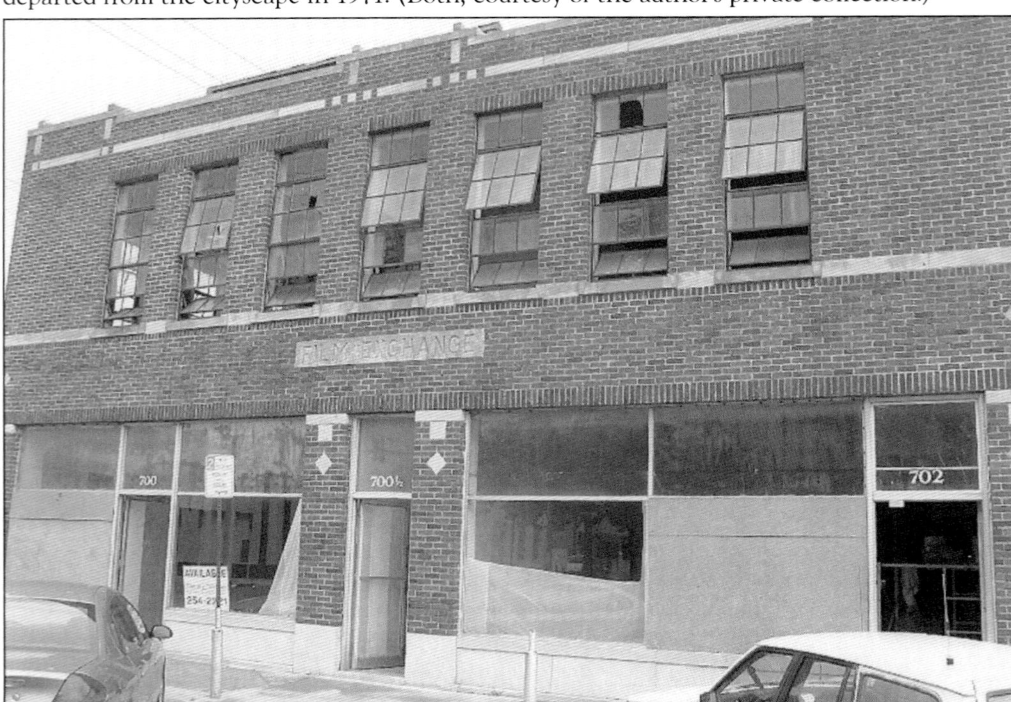

At right is the Oklahoma Theatre Supply Company at 628 West Sheridan Avenue shortly before it closed in 2004. The original facade and upper floor windows are hidden in this image by sheet siding applied some time in the early 1970s. (Courtesy of the author's private collection.)

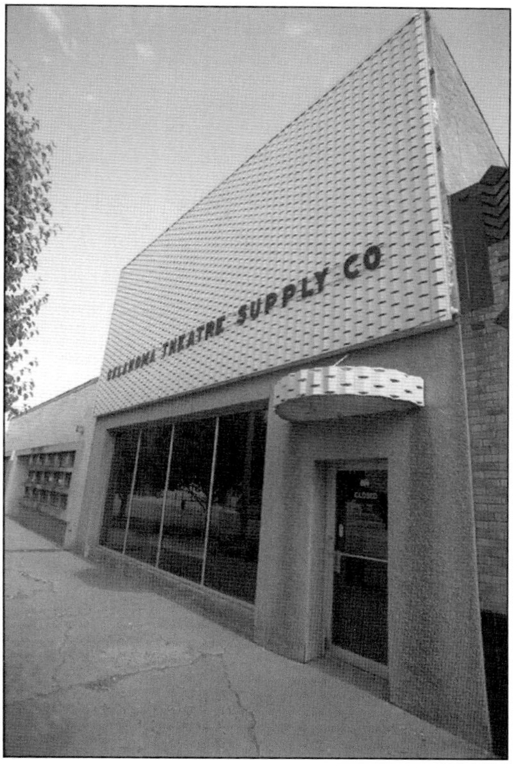

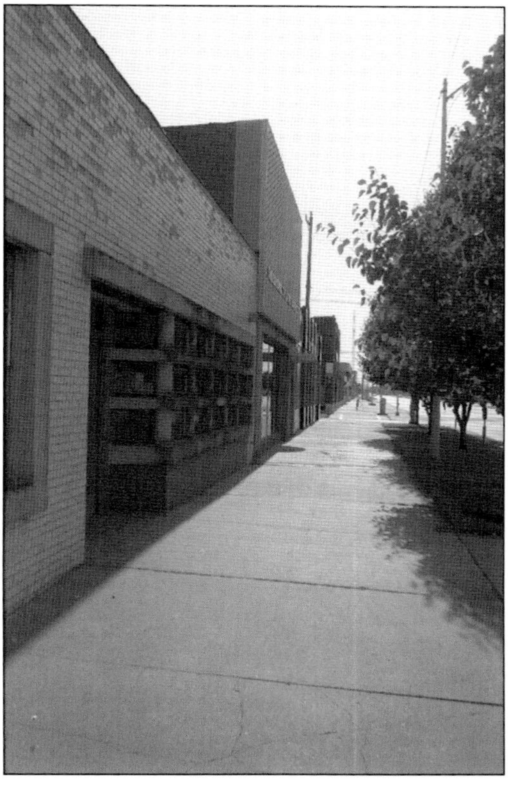

National Screen Service, Roland Theatrical Art Signs, and the Oklahoma Theater Supply operated from this 624 West Sheridan Avenue space. Next to movie studios, in the United States, the National Screen Service (NSS) had the most direct and profound impact on the movie paper advertising industry. From 1940 until the mid-1980s, the NSS was the "control center" for almost 90 percent of the movie paper distributed. In essence, the NSS turned movie paper advertising materials into an industry all its own. By the mid-1940s, most major studios turned over the production and distribution of all movie paper advertising to the NSS. The NSS produced, printed, distributed, and stocked all of the materials. (Courtesy of the author's private collection and historian Ed Poole.)

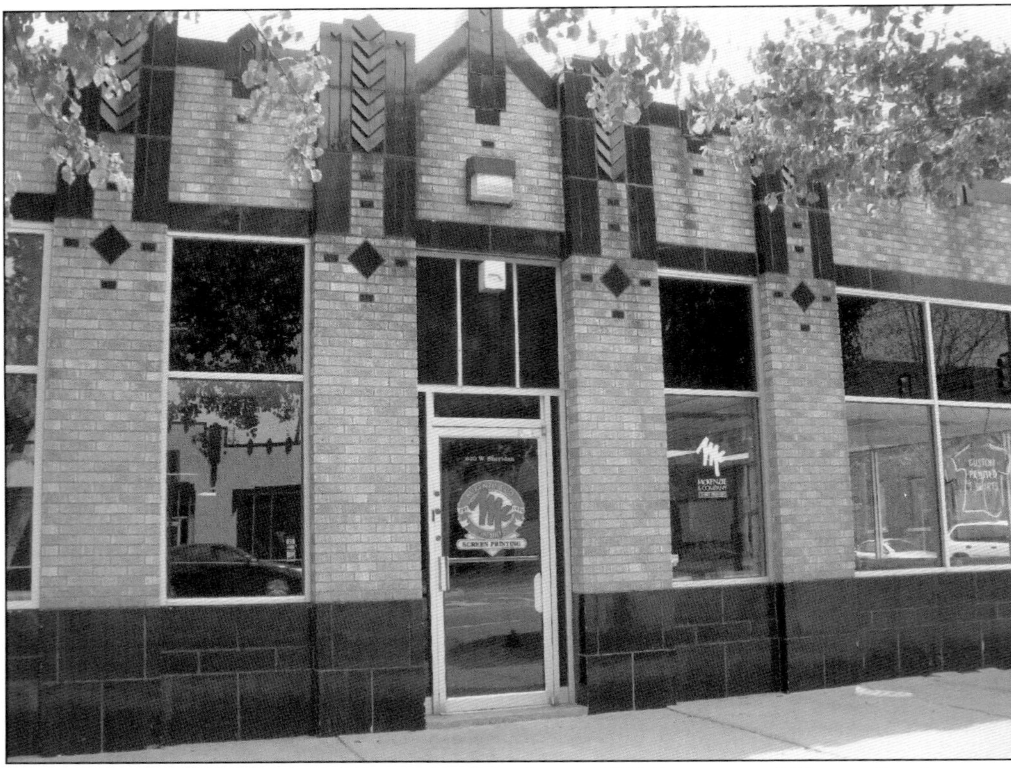

McKenzie & Company T-Shirts has occupied the former RKO Pictures and Warner Brothers space at 630 West Sheridan Avenue for more than 30 years. Amazingly, very little has changed from architect P.H. Weather's original design. However, during streetscape efforts, heavy equipment crews damaged tile work along the building's base. Below, the colorful interior is a stark, pleasant contrast to the Art Deco feel of the exterior. Three of the building's original film vaults are preserved and currently used for storage. Owner Jeff McKenzie states that his building has been tough to maintain in recent years and that it "may be Art Deco outside, but inside it is all shirts and ink." He further promises that if he can not print a better T-shirt, he will eat a bug! (Both, courtesy of the author's private collection.)

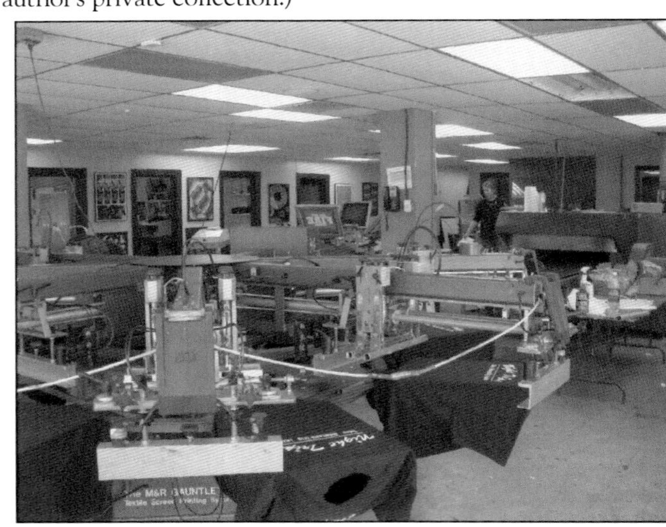

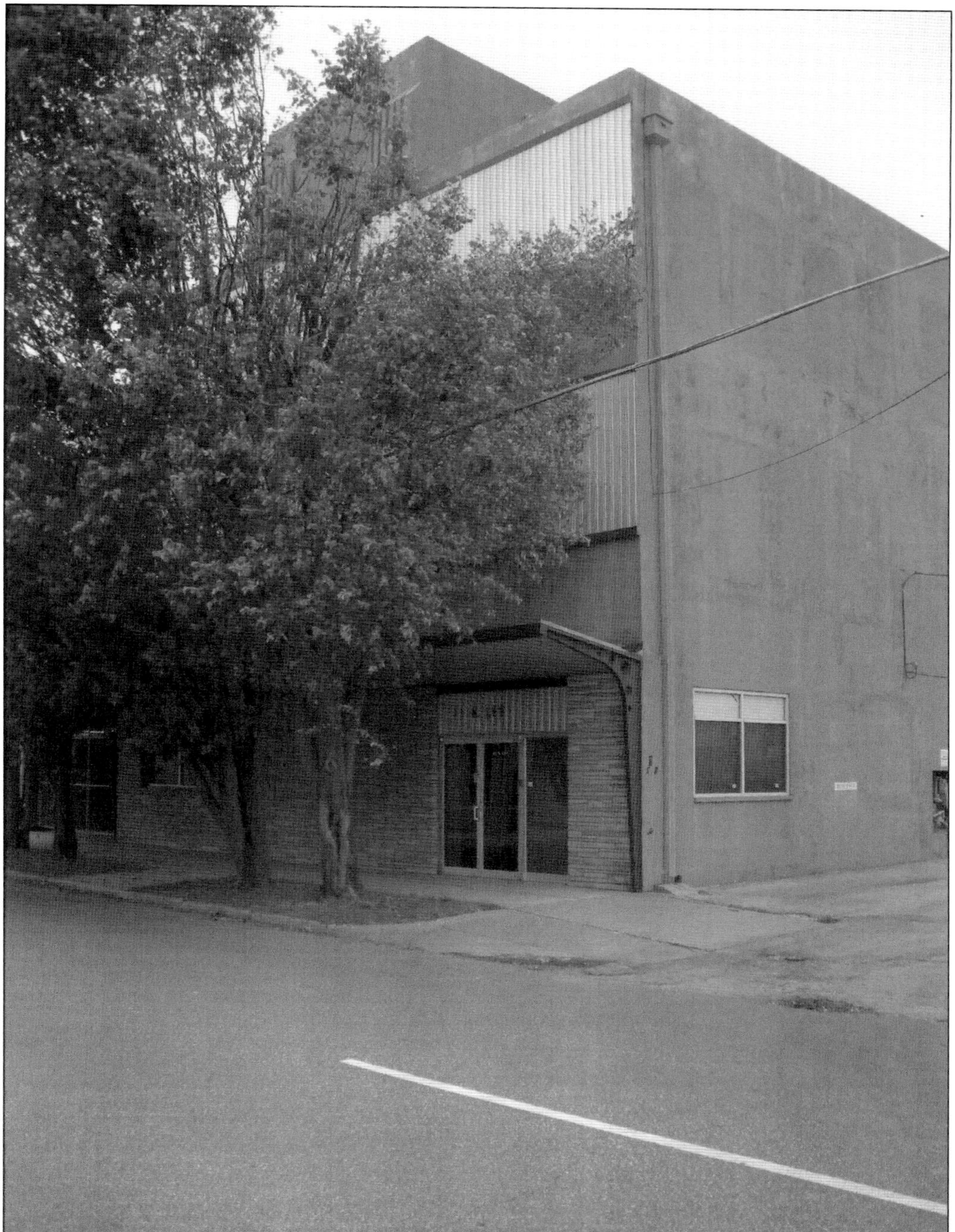

Here, the former offices of the Griffith and Video Independent Theatres empire sit almost hidden from view at 11 North Lee Avenue in Oklahoma City. Bands of stainless steel from the 1953 Video remodel still wrap around the building along with the addition of a gray paint scheme. The International Crystal Manufacturing Company, mainly because of the adequate parking to the west, occupied the building starting in 1984 until acquired by new owners in 2003. (Courtesy of the author's private collection.)

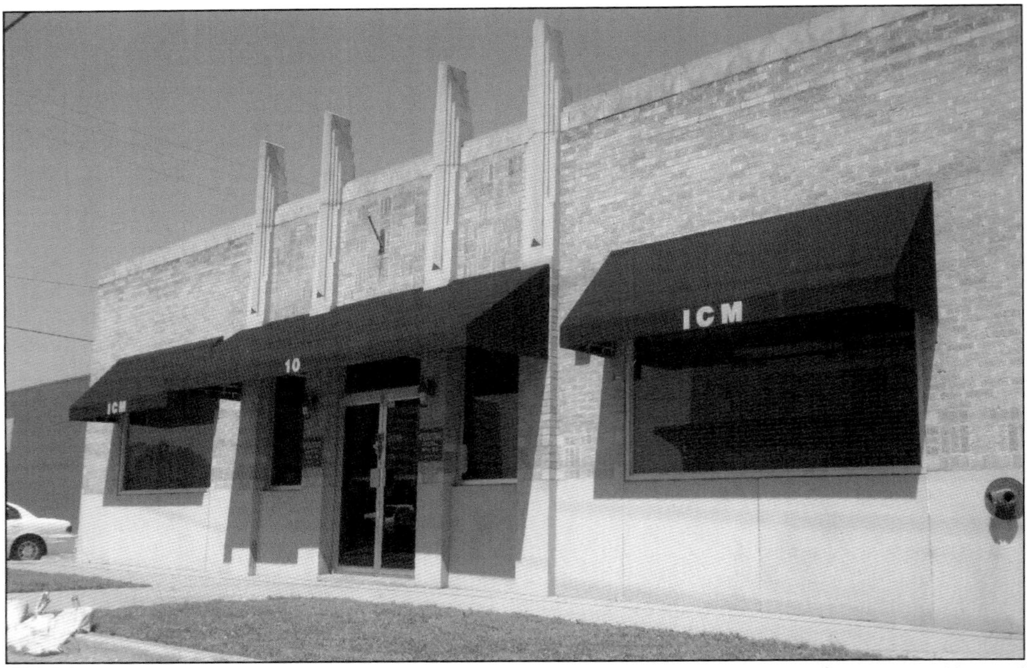

The location of 10 North Lee Avenue was home to 20th Century Fox for many years and hosted screenings in its own indoor theater. The screening room now serves as a break room, and the projection room is an office. All that remains are the original projection portholes. The International Crystal Manufacturing Company occupies this space and the former MGM and Poverty Row spaces. Below, one of three original film vaults remains. (Both, courtesy of the author's private collection.)

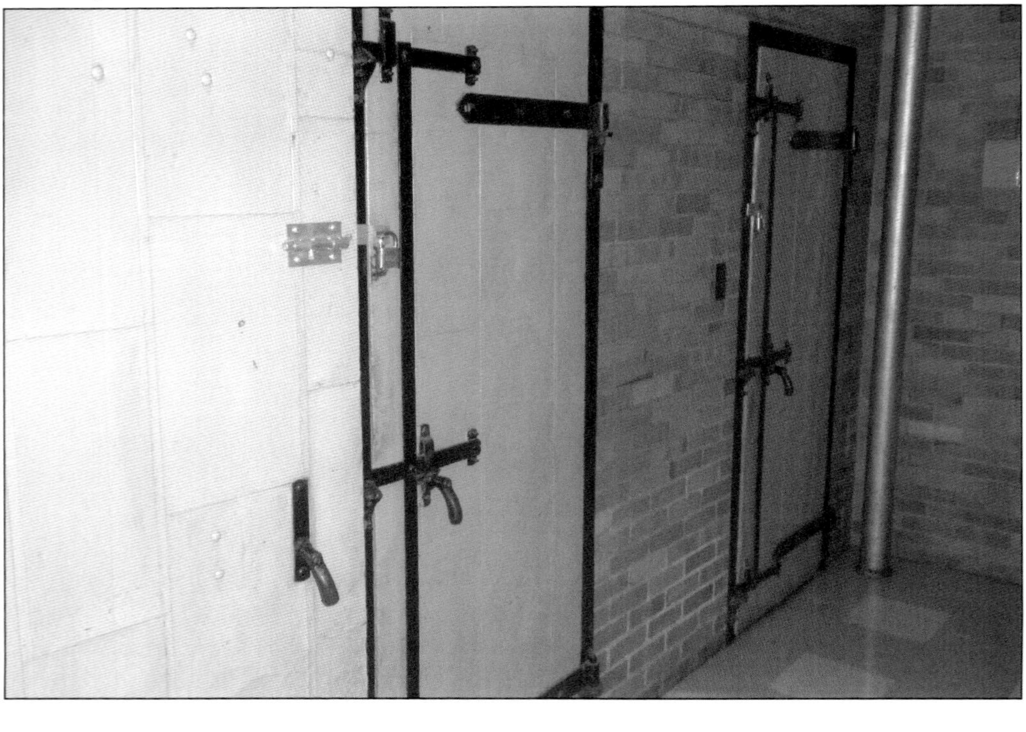

At right, the vault door is open and reveals that it is used for file storage. These vaults were a requirement of city building codes and were completely fire retardant and equipped with a sprinkler system. A second vault door stands open nearby with its interior surface festooned with 45 movie reel labels placed there by the projectionist as he checked out a film. Among them are *Shenandoah* and *Brides of Dracula*. (Both, courtesy of the author's private collection.)

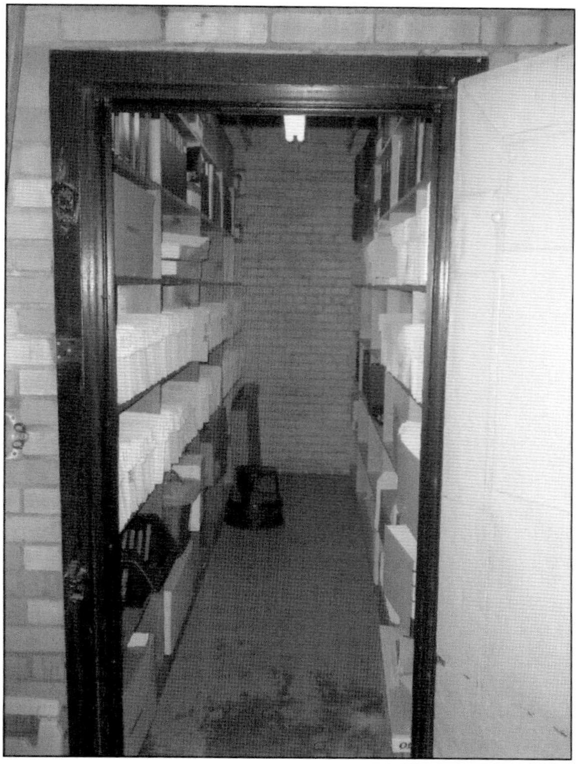

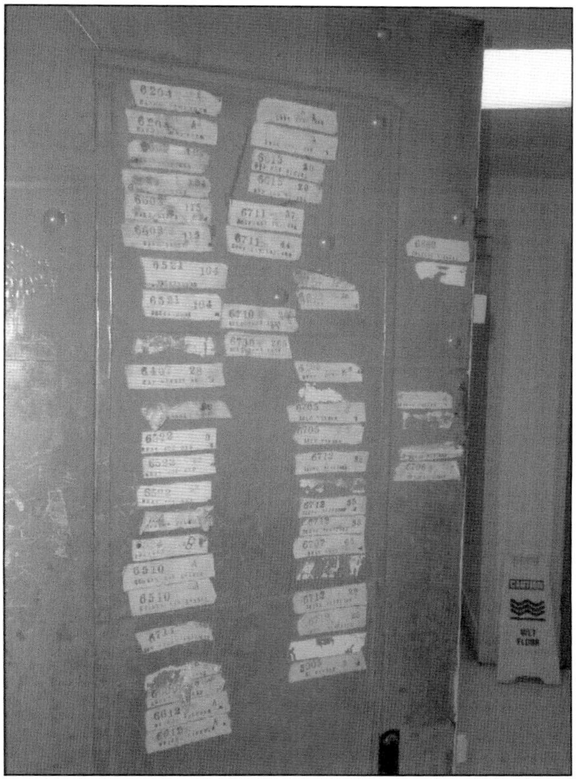

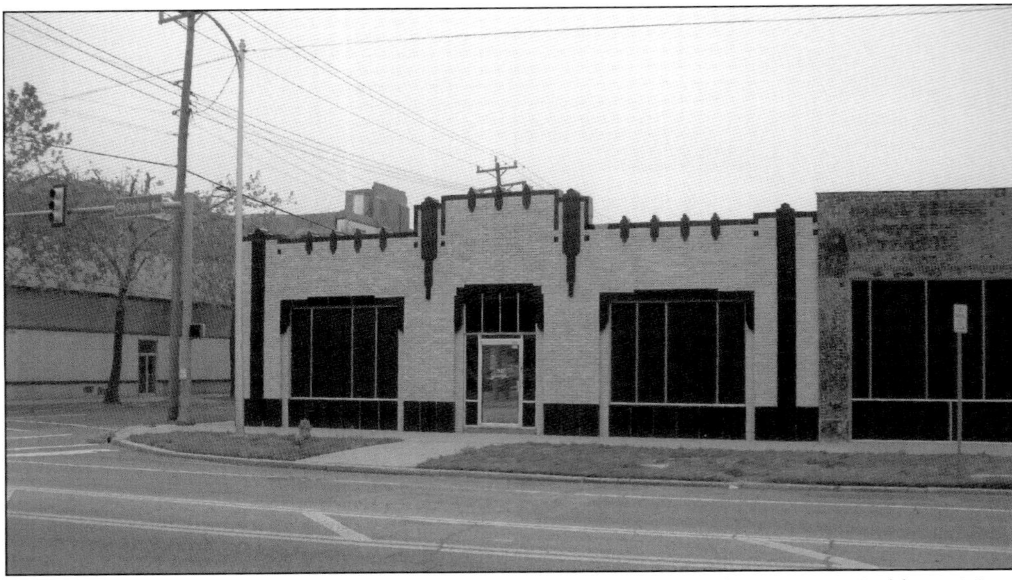

The International Crystal Manufacturing Company integrated the above Metro-Goldwyn-Mayer (MGM) building at 629 West Sheridan Avenue into its offices in the former 20th Century Fox building during the early 1980s. The building's interior was modified extensively to accommodate the company's needs, including the dismantling of both the Fox and MGM screening rooms. However, all former fireproof film vaults from both structures were kept intact for company record-keeping. They are among the only complete and unmodified film vaults left along Film Row. Other film vaults are located at 624 and 630 West Sheridan Avenue, while a small scattering of partial and deconstructed vaults reside in some of the original Film Row buildings. (Both, courtesy of the author's private collection.)

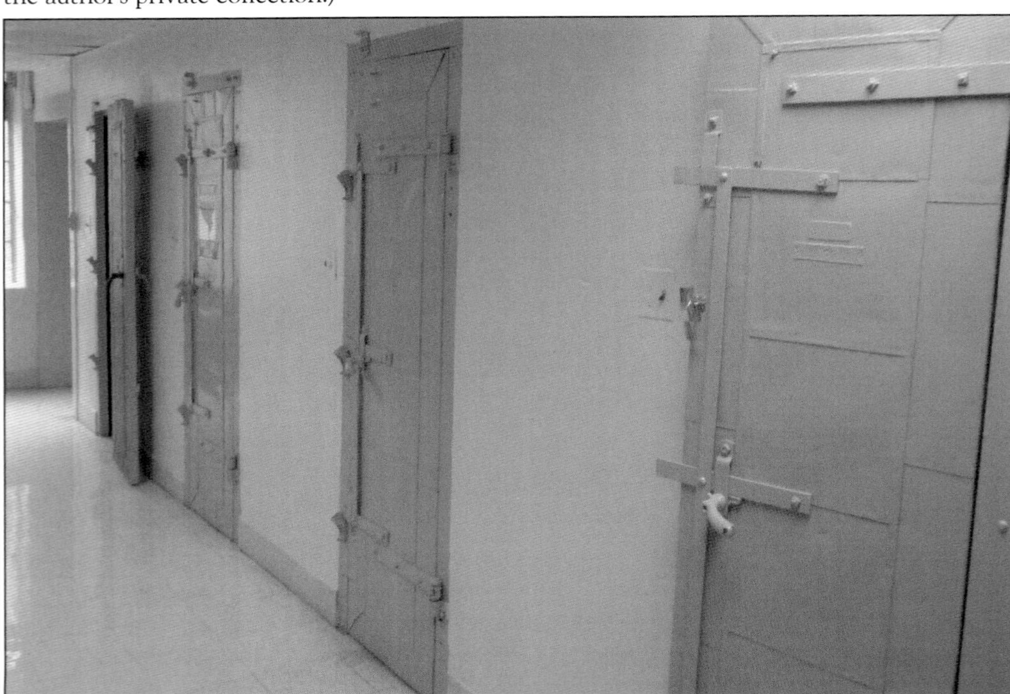

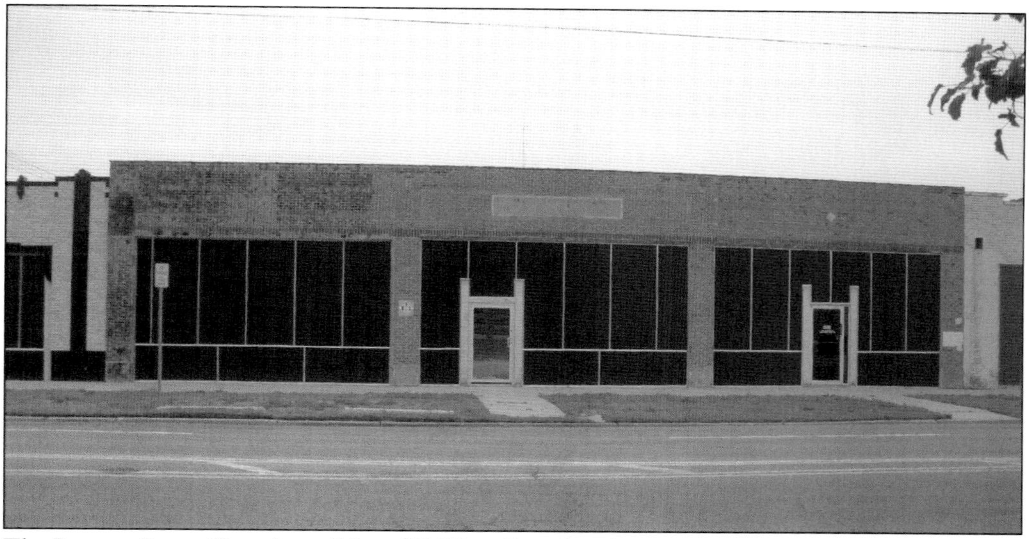

The Poverty Row offices from 619 to 625 West Sheridan Avenue were eventually integrated into the International Crystal Manufacturing Company's workspace. In this image, the former Tower Pictures, Monogram Pictures, Republic Pictures, Southwestern Theatres, Syndicate Pictures, United Artists, Universal, and Loew's film exchange windows are covered and no longer share glimpses into their past. Below, the southeast corner of Paramount Pictures' former redbrick facade has been revealed as stainless steel sheets are removed. On the corner facing right, efforts have not yet uncovered the former studio logo, now pictured on the following page and the cover of this book. (Both, courtesy of the author's private collection.)

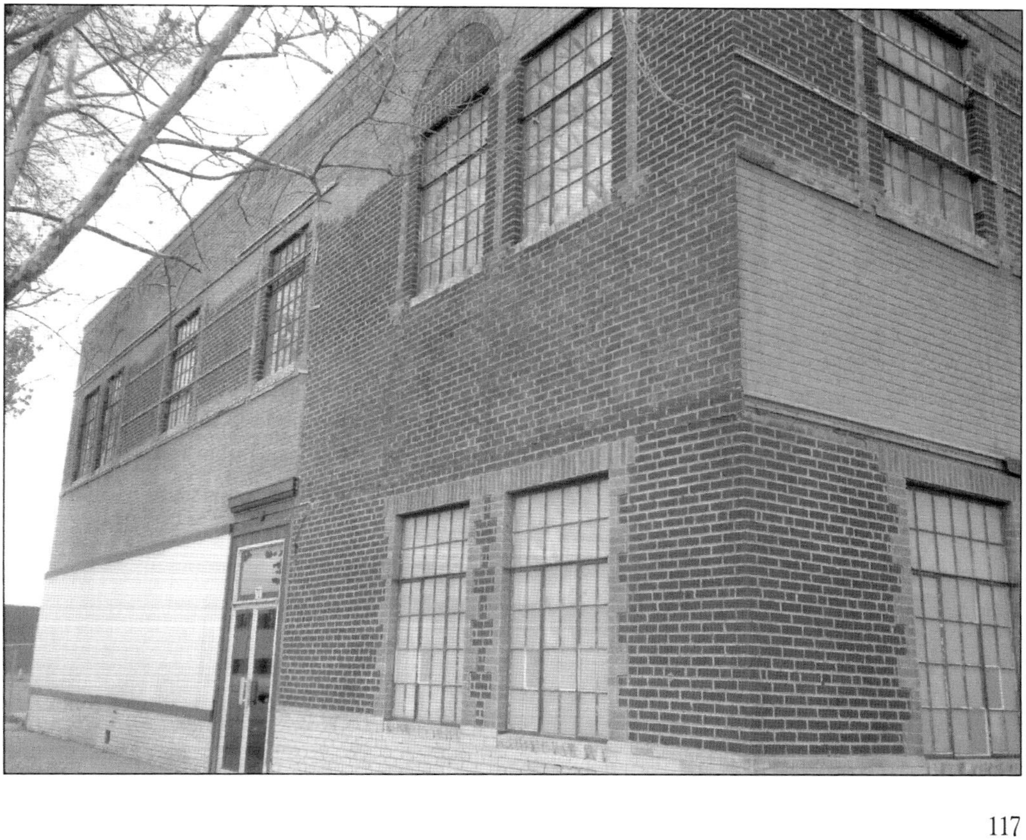

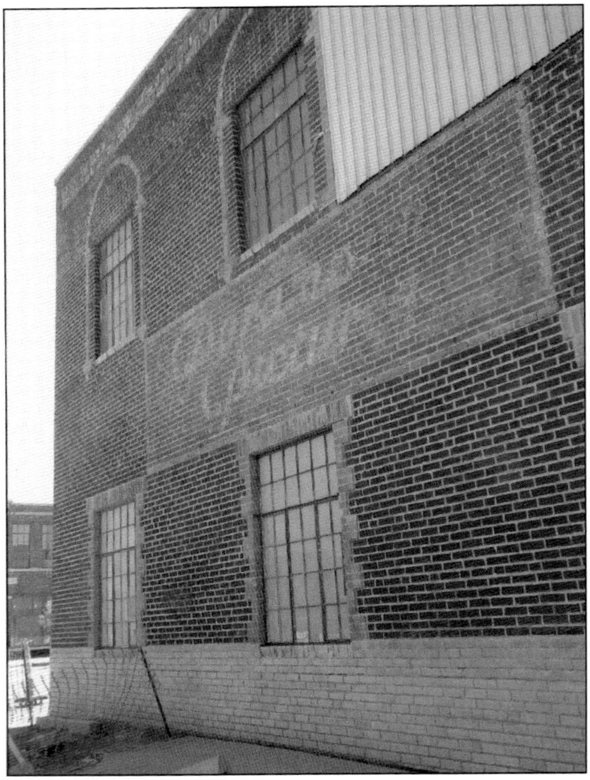

While stripping away gray paint and sheets of stainless steel attached to the building by Video Independent Theatres in 1953, property owners of the former Paramount Pictures building uncovered the studio's logo along the structure's southeast corner. This ghostly image is the only known signage to exist in the area from that bygone era and was once painted in vibrant colors. The Paramount Pictures name also appeared in large metal letters across the building's south facade and is now presumed lost. Lee Avenue has been stripped and prepared for new streetscaping in this image below. (Both, courtesy of the author's private collection.)

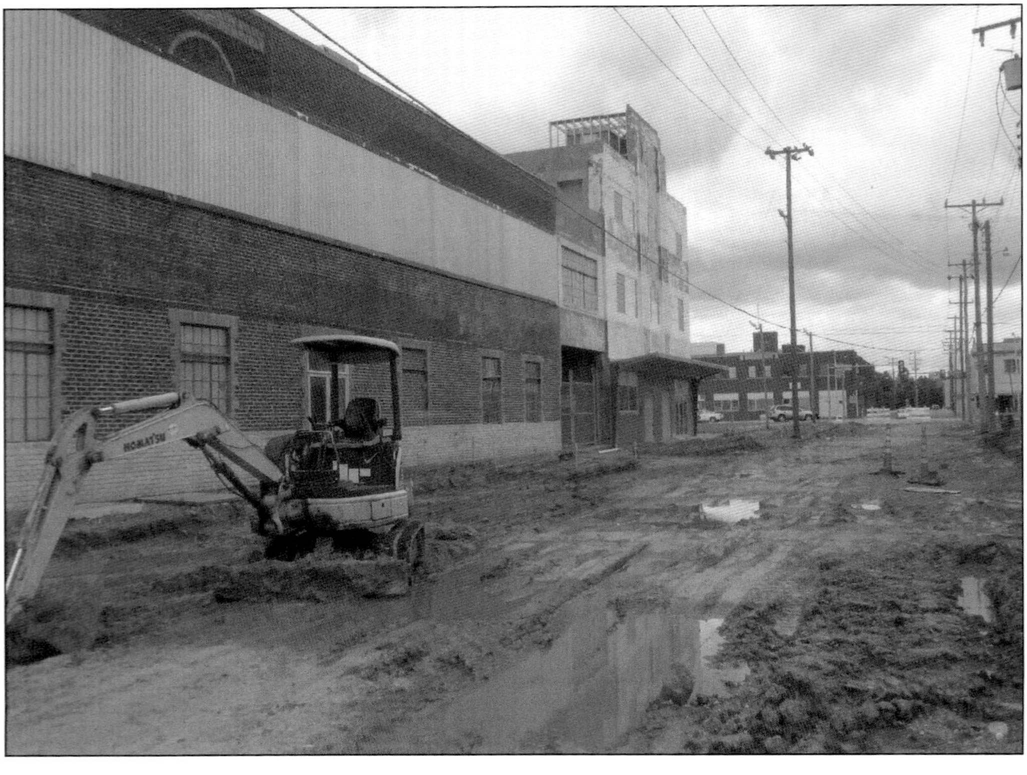

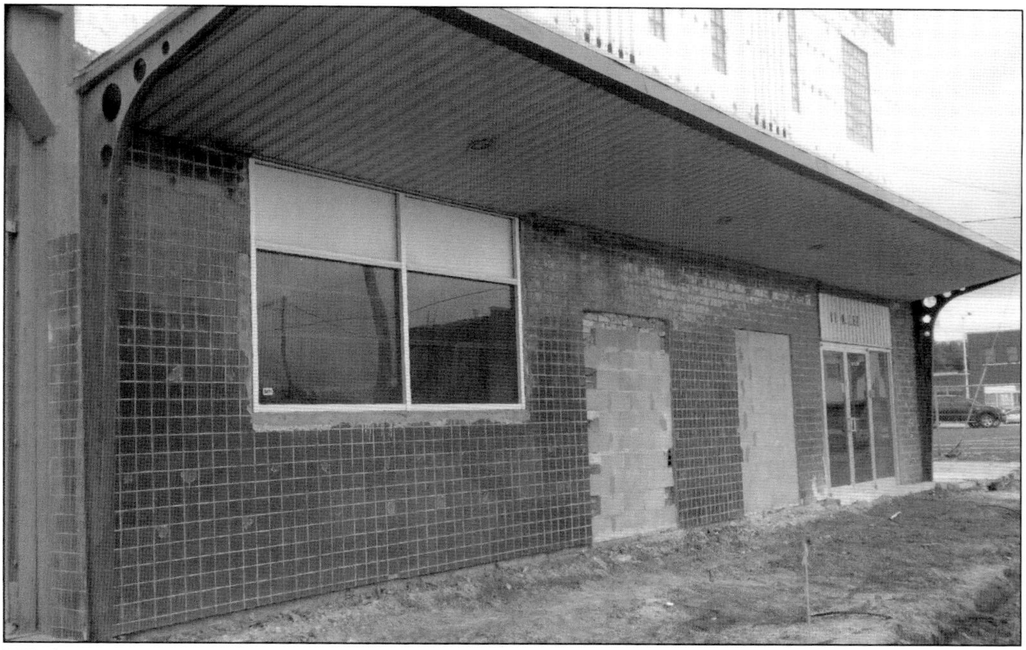

While property owners continued efforts to remove decades of paint and sheet after sheet of stainless steel encapsulating the former Paramount Pictures building, it was decided to remove the yellowed brick masonry from the 11 North Lee Avenue facade. Underneath was the crimson tile and former entrances to Griffith Theatres and the Film Coffee Shop. The tall frontage that was once adorned with the near three-story Griffith Theatres marquee was also revealed after removal of paint and stainless steel sheets resumed. Now, the Paramount and Griffith structures stand separate once more. (Both, courtesy of the author's private collection.)

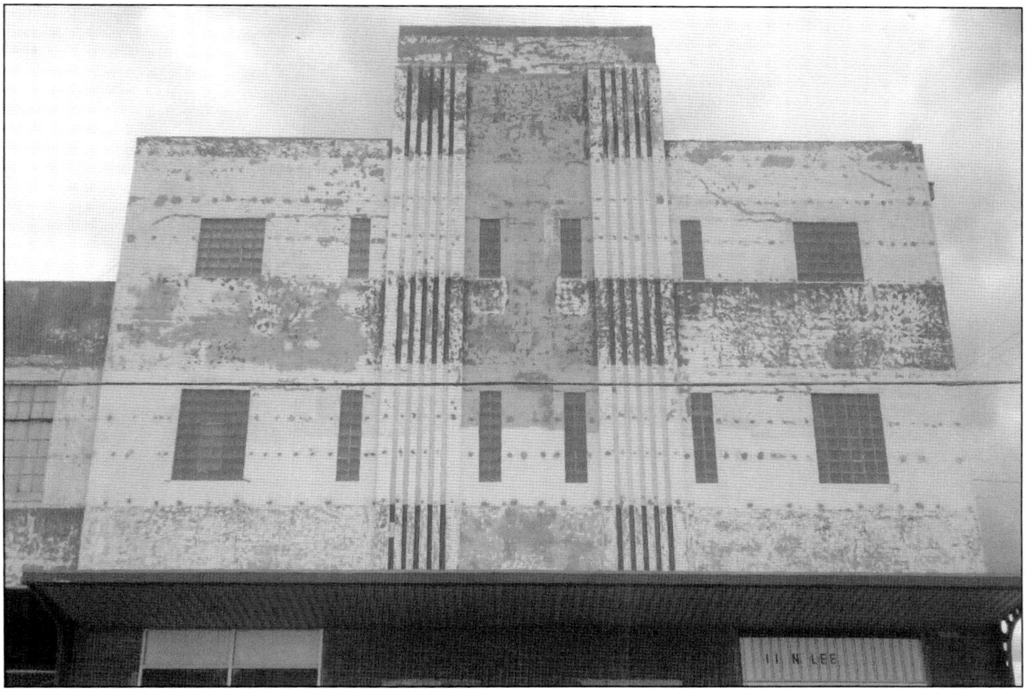

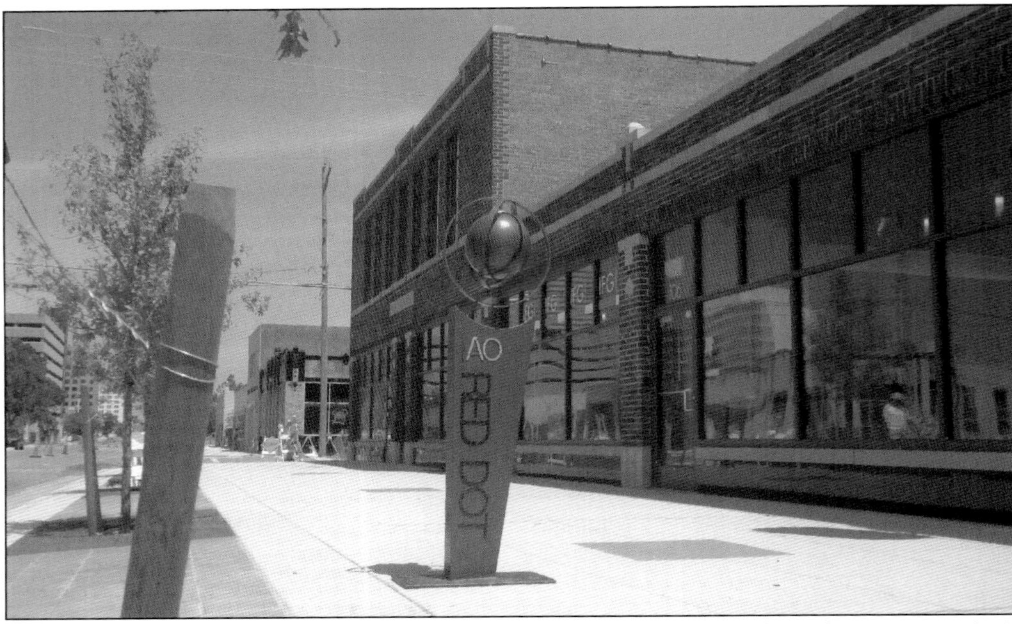

The former spaces at 704, 706, and 708 West Sheridan Avenue once hosted approximately 16 film exchanges that included Allied, RKO Pictures, Majestic Pictures, Altec, Oklahoma City Shipping and Inspection Bureau, and RCA Photophone, along with Goodall Electric Company Motion Pictures and the Oklahoma Theatre Supply Company. They are now home to the Insight Funding Group, a mortgage lender, and Individual Artists of Oklahoma (IAO), a grassroots contemporary arts organization and gallery. Above, the Red Dot sculpture marks IAO as the location of its annual art auction and sale to support the organization. The dark cobbled squares in this image are reserved for possible future film-themed embellishments, such as historical markers or Hollywood-inspired stars. Below, decades of grime have been removed from the building and its film exchange lintel as restoration and revitalization efforts prepare it for the 21st century. (Both, courtesy of the author's private collection.)

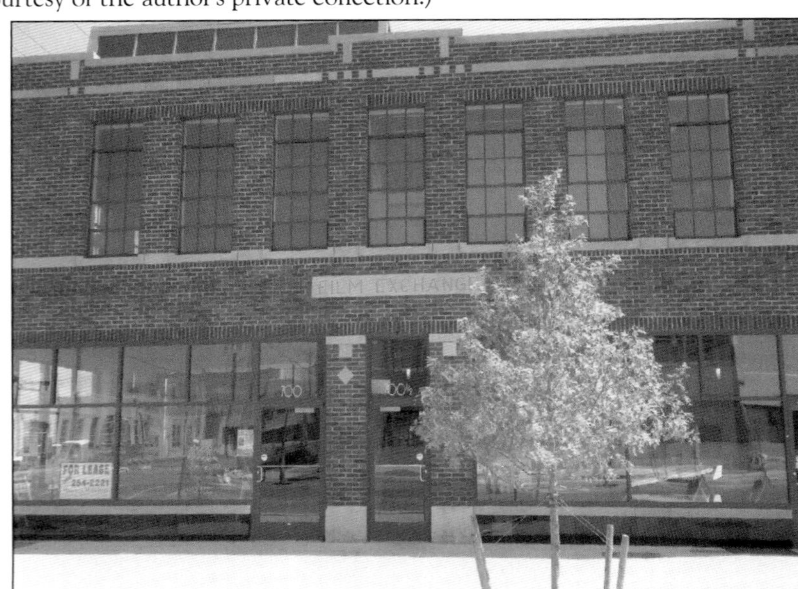

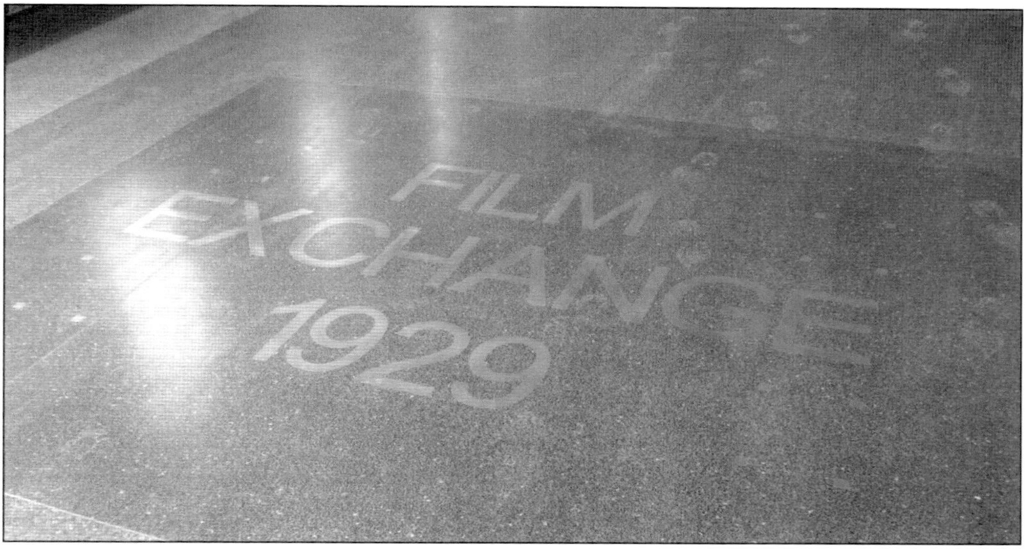

Revitalization and restoration efforts of the Sheridan Avenue Film Exchange building were important to the area's ultimate success. In the image above, the building and area history is celebrated by the addition of the unique floor inlay reading "Film Exchange 1929." This same inlay was incorporated into each of the building's entryways with the space address number. In 1929, film exchanges were still somewhat scattered across the cityscape but were converging on the 600–700 blocks of West Grand Avenue quickly, giving it the moniker of Film Row by the end of that same year. Below is a view of one of the large and newly restored skylights in 702 1/2 West Sheridan Avenue. (Both, courtesy of the author's collection.)

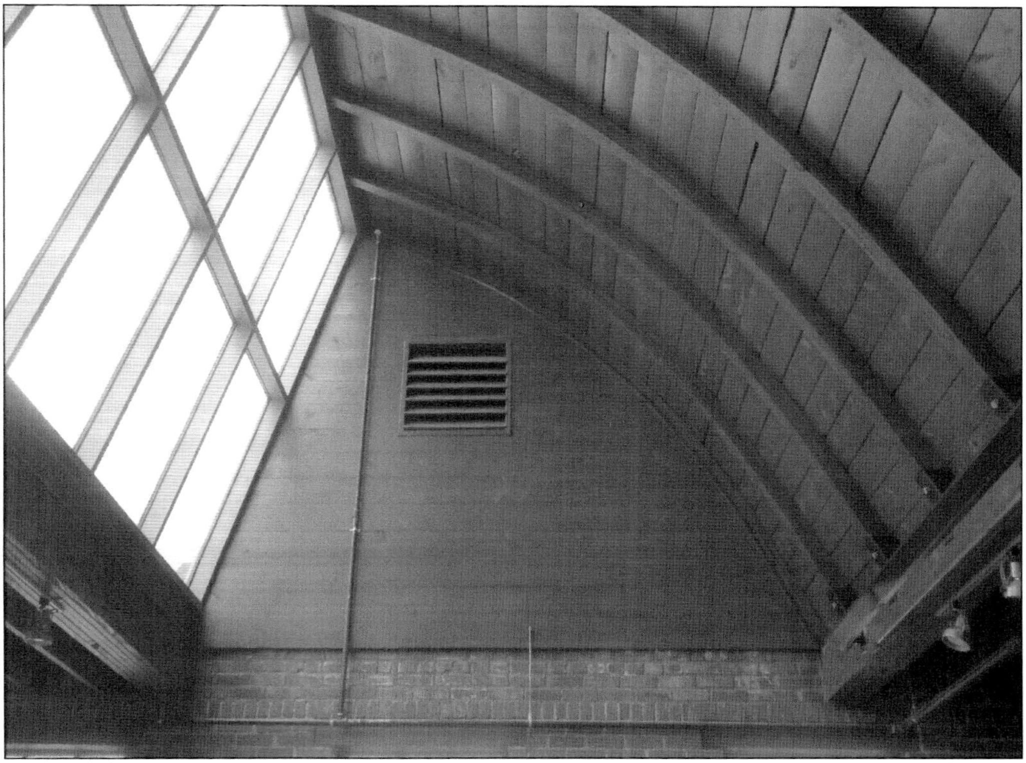

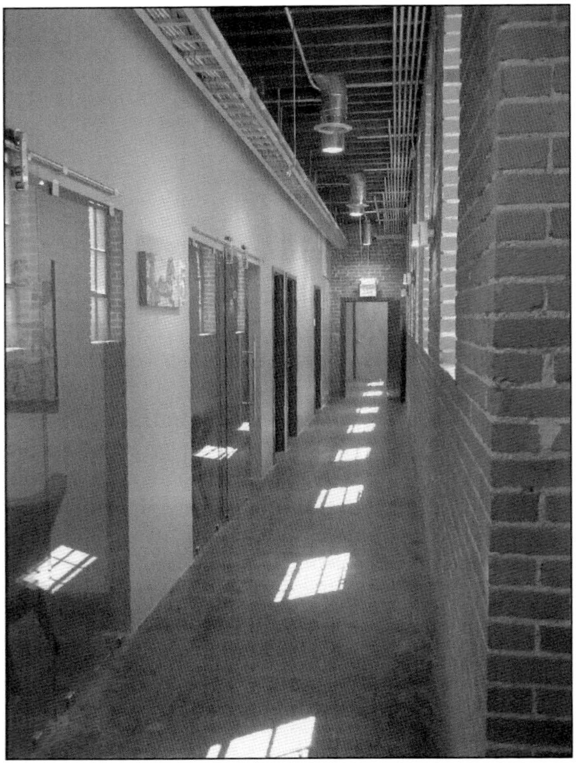

At left, the former 42-year home of Columbia Pictures at 702 West Sheridan Avenue is now occupied by Critical Mass Productions, a creative video editing, production, and post-production company in Oklahoma City. As seen in the image at left, the revitalization of the space was just as creative with the addition of sliding glass partition doors and film vault ruins converted into a useful kitchenette below. The original five film storage vaults located at the south end of the space were gutted some time in the past. (Both, courtesy of the author's collection.)

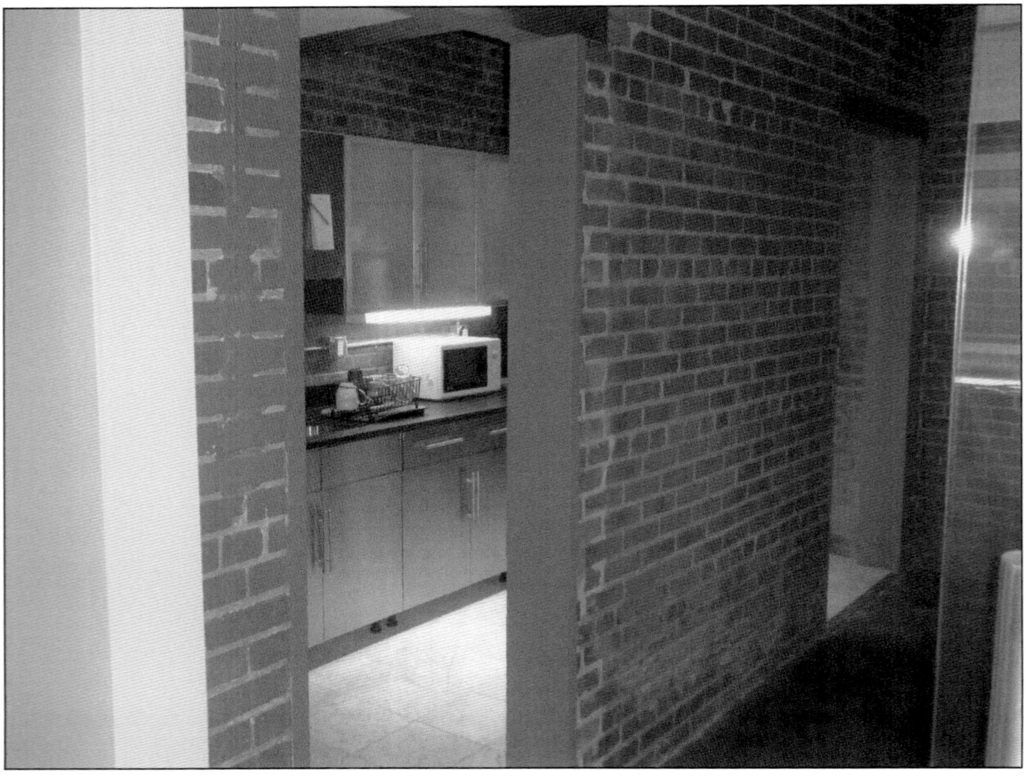

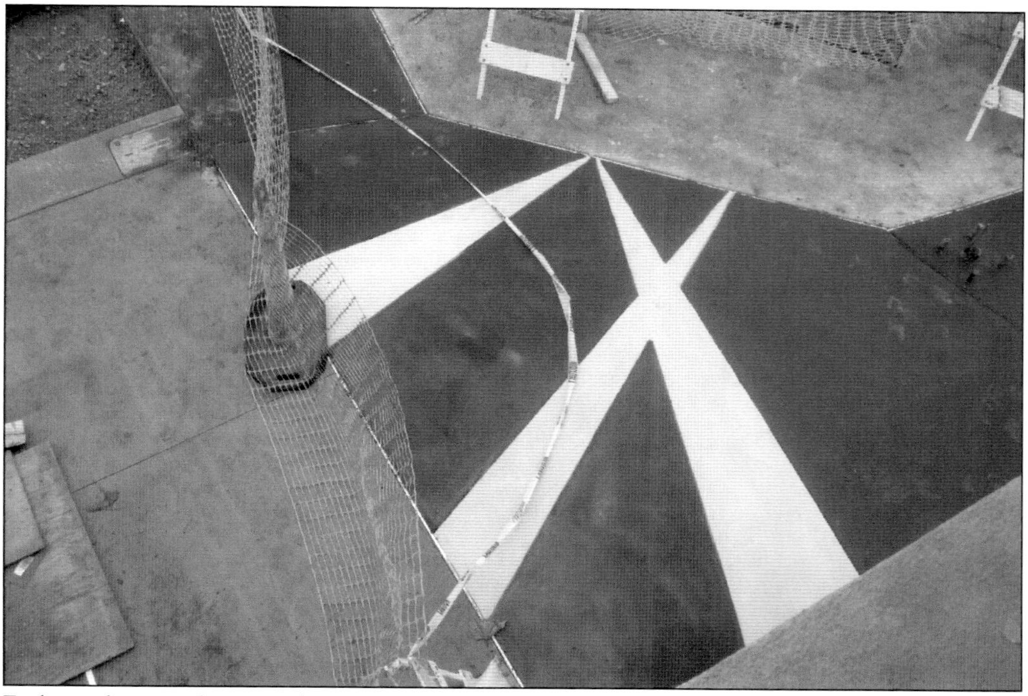

Early renderings of potential streetscaping for the Oklahoma City Film Exchange offered unique features that would identify to visitors that they had arrived on Film Row. The concept was innovative and the first of its kind used in Oklahoma City. In the image above, pedestrian ramps of colored concrete feature designs reminiscent of crossing film premier spotlights. The crosswalks below were constructed as large filmstrips that surround three intersections adorned with either a large reproduction of the spotlight or Hollywood-star motif. (Both, courtesy of the author's collection.)

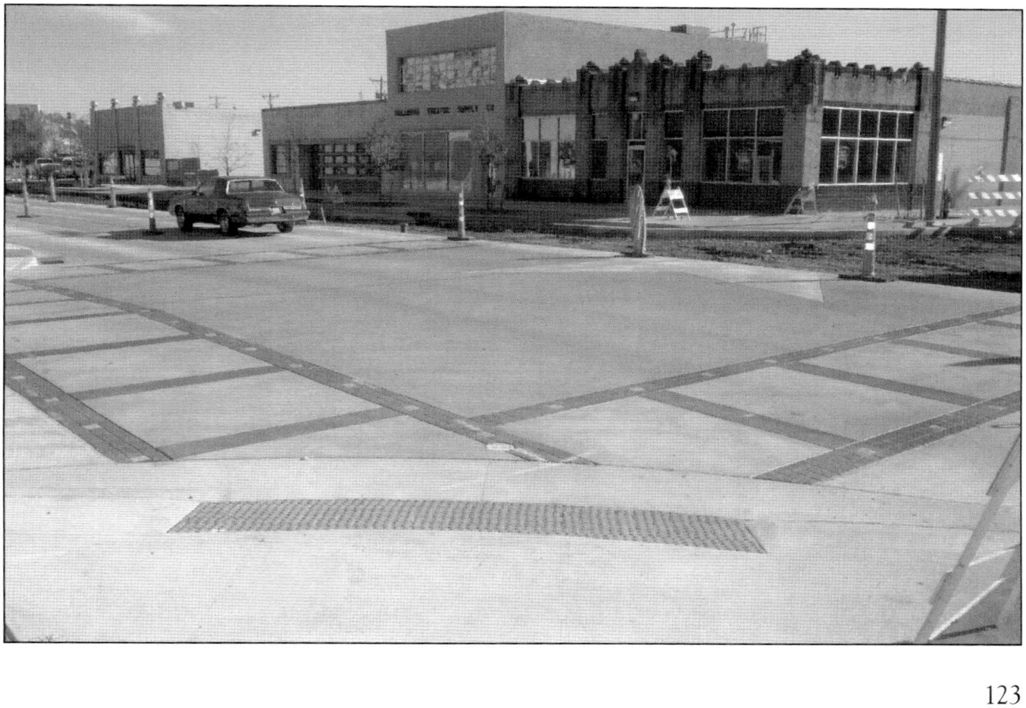

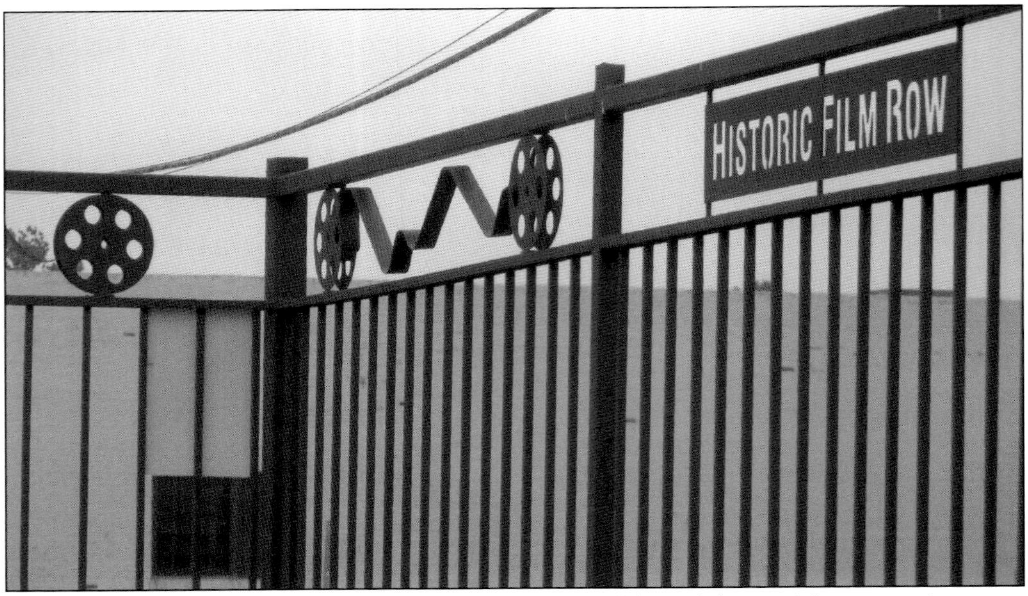

Early efforts by property owners defined the spaces and celebrated the area's history with custom embellishments, such as this iron fence featuring reels of film and studio names cut into mounted panels, as with the name "Historic Film Row" above. The alleyway stairs and access gates leading to the upper floors of the Film Exchange building are adorned with iron film reels in the image below. During the 1960s, an upper door along the right led to Challenger Studios, belonging to Native American artist J.D. Challenger. (Both, courtesy of the author's collection.)

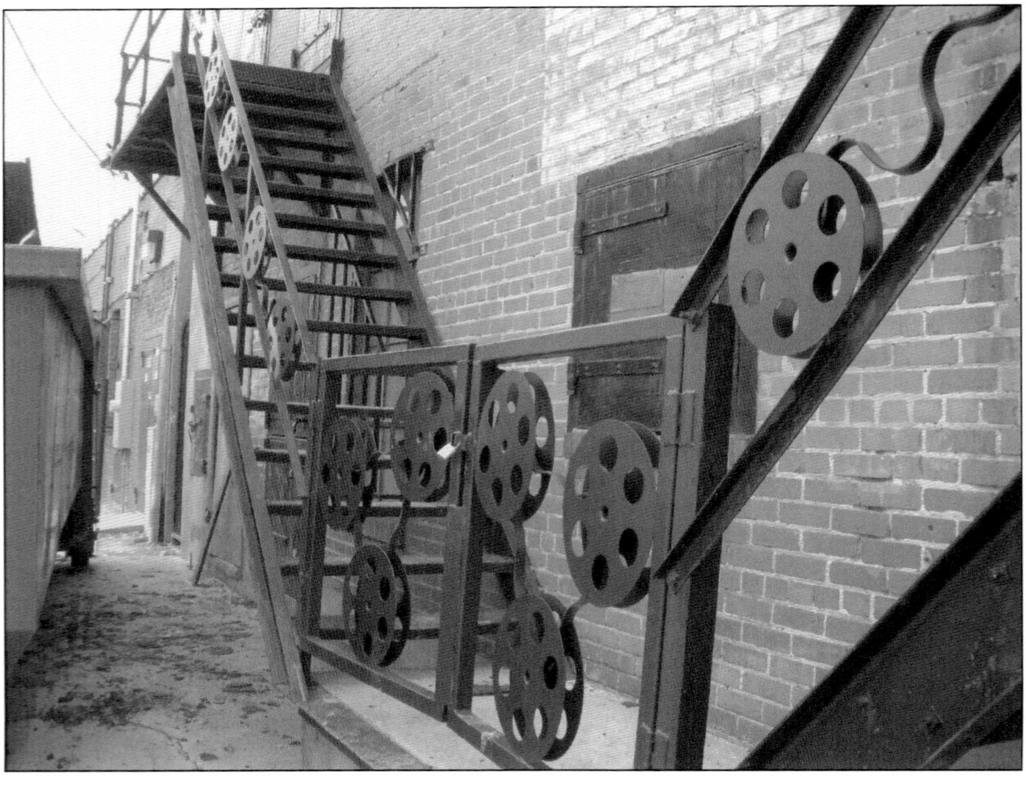

The former Oklahoma Theatre Supply Company offices at 628 West Sheridan Avenue were restored to their 1946 opening state in the image at right. The interior was modified slightly and almost immediately occupied by four architect and design groups. In the image below, the former showroom housing the wares of theatres and their projection rooms now serves as modern office space, with the missing display cases and shelving being the only significant change. In honor of Oklahoma Theatre Supply's tenure, the company's name remains on the restored facade. (Both, courtesy of the author's collection.)

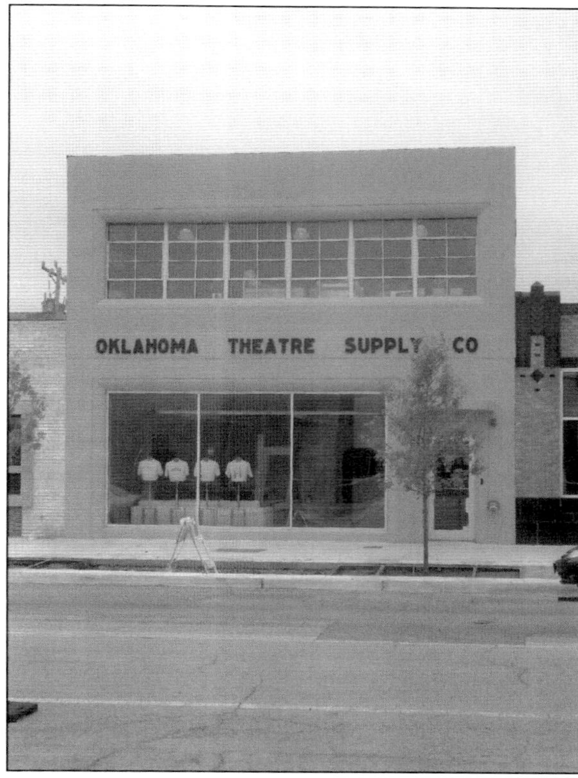

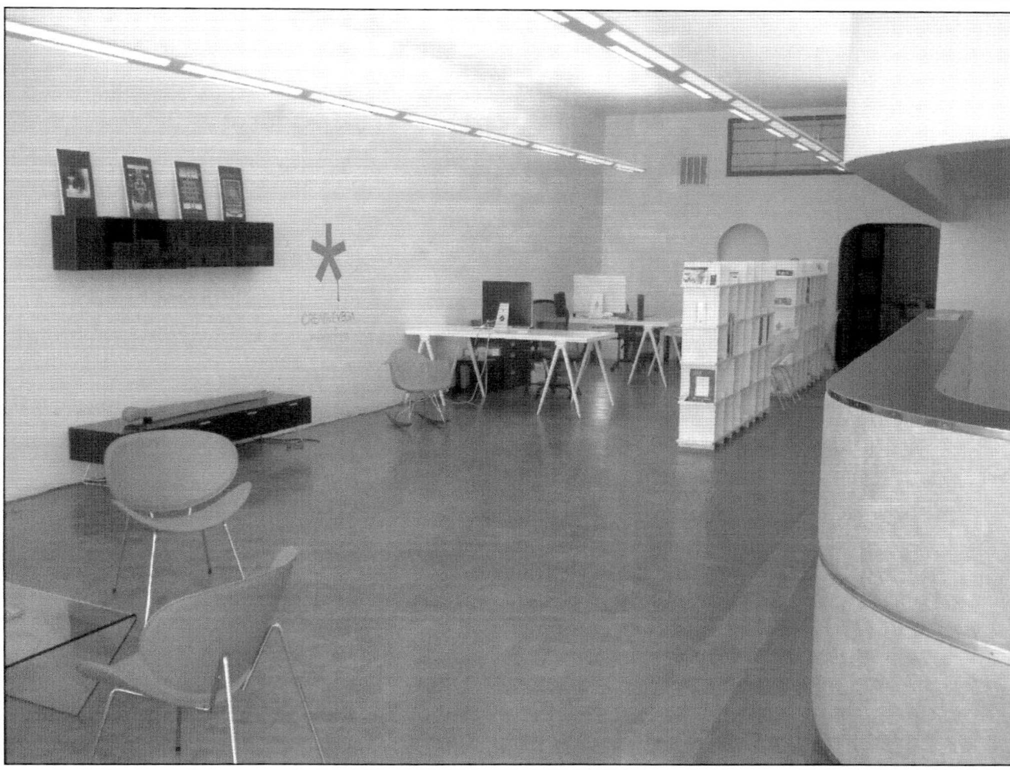

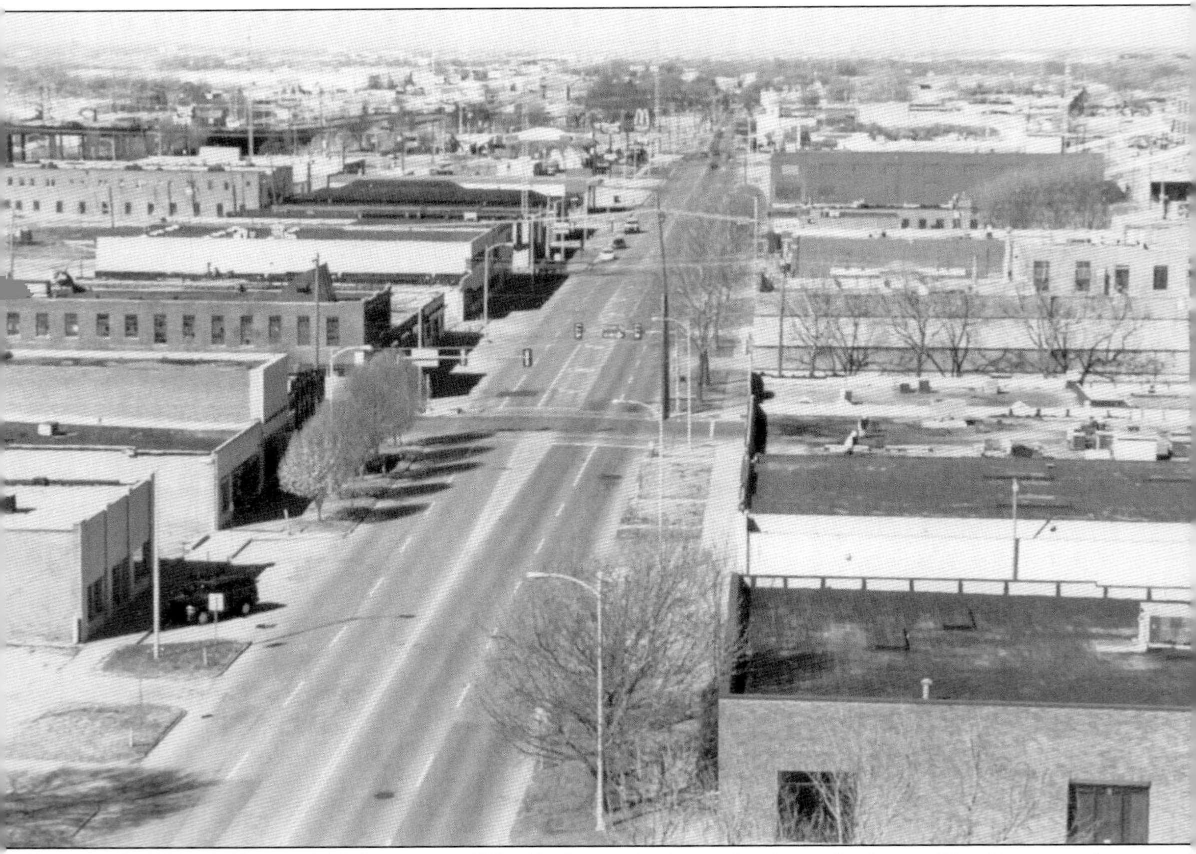

In 2004, the future Oklahoma City Film Exchange business district and Historic Film Row were but a dream. Since the 1970s, the vision of Skid Row being anything more than what memories knew it to be was difficult to overcome. As this photograph shows, this southwest portion of downtown was bleak and rarely ventured into, at times seemingly a ghost town. However, for nearly 50 years, the image of West Grand–turned–Sheridan Avenue was very different. During those golden years, studio film exchanges and their people, promotions, events, and products were part of the state and its capital's downtown cityscape. They ventured into its shops, cafés, and even its politics. Through the Great Depression era, Franklin Roosevelt's New Deal, World War II, poodle skirts, the civil rights movement, hippie culture, and *Raiders of the Lost Ark*, Oklahoma City's Film Row and its people provided the moving images that captured it all. (Courtesy of the author's collection.)

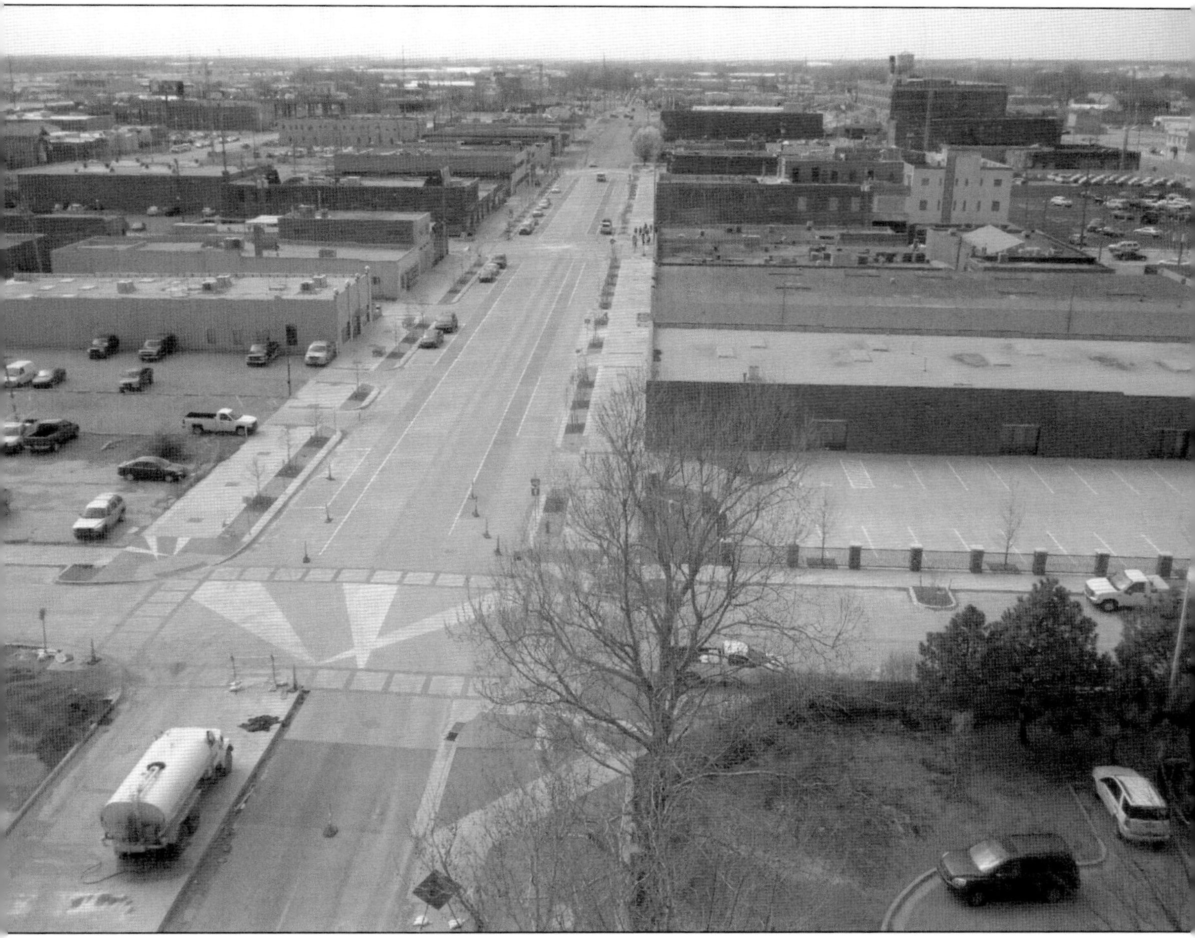

In 2011, the legacy of Film Row and its former exchange inhabitants has been preserved, revitalized, and made ready for future generations. The seedy streets from years past have been replaced with new bike lanes, sidewalks, and streetscaping. They are embellished with Shumard oak trees, cobbled paving, and custom film-themed pedestrian ramps and crosswalks. The historic buildings are home to numerous innovative and tax revenue–generating businesses, which in turn will continue stoking the fires that sustain the new Oklahoma City Film Exchange business district. Even now, the district's story continues as new ventures spread out from its West Sheridan and Lee Avenues core toward future development. In 1942, Film Row screened the Warner Brothers film *Casablanca* in one of the four screening rooms available. Looking along Sheridan Avenue and the future of Film Row nearly 70 years later, it may still be possible to hear actor Humphrey Bogart's voice carry on the wind, "I think this is the beginning of a beautiful friendship." (Courtesy of the author's collection.)